THE POWERS OF THE PAST

For my parents
Murray and Frances Kaye
with love, appreciation and admiration

THE POWERS OF THE PAST

*Reflections on the crisis and
the promise of history*

HARVEY J. KAYE
Ben and Joyce Rosenberg Professor
Social Change and Development
University of Wisconsin-Green Bay

University of Minnesota Press
Minneapolis

Published by the University of Minnesota Press
2037 University Avenue Southeast, Minneapolis, MN 55414
Printed in Great Britain

Library of Congress Cataloging-in-Publication Data
Kaye, Harvey J.
    The powers of the past: reflections on the crisis and the promise
of history / Harvey J. Kaye.
        p.   cm.
    Includes bibliographical references and index.
    ISBN 0-8166-2120-9. – ISBN 0-8166-2121-7 (pbk.)
    1. History–Philosophy.   2. Historiography.   I. Title.
D16.8.K34   1992
901–dc20   91-27359
                                                                CIP

CONTENTS

Prolegomena   **1**

  A personal and political introduction   1
  Outline of the work   6
  Intellectual debts and acknowledgements   8

1 The crisis of history   **12**

  The crisis in education   12
  Paradox 1: The demand for the past   18
  Paradox 2: Developments in historical studies   21
  Historians' responses to the crisis   34

2 The crisis of the grand-governing narratives   **40**

  Post-war settlement and grand-governing narratives   40
  Disruptions and discontinuities   50
  Again, the crisis of history   60

3 The use and abuse of the past   **65**

  Hegemony and history   65
  Class war from above   73
  The New Right and the past   82
  Thatcher's and Reagan's raids on the past   95
  The New Rights' historical education projects   105

4 The end of history? **120**

  A post-liberal and post-social democratic consensus? 120
  Refashioning hegemony 130
  The present as future 135

5 Breaking the tyranny of the present **145**

  The challenge 145
  The powers of the past 150
  Making history 161

NOTES 170

INDEX 199

PROLEGOMENA

I think you must like history as I liked it when I was your age, because it deals with men, as many men as possible, all the men in the world in so far as they unite together in society, and work and struggle and make a bid for a better life. All that can't fail to please you more than anything else. Isn't that right?

Antonio Gramsci in a letter to his son

A PERSONAL AND POLITICAL INTRODUCTION

When I was a child my grandfather would come over to our house almost every weekend and on those occasions he introduced me to the past – or at least what I took to be the past. Most often he would read to me from a collection of Old Testament Bible Stories. Other times he would tell me about coming to America as a Russian–Jewish immigrant and about growing up on the Lower East Side of New York City. My grandfather was a courtroom lawyer (a barrister) and he had a very special way of telling stories. Equally important, I later learned, was that he had been a young socialist before and during his years in law school. It is quite likely that his particular – no doubt 'political' – renderings of the Old Testament shaped my sense of the stories. What I heard from my grandfather was a history of exploitation and oppression but, equally, a history of dissent and struggle *and* exodus, redemption, revolution and liberation. I was captivated and inspired by the narrative he offered. Of course, I later came to understand that there is a significant difference between myth and history, indeed, that there exists an inherent antagonism between them, though not necessarily an uncreative one. Nevertheless, looking back I realize how deeply within me my grandfather imbued the sense that history matters intensely and, also, a commitment to the values of a radical-democratic socialism. Growing up and growing older has, in part, seemed to entail a process of recognizing this.

In spite of the mediocre and unchallenging history I was taught at school, I was determined to read it at university. To be honest, I was briefly tempted to pursue a BA in politics, but I remember being horrified by my first-year political science instructor, whom I otherwise admired for his intellectual commitment and enthusiastic teaching, when he remarked, in hopes of recruiting me to his discipline, that 'History is interesting, but it's just the background.' I doubt if I actually had a better definition to offer at the time, but his words so antagonized me that I immediately went over to the History Department to register as a major. I admit that following the first degree in history (1967–71) I did 'transfer' to the social sciences for, as an academic discipline, I found history somewhat reserved and constraining in those years; but I did so with the intention of still pursuing historical studies which appeared to be re-emerging in both political science and sociology. In fact, it was my experience that although history was tolerated – and many sociologists deferred in a superficial manner to C. Wright Mills' call for a historically grounded social science – actually to pursue a historical dissertation entailed a series of negotiations and confrontations with professors who, like my first-year political science instructor, comprehended history as simply the preface or introductory section.[1]

For several reasons I was committed at the time to Latin American Studies and, specifically, I wanted to write my doctoral dissertation as a historical sociology of landlord–peasant relations in Spanish America. What I had discovered of writings on the subject in social science were often absurdly ahistorical so I naturally turned to the work of historians. There I found that although attention had been given to the landlords' domination of the peasantry (no doubt because such relations were antithetical to the liberalism of North American and European scholars) and, increasingly, peasant resistance and rebellion, there was still little sense that the movement, the historical development of those polities and social orders were actually shaped by peasant and worker struggles. There were alternative historical models available in North America for the kind of work I wanted to pursue, for example, Barrington Moore's *Social Origins of Dictatorship and Democracy* which pioneered the historical–sociological enterprise for many of us, and the studies of Southern slavery by Eugene Genovese. And it was through the latter's writings in particular that I discovered the British Marxist historical tradition, for the path from Genovese led to Maurice Dobb and the question of the 'transition from feudalism to capitalism', then to Rodney Hilton and landlord–peasant conflicts, and onwards to Christopher Hill, George Rudé, Eric Hobsbawm and E. P. Thompson. Here, in the works of these historians, I not only came upon a range of ideas and insights for my dissertation, I re-encountered the kind of history to which my grandfather had, in his own way, introduced me twenty years earlier. It recounted both the experience of exploitation and oppression *and* the episodes of dissent and struggle; it was committed and passionate; and it was connected to a larger problematic. (Little did I know that its authors were in several cases themselves raised in Old Testament traditions!)[2]

Having been so persistently challenged on the issue, I had necessarily begun by this time to develop a sharper and more deliberate conception of the purpose and promise – better, the *necessity* – of historical study and thought, one which transcended both the problem of academic disciplines and the notion of history being simply the background. Moreover, I had increasingly come to believe that, although it offers no guarantees, the making of a *new* history – in the sense of a future different than the present, especially a history to be characterized by the ideals of liberty, equality and democratic community (the values which my grandfather had expressed through his storytelling) – requires that people not only be 'committed' and 'engaged' but, also, possessed of a deep and critical knowledge of the past and its relations with the present. I do not assert that the study of the past provides a clear and demarcated path to effective democratic (or any other kind of) political action. However, I do contend that critical historical study and thought are crucial: first, to the development of an awareness that, however tragic the dialectic which is history, the creation of polities and social orders characterized by greater freedom, equality and democracy is possible; and, second, to the pursuit of the essentially pedagogical process which I have referred to elsewhere, following E. P. Thompson's directive, as the *historical* 'education of desire' in which we reflect upon and inform our deliberations and agency with the experiences, struggles, and aspirations and visions which have preceded our own. To be clear about it – and I shall have recourse to this quote again – the best scholarly and educational practices are those which contribute most emphatically to the sense of history called for by Antonio Gramsci: 'an historical, dialectical conception of the world which understands movement and change, which appreciates the sum of effort and sacrifice which the present has cost the past and which the future is costing the present, and which conceives the contemporary world as a synthesis of the past, of all past generations, which projects itself into the future'.[3]

I have begun on an autobiographical note in order to explain the original motivation behind the present book. It might be said that I write to deliver a belated reply to those of my instructors and seniors who doubted or denied the centrality of history. Yet, even more importantly, I also offer this work as a response in essay form to my students and others who, smartly enough, have continued to pose the question 'What for, history?'. To the extent that it is limited to the by no means unimportant selection of a major or degree subject, or, beyond that, to the choice of a future livelihood, I leave the discussion to the academic advisers and career counsellors; but, on the good chance that the asking reflects intellectual and political concerns, this book presents my answers.

The initiative to address the issue of the purpose and promise of critical historical study and thought is occasioned, however, by more than a lingering desire to respond to a question I had answered only inadequately before. It is also instigated – in fact, the very contents of the book have been determined – by the persistent, though changing, 'crisis of history', the apparent devaluation and decline of history in schooling and the broader culture since the mid-1970s. Taking up university teaching in the latter part of that decade, intent upon cultivating and promoting critical study of past and present, I was surprised and disappointed to discover that, not long after I had completed my own undergraduate studies, students had begun to turn away from the discipline in a decided fashion and, too, that history had lost its commanding place in the curriculum. At first it was only historians themselves who seemed to take any notice of and be concerned about the retreat from historical education, but by the early 1980s the 'crisis' had become a major public issue involving not only the problem of history in schools and universities but, also, the place of the past and history in the wider arenas of political and cultural life. Indeed, as I shall discuss, the crisis was to be placed directly on the political agenda in both the United States and Britain (and elsewhere in the West and beyond). In this way the question of the purpose of history acquired added meaning and urgency, especially since those groups most aggressively proclaiming the existence of the crisis and calling for the radical revision and renewal of historical education, the American and British New Right and neo-conservative forces which had themselves emerged in the course of the 1970s, were themselves advancing renditions of 'the past' and its relation to the present and, also, a conception of the value of historical study and thought which looked not towards their making critical contributions to the further development of liberty, equality and democratic community but, rather, to their serving the powers that be and supporting, at best, the status quo.

Recognizing their own marginalization, historians, as we would expect, have not failed both to offer explanations of the crisis and to propose strategies by which history might be returned to the centre of educational and public life. Unfortunately, regularly missing from their analyses and proposals is adequate consideration of the connection between the crisis and the larger contemporary historical developments with which it has been bound up. Absent in particular, I will argue, is an acknowledgement of the *political* components of the crisis, that is, both the circumstances which came to be comprehended as a 'crisis' and the manner in which they were actually articulated as such. As a consequence, historians also seem to be failing to realize that what is at stake in our response is not merely the *status* of the discipline but, again, the very purpose and promise of historical enquiry and, ultimately, the vision(s) of past, present and possible futures to prevail in our public cultures.

OUTLINE OF THE WORK

Following these Prolegomena the book is divided into five chapters. In the first I survey the crisis of history, highlighting the paradox that at the very same time that history has been under siege in schooling and education, and historians have experienced a sense of marginality in the larger culture, there has been a tremendous surge of popular interest in the past and historical scholarship itself has been effervescent. Noting the analyses and proposals put forth within the historical profession suggesting, in most cases, worthwhile, but essentially adaptive, strategies or tactics on the part of historians, I point out that, unfortunately, in most instances these and related responses to the crisis ignore or avoid the fundamental and crucial questions of the purpose and promise of historical study and thought. Further, by insufficiently addressing contemporary historical developments, they fail to recognize, first, the political origins and character of the crisis and, second, as a consequence, that it calls for a more critical conception or vision of historical practice than those they afford.

In Chapter 2, I present the argument that the developments characteristic of the crisis of history are actually the product of a series of political and economic developments in the United States and Britain (and beyond) in the 1960s and 70s which had the effect of undermining the respective liberal and social-democratic national 'consensuses' and their associated 'grand-governing narratives' – the visions of past, present and possible futures by which we make sense of and orientate our individual and collective experiences and endeavours – which shaped and informed American and British historical consciousness and perspective in the decades following the Second World War.

In Chapter 3, I look even more directly at the connection

between history and politics. Following a brief discussion of the relation between the grand narratives and power and ideology, or, what might be termed the problem of 'hegemony and history', I relate how the developments associated with the crisis of history actually came to be defined *as* a crisis in the course, and as a consequence, of the formation and ascendance to power of the American and British New Rights in the 1970s and 80s. Referring in particular to the words and programmatic initiatives, especially those in the area of historical education, enunciated by Ronald Reagan and Margaret Thatcher and their respective political comrades and colleagues, I explain how the use and abuse of the past have been central to their efforts to refashion capitalist hegemony in the United States and Britain.

Chapter 4 brings us to contemporary developments. After consideration of the degree to which the New Rights have (or have not) accomplished their political aspirations, I look at how conservatives and the powers that be have sought to incorporate the dramatic and revolutionary developments in Eastern Europe and the Soviet Union to their projects by defining them as 'the triumph of capitalism' *and* 'the end of history'. Such efforts, I contend, represent continuing campaigns on their part to develop new grand-governing narratives in support of post-liberal and post-social-democratic consensuses – a project implying a particular supporting role for historians.

In response and opposition, I call in Chapter 5 for a renewal and reassertion of the *radical-democratic* vision of the purpose and promise of historical study and thought, that which drew so many of us to the discipline in the 'sixties'. Influenced by the 'Western' and British Marxist historical traditions, and imbued with our own intellectual and political involvements and aspirations, that vision conceived of historians as having a significant part to play as citizen-scholars in the formation and/or reformation of political and social thought and, thus, in the actual *making* of history. In these terms, I propose that historians see themselves as critical intellectuals, capable through their practices of invoking *the powers of the past*: perspective, critique, consciousness, remembrance and imagination. Finally, I close by returning to consider the question of the crisis in historical education, the possible development of new grand narratives truly alternative to those historically engendered, and the contributions, when connected to and engaged in the struggles of working people and the oppressed past *and* present, which historians might yet be able to make towards the development of a more democratic history.

INTELLECTUAL DEBTS AND ACKNOWLEDGEMENTS

It should be evident that this book is motivated by both academic and political concerns. That is, it represents not only a reply to the perennial question, 'What for, history?', but, also, a contribution to, or intervention in, the debates over the actual future of historical study and thought in schooling and public life, indeed, over the future shape of public and political life itself. I must say that it has been written with my own history and social science students in mind for they have been hearing these thoughts in the course of their development. At the same time, as a product of my own personal and intellectual biography, I have always intended that the work should speak to both American and British audiences (thus, I have tried to be clear about my terms, e.g. lawyer/barrister). This is not simply to increase the potential readership but, rather, as I hope to show, it is because of the striking parallels between the United States and Britain regarding the crisis of history, the ascendance of the New Right, and the connections between the two. I have not been unaware of the difficulties, nor am I confident that I have transcended them. Nevertheless, I am hopeful that it may have provided for productive results. Still, I should add that I make no claim to dramatic originality. The ideas and ideals presented here have been expressed before by different authors in a variety of ways and in my review of such writings I have often found myself in sympathy and, allowing for certain reservations, agreement with numerous of my predecessors (but, equally, antagonized by others!); an experience which has been, in one sense, reassuring for it has afforded me – in the midst of seemingly original problems – a sense of continuity and comradeship.

My intellectual debts and inspirations are many and diverse, ranging, one might say, from the secular to the religious (as my autobiographical remarks, in part, reveal). In particular, however, my ideas are derived from my continuing work on the British Marxist historical tradition; recurrent encounters with the beautifully evocative 'Theses on the philosophy of history' by Walter Benjamin, the German–Jewish thinker and critic who died in 1940 while fleeing the expansion of Nazism; and persistent exploration of the prison writings of the Italian Marxist, Antonio Gramsci, who spent the last ten years of his life shut away, but not shut down, in the gaols of Mussolini's Fascist regime.[4]

Writing is a most personal and sometimes lonely activity. Yet the effort to think through and put ideas to paper has always required, for me at least, conversation and argument with colleagues, students and friends who are willing to listen, converse and dissent. The ideas and arguments which I present here were first tried out in a series of articles which appeared in *Socialist Register 1987* (Merlin Press), *The Times Higher Education Supplement*, and *The Chronicle of Higher Education*. I thank the editors of those publications with whom I worked, especially, Ralph Miliband, Leo Panitch and John Saville (*Socialist Register*), Brian Morton (*THES*), and Karen Winkler (*The Chronicle*), for affording me those opportunities. Regarding the actual book project, my editor, Farrell Burnett, was consistently helpful and encouraging.

A great number of other people contributed to the making of this book. In particular I must acknowledge the intellectual and comradely influence of Henry Giroux, Ellen Wood, Victor Kiernan, Daniel Singer, Carl Chinn, Roy Lowe, Terry Brotherstone, Ron Baba, Anthony Galt, Craig Lockard, Jerry Lembcke, David Lowenthal, Ray Hutchison, Dave Jowett, Hugh Miller, Stephanie Cataldo, Eve Mueller, Jody Krejcarek, Susan Jackson and Greg Widen. All may not agree with what I have come to say, but then they should write their own books on the subject so I can try to influence or dissuade them!

I should also record my appreciation of the Department of Social Change and Development at the University of Wisconsin-Green Bay which has been my academic home for a dozen years now. Encouraging, and regularly demanding, the crossing of disciplinary boundaries by faculty and students alike, it has been and remains a most stimulating and engaging environment in which to work.

At the same time, I want to note the scholarly and friendly welcome afforded me by the Institute for Advanced Research in the Humanities and the School of History at the University of Birmingham, and to thank the Institute for awarding me a Visiting Fellowship in support of a sabbatical in England in 1987. That experience was crucial to the writing of this book.

Most important of all, however, has been that oft' cited threesome, my family, Rhiannon, Fiona and, especially, Lorna. Without their enthusiasm and never flagging support, emotionally and materially, this work would never have been accomplished. The book itself is dedicated to my parents, Murray and Frances Kaye, whose love and presence is felt in all my endeavours.

Finally, I am not oblivious to the fact that these introductory remarks have been punctuated by words such as 'belief' and 'commitment'. In the course of writing this work I came upon a set of lectures by the renowned scholar of Jewish history, Yosef Hayim Yerushalmi, published under the title *Zakhor*, the Hebrew word for 'Remember!'. In the lectures Yerushalmi examines Jewish history and Jewish collective memory in the light of this biblical commandment. He observes that, perhaps, the history and memory of the Jews, even more than those of other peoples, stand in tense and problematic relation to one another; and, in the fourth and final lecture, 'Modern dilemmas: historiography and its discontents', he describes how 'Modern Jewish historiography began precipitously out of that assimilation from without and collapse from within which characterized the sudden emergence of the Jews out of the ghetto [in the course of the revolutionary 'long nineteenth century']. It originated, not as scholarly curiosity, but as ideology, one of a gamut of responses to the crisis of emancipation and the struggle to attain it.' He proceeds to offer the poignant reflection that 'The modern effort to reconstruct the Jewish past begins at a time that witnesses a sharp break in the continuity of Jewish living and hence also an ever-growing decay of Jewish group memory. In this sense, if for no other, history becomes what it had never been before – the faith of fallen Jews.'

I am not a historian of Jewish life, yet I cannot deny that Yerushalmi's words may well have captured my more generic commitment to historical study and thought and in that very same sense I imagine that he has articulated the universal dilemma of modernity except that not all of the 'fallen' have sought to engage 'history' as their alternative.[5]

CHAPTER 1

---------- · ----------

THE CRISIS OF HISTORY

The crisis consists precisely in the fact that the old is dying and the new cannot be born; in this interregnum a great variety of morbid symptoms appear.

Antonio Gramsci

THE CRISIS IN EDUCATION

First emerging in academic circles in the 1970s, by the mid-1980s the 'crisis of history' had become a matter of public debate, a frequent subject of editorial commentary and articles in newspapers and magazines, and even, as we shall see, an item on the political agenda. Participants in such discussions in both the United States and Britain anxiously declaimed that historical study and thought were in serious 'decline and fall' in their respective countries if not across Western society. Fritz Stern's words seemed to sum up the situation best from the historian's vantage point: 'It may be part of our professional and social predicament that at the very time when historical knowledge is of critical importance it is in fact neglected.' (Though we may well wonder when historical knowledge would *not* be of critical importance!) Put more bluntly, it appeared to many as if the thesis that history is irrelevant – or, as Henry Ford had once so eloquently declared, 'History is bunk!' – had come to prevail.[1]

Media attention, as we would expect, was to be focused most directly on schooling and education. Quoting teachers' first-hand accounts and various local studies, columnists and journalists in the United States reported that not only couldn't 'Johnny' read, write and calculate adequately, he was learning very little American and world history and geography. And they then regularly proceeded to hypothesize what ills this portended for both national culture *and* national security. Writers and critics in Britain – with apparently far more history at stake – were equally agitated and concerned about present and future generations being ignorant of the major events and personages which had shaped the 'British' past. (And, likely cited as evidence of the 'civilizational' as opposed to the merely national–specific character of the crisis, it was reported in the English-language press how even in France – where it was always assumed that the 'storming of the Bastille' was firmly implanted in the consciousness of every *citoyen* – it was discovered that two out of every three children entering secondary education could not cite the dates of the French Revolution.[2])

Further supporting evidence was forthcoming in the form of test results, interviews and surveys, all of which seemed to confirm the expectation that in general students were poorly informed about their national pasts and world history (though it should be added – which is not to belittle the findings – that there was practically nothing to show that they were actually *less* so informed than their elders and predecessors). Other indicators of the crisis were offered, intended to serve as both evidence and explanation. For example, it was regularly noted that in the aftermath, or wake, of the 1960s, courses such as Western Civilization and American History which had long been required in the general education (foundation-year) programmes of most American colleges and universities had been shifted to the elective (optional) list and that the number of undergraduates majoring in the subject had fallen dramatically. (Peaking in 1970–1 at about 44,000, the number of BA degrees awarded in 1985–6 had dropped to only 16,000!) Though the structure and curricula of education are quite different in the United Kingdom, similar kinds of things were accounted of history in British schools and universities. Also, in both the United States and Britain it was continually pointed out that either 'humanities' or 'social studies' had taken the place traditionally held by history at all curricular levels and, moreover, that where historical education had survived it had often come to involve less the provision of a coherent narrative, or even core subject, and more the selection of special topics organized around themes or 'problems'.[3]

For many the crisis was traceable directly to the campus rebellions of the late 1960s and student demands to make education more 'relevant', later persisting due to the paranoia and/or pragmatism of the 1970s and 80s and the increasing desire on the part of young people to be made more employable or 'marketable' (that is, calls for relevance gave way to those for utility and practicality expressed most straightforwardly in the now familiar question 'What can I do with a degree in history?'). There are problems with this 'explanation' of the crisis. First of all, as revealed by the statistics of history degrees awarded, student interest in historical studies actually increased in the course of the 1960s, reaching its zenith (at least in America) in the very years of heightened student radicalism! Second (as we shall see in the next chapter), although the decline in students choosing to pursue a degree in history was clearly related to economic developments, specifically employment prospects, the question remains as to why students actually turned away from history in particular. That is, the possibility of employment had always been a reason for pursuing higher education and a degree in history had not previously been perceived to be a hindrance to securing a job after graduation. What had changed? And, finally, why did academic 'authorities' choose to respond to the student rebellions and anxieties by fragmenting history and/or reducing or completely dropping it from the general education curriculum as opposed to maintaining and insisting all the more on the necessity and value of historical education?

Undeniably, there were historians who had perceived the makings of a crisis in the early to mid-1960s – and one by no means limited to schooling. In 1964 the American cultural historian, Warren Sussman, regretfully observed that 'The last two decades in America have been marked by a singularly antihistorical spirit among the leading figures of our intellectual life': and, about the same time, Hayden White, an historian of European ideas, wrote in an article titled 'The burden of history' of how the discipline had been drummed out of both the sciences and the arts. In a very similar fashion to that of his American colleagues, the British historian, J. H. Plumb, wrote of a 'crisis of history' (his own term). Acknowledging that historians and their endeavours were numerous and multiplying and that the profession was 'strictly organized' and 'powerfully disciplined', Plumb nevertheless contended that this could offer but little comfort because the discipline 'possesses only a modest educational value and even less conscious social purpose'. The 'historian's dilemma' was that in spite of its apparent successes there was still a 'lack of faith in the ultimate value of historical enquiry'. (He would return to this a few years later in his book, *The Death of the Past*.)[4]

Anxious voices and predictions of an impending, if not already transpiring, crisis were, however, relatively few in this period for the 1960s witnessed almost continuous growth for academic history, not only in terms of student numbers but, also, for the professional historian, in resources and teaching and research opportunities. Consider the simple fact that higher education in both the United States and Britain was expanding rapidly in these years by way of both the enlargement of existing institutions and the establishment of new colleges, universities and polytechnics – and history was expanding with it. All this provided a sense of heightened status for the discipline. Yet, perhaps, C. Vann Woodward expressed the sense of the times most clearly in his 1969 Presidential Address to the American Historical Association Convention. Describing the post-war years as a 'boom period' for history and its practitioners – the demand for historians' scholarly and pedagogical skills had never been greater and, in turn, they had never been so productive – he proceeded to remind his colleagues that this might not be a permanent state of affairs. Indeed, he presciently warned of leaner times ahead entailing lower enrolments, reduced resources and fewer jobs for historians. This would be due, he proposed, not simply to student preferences, but, all the more, to the declining intellectual and social status of history and historians.[5]

Of course, it might be replied that historians themselves have a vested interest in the prosperity of the historical discipline and historical education and, therefore, they might never be satisfied. But we should not completely discount these early prognoses of a crisis, for the rapidity and extent of the devaluation and collapse of the prevailing models of historical education which took place during the next several years surely suggest that a crisis of confidence and commitment to the subject was brewing, at the least regarding its constitution and, too, that deeper and more extensive forces were at work. (It should be noted that the persistent reference to 'the sixties' in so many of the pieces treating the problems of historical education has grounded and signalled not simply an historical hypothesis as to their origins but, also, as will be discussed in Chapter 3, a 'political' problematic harnessed to a broader agenda by the New Right in both Britain and the United States.)

Interpretations of the crisis have been rendered in which the decline of history in schooling and the academy is, or might be, perceived as merely a reflection of grander social and cultural transformations. American education and cultural critic, Henry Giroux, has linked the 'death of history', both in schools and out, to the continuing development of industrial capitalism and, more specifically, the concomitant expansion of the 'culture of positivism' – a reified form of rationality linked to scientific and technical progress which effectively 'suppresses the critical formation of historical consciousness'. This is not, Giroux makes clear, an autonomous and apolitical process as the discourse, or content, of the culture of positivism 'itself' proposes, but, rather, is bound up with a particular pattern of 'ideology and social control'. On a more extensive plane, the English writer, John Berger, in *Pig Earth*, a novel in the form of a collection of stories, poems and essays on the disappearance of peasant life, ties the demise of historical thinking to the modern, and even more generic, 'culture of progress' characteristic of both capitalism and socialism. Writing in particular of the former, for his territory in the novel is Western Europe (namely Alpine France), he states: 'Finally, there is the historic role of capitalism itself, a role unforeseen by Adam Smith or Marx: its historic role is to destroy history, to sever every link with the past and to orientate all effort and imagination to that which is about to occur.' Yet, on a still grander scale, the intellectual historian, Walter Adamson, refers to an observation made by Karl Deutsch that 'if we consider the world-historical aggregate figures, 1955 was the approximate crossover point at which more than half the world became literate and more than half the world ceased to live off the land'; leading Adamson himself to proffer that 'If ours is a time of unprecedented difference and consequence, then one might expect a flight from history in both existential and more narrowly intellectual terms. That this is the case is all too familiar . . .'[6]

Such arguments are compelling. There is much to be said for analyses which situate the devaluation of historical education and the historical discipline within a more universal denial of the past and historical thinking – an experience diagnosed by Russell Jacoby as 'social amnesia – memory driven out of mind by the social and economic dynamic of society'. The modern world of social change and development does, indeed, make the relation between past and present problematic for, as Marshall Berman describes it: 'To be modern is to find ourselves in an environment that promises us adventure, power, joy, growth, transformation of ourselves and the world – and, at the same time, that threatens to destroy everything we have, everything we know, everything we are. . . . To be modern is to be part of a universe in which, as Marx said, "all that is solid melts into air".'[7] Nevertheless, if the crisis of history ought not to be too readily reduced to a product of student rebellions and anxieties, neither should it be too readily and too simply conflated with the dynamic of modernity, capitalist or otherwise. For a start, the movement of modernity both undermines and *liberates* historical consciousness thereby 'empowering' the historical enterprise itself. Furthermore, however much the evolving processes of modernization continue to transform British and American lives, it would be absurd to ignore the fact that the changes and developments we associate with such processes have characterized Britain and America for many a generation and that at least for several of them academic history had thrived. In other words, it is not 'modernization' as such which has created the contemporary crisis of history. Both the events of the late 1960s at one end of the scale and the processes of 'modernization' at the other represent important reference points for comprehending the emergence of the crisis, but they are insufficiently historical;

the former do not make intelligible the depth or extent of the crisis, the latter do not account for its timing, and neither explains its paradoxical character.

PARADOX 1: THE DEMAND FOR THE PAST

A most evident and, to historians, frustrating paradox has been that at the very same time that historical study and thought were seen to be slipping to the academic and cultural peripheries, there were arising both a tremendous popular demand for 'the past' and, in response, a vast assortment of public and private initiatives to supply 'historical' presentations and representations. Speaking of the phenomena in America, the historian John Lukacs has referred us to such things as the following: from 1950 to 1980 local historical societies doubled in number to a total of 3,000. During the same period 'popular histories' frequently achieved greater hardback sales than fictional works. And in recent years a new 'historical' literary genre has appeared and joined the bestseller ranks; entailing the merger of fictional narratives and the historical past it is best exemplified by *Ragtime* and *Roots*. Moreover, based on these historical and literary works, or developed from 'original' ideas, television and film renditions of history and the past have been produced capturing the popular imagination and occasionally breaking the records for numbers of viewers (most spectacularly, the mini series *Roots* and *Holocaust*). In a different though related vein, there have been the public television successes of programmes like the British historical soap opera *Upstairs, Downstairs*.[8] To these we might add: the development of historical restorations and recreations, from single old homes to entire towns and city sections; the related process of gentrification in which the upper middle classes first colonize and then 'take over' what had been viewed as old and declining neighbourhoods; the construction of museums, monuments and memorials (most dramatically, the Vietnam War Memorial in Washington, DC, and the Museum of American Immigration situated at the restored Ellis Island complex in New York harbour); the staging of both historical re-enactments (most usually, but not only, famous battles of the Revolutionary

War for Independence and Civil War) and rededications (such as Liberty Weekend in celebration of the 1986 Centennial of the Statue of Liberty); and, tied up with and recording all of these activities, the publication of magazines featuring historical topics (including not only the revamped *American Heritage* and a selection of military history titles, but also a host of others catering to an extraordinary array of interests in 'the past' and 'tradition').[9]

Strikingly similar things have been occurring in Britain. Indeed, so phenomenal has been the growth of undertakings and enterprises presenting and representing the past that observers and critics have come to refer to it all as the 'Heritage Industry'. This growth sector of the cultural economy has built on existing institutions and practices, yet in many ways it has represented a 'new' departure. Extending in temporal terms from the Roman and 'pre-conquest' periods to the twentieth century itself, and ranging across the spheres of human activity from the scientific and technological to art, design and 'culture' and taking in, of course, the politico-military, the heritage industry has sought to portray not only the 'momentous', the highpoints of the past, but, also, the pursuit of everyday life. And, in a 'democratic' fashion, it has incorporated into the 'National Heritage' not merely the lives and cultures of the elites, aristocratic and bourgeois, but, equally, peasant, lower middle- and working-class experiences. Thus, taking account of just museums, not only do we have the great national institutions in the capital such as the Victoria and Albert, the Imperial War Museum, and the British Museum, along with their provincial counterparts, *and* a widespread assortment of historic homes, country houses, and castles being made accessible to the public, but also there has been the creation of many more new museums in city and country, some along the lines of the traditional ones, and others offering more 'direct', and, even, 'hands on' experiences (museologists apparently refer to the older and newer types respectively as 'dead' and 'living' museums). Consider – among the more significant operations – the Museum of London in the Barbican, the Wigan Heritage Centre, the Jorvik Viking Centre in York, and the open-air museums like the Black Country Museum in Dudley and the Welsh Folk Museum near Cardiff.

David White opened his 1987 article on 'The born-again museum' with the following words and remarkable statistics: 'The business of looking backwards has never looked better. It is estimated that, on average, one museum opens every fortnight in Britain. Over the last 20 years, the number of museums has more than doubled from around 800 to more than 2,000.'[10]

In the midst of all this, American historian and author of *The Culture of Narcissism*, Christopher Lasch, offered the sobering reminder that 'there is history that remembers and history that arises from a need to forget.' To many critics in both Britain and the United States, the heightened appetite for the past reveals not so much an engagement with history as either nostalgia and/or a means of celebrating the present. That is, the demand for 'things gone by' and its massive provisioning are actually the means by which we attempt to 'deny the past's inescapable claim on the present' or, as the historical geographer and author of *The Past is a Foreign Country*, David Lowenthal, has remarked: 'A past nostalgically enjoyed does not need to be taken seriously.' Echoing sentiments also expressed in Britain, Lasch has declared that 'If Americans really cared about the past, they would try to understand how it still shapes their ideas and actions. Instead, they lock it up in museums or reduce it to another object of commercialized consumption.'[11]

Granted, vast quantities of 'the past' should not be mistaken for history. None the less, we should avoid dumping all such efforts and projects into one barrel marked nostalgia, entertainment and bogus history or fraud. Moreover, we should not too quickly equate the pasts being supplied with either the original needs and desires which instigated their production or the ways in which they are perceived and understood, for much of the growth of interest in the past may well be expressing deeply felt needs, aspirations and, even, commitments both to secure and communicate past experiences and to comprehend the relations between past and present. In this very sense we should also beware the too easy derogation of nostalgia, especially (as I hope to make clearer in the next chapter) in the light – or shadow – of the perceptibly dramatic *discontinuities* in our contemporary experience. In essence, Lasch himself warns of this when he writes that 'What is needed is not an explanation of our nostalgic national condition but an explanation of the widespread *preoccupation* with nostalgia in the intellectual community and mass media. . . .' His own theory, and one with which I am most sympathetic, is that the critics of nostalgia are themselves so discomforted by contemporary developments that they 'seek to reassure themselves that evidence of cultural decline is really [just] evidence of nostalgia'. In contrast to those 'who set cultural fashions', Lasch contends, 'ordinary men and women live in a world in which the burden of the past cannot easily be shrugged off by creating new identities or inventing usable pasts.'[12] In short, though it might mean that the historical discipline is less likely to inform such thinking, the devaluation of historical education does not mean that people do not develop, or seek to develop, meaningful notions and understandings about the past and its relation to the present (having real consequences). Along with the need for more critical analyses of our current nostalgia-inducing political, economic and cultural circumstances, what this directs our attention towards is not so much the problem of the *decline* of historical consciousness and perspective as the question of their form and content and the ways in which these are shaped.[13]

PARADOX 2: DEVELOPMENTS IN HISTORICAL STUDIES

What has been all the more ironic and galling to historians about the crisis is that in these very same years historical studies by (almost) all accounts have been flourishing. The primary reason was the sudden expansion in the 1960s and, then, in the 1970s and 80s, the rise to predominance, if not pre-eminence, of 'social history' within the discipline. Admittedly, social history was by no means an original development of the 1960s. A *social* approach to the study of the past – in contrast, that is, to the more narrowly drawn political, diplomatic, and military historiography which prevailed for many a generation (from 'Thucydides to Ranke' says Georg Iggers, though we could easily extend it well beyond that) – can be traced back to at least the turn of the century with recognizable roots even deeper in the nineteenth century (Marx and, especially, Engels among others). For example, in Britain in the first decades of this century there were, most notably, the studies of the social consequences of the Industrial Revolution by the Liberal-Left intellectuals, John and Barbara Hammond, and the histories of trade unionism and the British State by the Fabian socialists, Sidney and Beatrice Webb. Also, there was the work over several decades of the (Christian) socialist historian and essayist, R. H. Tawney, on the development of capitalism and the many writings by the guild socialist, G. D. H. Cole, on labour history and related subjects. Moreover, paralleling and intersecting with the efforts of the Hammonds, Webbs, Tawney and Cole, whose studies were very much bound up with the evolving politics of the British Left and the labour movement, was the development of the specifically academic or 'professional', and more 'conservative' scholarship of economic historians – who established themselves as a related but separate university discipline in Britain (the journal of which, *Economic History Review*, originally published social history articles as well).[14]

Across the Channel at the turn of the century, the French philosophy-trained historian, Henri Berr inaugurated the *Revue de synthesis historique* proclaiming the pursuit of an integrative approach to history with social and cultural experience at its core. This was an aspiration to be sought all the more aggressively and successfully by the great medievalist, Marc Bloch, and the early modernist, Lucien Febvre, who, together, founded the *Annales d'histoire economique et sociale* (the *Annales*) in 1929. From the journal's inception, Bloch and Febvre sought to enlarge the focus of historical enquiry and, through an engagement with the work of social scientists, to extend the horizons of history beyond political events to social structures, practices, and world views or, as the *annalistes* themselves say, 'mentalities'. But not only through the *Annales* did social history take form in France. Concurrently, the historiography of the French Revolution was being refashioned by Georges Lefebvre, whose commitments to a Marxian analysis and contemporary working-class struggles led him beyond the usual practice of merely assuming the presence and participation of 'the people' to the task of actually exploring and recovering the experiences and actions of the peasants and labouring classes in the revolutionary upheavals.[15]

In the United States, too, there were initiatives in the early years of the twentieth century entailing or projecting a more *social* history. Frederick Jackson Turner by example and the 'progressive historians', James Harvey Robinson and Charles Beard, all the more formally, called for a 'new history' which, attentive to the work of social scientists, would be more capable of addressing the social issues of the day and, thus, of contributing to public discourse and debate.[16]

None the less, the 'take off' of social history occurred in the 1960s and, while drawing on these respective national foundations, it is arguable that it was an international development influenced in particular by two distinct groups of historians. The first was the generation associated with the post-war revival of the *Annales* under the direction of Fernand Braudel, the grand scholar of the Mediterranean world. Joined by a younger cohort including, among many others, Emmanuel Le Roy Ladurie, Georges Duby, Pierre Goubert, Jacques Le Goff, and François Furet, Braudel, in the spirit of Bloch and Febvre, declared the ambition of the *Annales* to be the making of a 'total history' encompassing economic, social, cultural and, even more emphatically, material and environmental structures and experiences. (This was at the expense, as it was widely to be recognized and criticized, of the 'political' in all its variety and complexity, and represented something of a break with the intellectual concerns of Bloch at least.) Also, in the tradition of the pre-war *Annales*, history was to be symbiotically linked with the social or 'human sciences'. Simply stated, the 'Annales school' produced a phenomenally voluminous and innovative body of scholarship and, in the process, established the *Annales* as the premier historical journal in the world.[17]

Mentioned early in the Prolegomena, the second, and actually more significant, influence among the first wave of British and American social historians in the 1960s was that generation of British Marxist historians including Rodney Hilton, Christopher Hill, George Rudé, V. G. Kiernan, Eric Hobsbawm, John Saville and E. P. Thompson which had begun to take shape in the years 1946–56 when they were all members of the Communist Party Historians' Group. Intellectually and politically committed to reconstructing the academic and popular understandings of the making of modern Britain, the Marxist historians were especially intent upon revealing and portraying the experience and agency of the 'common people' in, and their contributions to, that story. In contrast to the *annalistes*, the British Marxists never gave up a primary interest in political relations and experiences – power and struggle – though they necessarily sought (and succeeded in so doing) to revise and expand the conception of the 'political' which had been the legacy of the traditional political historiography. At the same time, although they themselves worked from the grand hypotheses originally advanced by Marx and Engels, they were eager to maintain a dialogue with both non-Marxist historians and, very much like the *annalistes*, Marxist and non-Marxist social scientists; and, in that very spirit, in 1952 several of them founded what is now, arguably, the leading English-language journal of social history, *Past & Present*.[18]

Obviously, the field of social history has been continually shaped by both academic *and* political currents and concerns. Indeed, it would appear that it has been perennially associated with the politics of the Left. However, while there is much truth to that, it would be a mistake to assume that the field has been co-equal with Left, socialist or 'radical' historiography – as the case of the *Annales* school reveals. In this respect, it should also be noted that the original post-war champions of a 'new social history' in the United States were actually poised against 'the Left'. Citing as examples the work of (the 'consensus historians') Richard Hofstadter, Oscar Handlin, Daniel Boorstin and (the historical sociologist) Seymour Martin Lipset, Sean Wilentz has observed that 'much of today's new history – the new social history in particular – originated not as a revolt against tradition but in the efforts of 1950s liberals to supplant the legacy of the Progressive historians and of 1930s Marxism.' As Peter Novick explains, the major intellectual influence on these post-war social historians was the German sociologist, Max Weber, whose 'model of society was attractive as an alternative to Marxism. A somewhat oversimplified version of [Weber's] doctrine of "value freedom" in scholarship, and the substitution of "neutral" for evocative language was widely endorsed by social scientifically oriented historians.' Still, while social history ought not to be equated with the Left or radical history, it was the field chosen by many of the new, younger, politically Left historians of the 1960s both in Britain and the United States. Referring to the American case, Novick writes: 'The great majority of young radical historians entered into one or another subdivision of social history . . . While a great deal of new social-historical scholarship beginning in the late 1950s, was informed by Parsonian sociology and by "modernization theory", social history remained, as it always had been, relatively hospitable to young radicals.'[19]

The point is that even if many of those who were to become social historians were not politically motivated to do so, and even if social history 'never became the center of a left bid for intellectual hegemony', it remains that the great energy and dynamism of social history commencing in the 1960s was due in great part to the entry into the field of a generation of scholars who were sympathetic with, inspired by, and/or themselves engaged in such struggles as the campaigns for civil and social rights for racial and ethnic minorities and the poor, the antiwar and anti-imperialist movements, the movements for women's rights and equality, and the labour movement. Moreover, they brought these concerns and experiences to their research and teaching. Though not limited to particular organizational and publishing initiatives, the intimacy between history and politics for this generation was most clearly and deliberately expressed in such endeavours as *History Workshop* in Britain and *Radical America* and *Radical History Review* in the United States. Though their particulars differed, they shared a conception of history and historical practice which, hostile to the 'academicism' and 'professionalism' increasingly characteristic of the discipline, envisioned a broadening or, more honestly, a *reformation* of both the scholarly and pedagogical agendas.

The History Workshop movement originated in 1966 at Ruskin College (a trades union and adult education institution in Oxford) among a group of 'worker-historians' whose politics were avowedly socialist and whose intellectual interests were in labour history. As Raphael Samuel, a Ruskin tutor and leading figure of the movement, recalls, the Workshop's formation and development were shaped by the writings of the older British

Marxist historians *and* 'a series of left-wing stirrings common to Britain and Europe in the later 1960s', referring specifically to the heightened worker militancy of the period, the student revolts, and the emerging women's movement. A sign of its success in becoming a national movement, or network, was the inauguration in 1976 of *History Workshop Journal* (subtitled *a journal of socialist historians* but later amended to *socialist and feminist*) edited by a collective composed of both veterans of the original Ruskin Workshop and university-based historians. The editorial in the first issue of *History Workshop* stated that 'concerned at the narrowing of the influence of history in our society, and its progressive withdrawal from the battle of ideas' the purpose of the journal 'Like the Workshops . . . [is] to bring the boundaries of history closer to people's lives'. That is, it was 'dedicated to making history a more democratic activity and a more urgent concern'. This was to be accomplished by encouraging and recruiting the participation and publication of non-academic historians; by attending to those subjects which related most directly to the lives of the common people and were generally ignored (at the time) by the mainstream historical publications; and by keeping the journal accessible to (readable by) working people.[20]

Radical America was started in 1967 by Paul Buhle and a group of other graduate students at the University of Wisconsin in Madison as a cultural project of the Students for a Democratic Society (SDS). Of note is that the University of Wisconsin had a tradition of 'leftward' historiography. American labour historiography had developed there in the inter-war years under the leadership of John R. Commons in the Economics Department. Liberal in its politics, the 'Commons school' or 'Wisconsin tradition' focused on trade unionism and collective bargaining, and it was this institutional framework which became the original paradigm of labour studies in America (as it was in Britain). Also, the History Department (where Frederick Jackson Turner spent the first part of his academic career) had been a ' "Progressive" holdout against more conservative historiographical currents' which had come to prevail elsewhere in the years after the Second World War. And it was in this setting that an early band of New Left graduate students in history had founded *Studies on the Left* in 1959 (moved to New York City in the early 1960s, it survived for a few years thereafter). Under the tutelage of the radical-revisionist historian of American foreign policy, William Appleman Williams, the intellectual thrust of the journal was to re-examine and reveal the socio-political and ideological origins of the 'American corporate-liberal state'.[21]

Nevertheless, *Radical America* distinguished itself from its predecessors. In contrast to *Studies on the Left*, *Radical America* set itself the task not of unveiling power structures but of recovering the social and political roots of American radicalism and socialism; and, in contrast to the Commons school of labour history, it did not limit itself to organizations and institutions (indeed, its articles were regularly critical of 'organized labor') but, rather, inspired by the work of the Marxist historians, black Anglo-Caribbean, C. L. R. James, and Englishman, E. P. Thompson, its editors and contributors pursued an even broader social history emphasizing working-class struggles, the organized and the 'spontaneous', in both public and industrial settings. Moreover, of importance to both social historiography and the development of women's studies, the editors of *Radical America* sought to promote research and publication of women's history from a socialist-feminist perspective. The purpose of the journal, however, was not only historical. The scholarly redemption of American radical and socialist movements was intended to contribute to the making of a contemporary New Left politics which might, through broader alliances with the American working class, transcend the inherent limits of the new social movements of the 1960s.[22]

Whereas *Radical America* was, and has remained, a political magazine with a strong interest in history, *Radical History Review* is a politically committed *historical* studies journal. Organized in 1974, the Mid-Atlantic Radical Historians' Organization (MARHO) which publishes the *Review* brashly presented itself as an alternative to the American Historical Association – its declared goal being to 'subvert' and 'destroy' the ideology and practices of 'professionalism' (and thereby aid in undermining the 'interests' which they served). Affirming an interest in cooperating with social scientists of a similar persuasion, MARHO's founders nevertheless insisted on the imperative of the autonomy

of the historical discipline, at the same time articulating their
radical-democratic hopes and aspirations for historical study and
thought:

> History is practically the only academic discipline in which the
> possibilities of human experience, the creativeness of human
> action, is still a major object of study; and for which general
> literacy is the only prerequisite for accessibility. This distinctive-
> ness is decisive and should be cultivated. Historians are best
> situated to show not only that liberation is necessary, but also that
> it is possible.[23]

History Workshop, *Radical America* and *Radical History Review*
were the most significant collective initiatives of the younger Left
historians of the 1960s and early 1970s. Their stated goals were to
be far from accomplished, but their insurgencies and their
labours were critical to the changes which have been effected in
the discipline these last two decades (and, as I shall argue later,
their aspirations remain compelling, if not essential).

The original, very much politically motivated, spirit of social
history in the 1960s engendered a veritable flood of social
historiography in the 1970s and 80s which, though still rebellious
in character (most enthusiastically so, women's history which
really came into its own in these years), was pursued *within* the
rapidly expanding horizons of an evolving and increasingly
receptive historical discipline. At the most generic level there are
three related features which have characterized the growth and
development of social history and, with it, the exuberance of
historical scholarship in this period. First, social historians have
pursued an extensive engagement with the social sciences
involving the incorporation of methods and theories formulated
in those disciplines. Though not always done so smartly, when
not taken up crudely or slavishly the approaches and ideas
garnered have been fruitful in the exploration of new problems
and sources and the reconsideration of old ones. Most obvious in
this respect was the growth of 'quantitative' history, made all the
more feasible by advancing computer technologies and their
increasing accessibility; but along with quantitative methods and
studies should be noted oral and visual approaches and studies,
and archaeological and material sources, all of which have led to

the establishment of new types of archives (though here, as elsewhere, it should be indicated that such techniques were hardly unknown to historians before this time).[24]

Although in the early days it may have seemed that historians were the suitors, the last twenty years have also witnessed a definite renewal of *historical* social science entailing both synthetic and primary studies. An obvious register of the mutuality of the history–social science affair has been the collaborative establishment of interdisciplinary centres and programmes at a growing number of universities and, more significantly, the creation of journals dedicated to social history/historical social science. Along with the pioneers, *Annales* and *Past & Present*, and their American counterpart, *Comparative Studies in Society and History* (1959), there are now (in English alone) the *Journal of Social History*, *Journal of Interdisciplinary History*, *Social History*, *Social Science History*, *Review*, *Journal of Historical Geography*, *Journal of Historical Sociology*, *Continuity and Change*, and the aforementioned *History Workshop* and *Radical History Review* (plus, of course, the older English and American journals, *Economic History Review* and *Journal of Economic History*) – not to mention both the great number of area, women and other interdisciplinary studies periodicals publishing such work *and* the definite increase in recent years of historical articles in the principal social science disciplinary publications.[25]

The second major feature of the rise of social history has been the seemingly unrestricted expansion in the variety of topics considered acceptable and even worthy of historians' attentions. At the outset the growth of social history entailed, in particular, challenging the presumptions and assumptions of the prevailing political and economic historiographies regarding a whole array of public experiences such as economic development and social change, collective behaviour and ideology, social movements and revolutions, work and industry, population and urban growth, and education, poverty and crime. Armed with 'sociological' perspectives and approaches, in this first period social historians were essentially concerned with questions of class, race and, to some extent, ethnicity (this refers particularly to the American scene). In the course of the 1970s and 80s, however, even as these areas of study continued to grow and develop, new and original

areas of enquiry were opened up posing questions of gender and,
in place of sociology, drawing on anthropological perspectives.
Such areas have included the family and life cycle, household and
property arrangements, intimacy and sexuality, and madness and
deviance. Indeed, it is arguable that historians now address
practically the entire range of human experience. On this we
might quote Arthur Marwick's remark in the latest edition (1989)
of his masterful introduction to historiography, *The Nature of
History*. In closing the chapter in which he surveys twentieth-
century developments he writes:

> Has this chapter rushed too quickly from one historian, one type
> of history to another? Have I left no clear impression of what is
> distinctive about the history of the late 1980s? The apparent
> shapelessness has been deliberate; there is no universal fashion, no
> accepted party line, no unbroken formation of 'New Social
> Historians'. However, if I have to single out one distinctive trend
> as we approach the 1990s, it would be the move from public
> history to private history.

And we might briefly add that the ecumenicalism – or,
depending on one's view, imperialism – of social historians has
led them to explore not only subjects long associated with the
social sciences but also those usually left, in one direction, to
students of science and, in the other, to those of the arts. For
example, a social history of the 'environment' might take up
issues of ecology and/or aesthetics.[26]

Yet the third major feature of the socialization of historiography (already intimated in what has been said thus far) has been
the *democratization* of the past associated with the development of
'history from below' or 'history from the bottom up', that is,
history written from the perspective of the lower orders and
informed by, as Barrington Moore once put it: 'sympathy with
the victims of historical processes and skepticism about the
victors' claims'.[27] Though proposing, as the preposition *from*
denotes, more a 'perspective' than a specific 'content', history
from below in actual practice has meant that whereas the classical
histories had almost consistently focused on and related the
experience and action of the elites and ruling classes, social
historians have regularly sought to recover the experience and,
also, though admittedly less often, the agency of peasants, slaves,

workers, women and others who had previously been considered peripheral to the 'essential' historical record. This alteration in the angle of historical vision has likewise instigated new research into, and a consequent reconsideration of, the experiences of the non-European peoples in their confrontations and continuing engagements with, most obviously, the imperial and colonial powers of the North Atlantic world (and, very much a product of this work in 'Third World studies', there has arisen 'global' or 'World History' which now competes with 'Western Civilization' for the latter's already tenuous place in American general education programmes).[28] Put most simply (and crudely), we might say that history from below has meant that social history, understood in the old-fashioned sense as 'history with the politics left out', now takes in not only the 'lifestyles of the rich and famous' but also those of the common people; political history, not only the actions of the rulers but also those – for and against – of 'the people'; economic history not only the activities of the owners and traders, but also those of the labourers; and cultural history, not only the ideas and thoughts of the intellectuals and their patrons but also those of the popular classes.

Again, although originating prior to the 1960s and 70s, and reflecting far more than the efforts of a single generation, it is arguable that the impressive growth of social history as 'people's history' in those years and since has been due in great part to the aspirations and efforts of social historians who were then students or perhaps just entering into academic careers. And it has not gone unnoticed by both supporters and detractors alike that the advancement of social history and, especially, the rethinking of the past from the bottom up have been carried on mostly by scholars on the Left – progressive liberals, socialists, radicals and feminists – leading at least one historian to suggest that 'what we now perceive as "the crisis of history" is merely the coming to an end of the function of history as elite ideology' (an observation we should definitely keep in mind).[29]

It may be an exaggeration to speak of social history being 'hegemonic' in the discipline, but not a gross one. In any case, after two decades of ascent and paramountcy, it should not be surprising that social history has become not only the renewed target of 'external' attack but, increasingly, the subject of criticisms, doubts and efforts at 'new' departures from within. The best known outside critics have been Geoffrey Elton, now Regius Professor of Modern History at Cambridge, and Gertrude Himmelfarb, a distinguished American historian of modern Britain. Elton's hostility was first expressed back in the late 1960s and has even appeared to mellow somewhat in the past several years – at about which time Himmelfarb went ever more on the offensive. Their common attacks have been twofold. The first is evidently politically motivated (and, in both cases, has been linked to conservative or neo-conservative agendas as will be discussed in the next chapter). Highlighting the Leftist political commitments of certain of the social historians they contend, or at least imply, that this makes their scholarship of dubious quality. The second is more intellectually grounded; that is, they have attacked the 'new' social historians for eschewing or rejecting the *political* dimension of history and, supposedly due to social historians' subservience to the social sciences, the narrative form in which it was traditionally presented. The latter concerns are not unreasonable though Elton's and Himmelfarb's notion of 'the political' is too narrowly construed and limited to the politics of the elites and, partly as a consequence, their criticism has been expressed in too blanket a manner for it is hardly true of all practitioners of social historiography, perhaps least so of those towards whom they are most politically hostile.[30]

Indeed, there also have been social historians – most assertively, from the Left – who have expressed those very reservations and criticisms about the directions being taken in the field in the course of the 1970s and 1980s. For example, the most pointed attacks against social history's turn away from the political were first made by the Marxist scholars, Elizabeth Fox-Genovese and Eugene Genovese. Directly targeting the post-war *Annales* school, along with a host of Anglo-American developments, for their acritical procurement of the methods and theories of the post-war Cold War social sciences which ignore or avoid questions of class, power and struggle, the Genoveses also took aim at other, supposedly 'radical', historical currents which, so eager to recover and 'celebrate' the experience and creativity of the lower classes, end up removing their subjects from the very *political* and *politico*-economic relations of exploitation and oppression which determine their lives. They did not reject an engagement with the social sciences; the question was *what kind?* of social science. Nor did they oppose history from the bottom up (they were themselves respected practitioners of it!); it was a matter of not reducing it to history *of* the bottom, that is, without the context of the structures and agencies of power and authority. The Genoveses explained:

> For the moment, we would call attention to the words with which the distinguished conservative scholar Eric Voegelin opened his challenging multivolume work *Order and History*: 'The order of history emerges from the history of order'. Or, in our decidedly less elegant Marxian language: history, when it transcends chronicle, romance and ideology – including 'left-wing versions' is primarily the story of who rides whom and how. To the extent that social history illuminates this essentially political process, we should all aspire to be social historians.[31]

Along with 'foreign' and 'domestic' criticisms, self-doubts have also been registered by some of the central figures, the 'movers and shakers', of the field. In fact, we find Lawrence Stone, an English historian (transplanted to America in the mid-1960s) who had long been a, perhaps *the*, leading proponent, promoter, and practitioner of the 'new' in social history, intimating as early as 1976 that after such a 'fruitful and creative period . . . the future looks less promising'. But it is not until the mid-1980s that a real sense of crisis arises in social historiography. For example, in 1985, reflecting on the fabulous accomplishments thus far, the editor of an important volume surveying 'The worlds of social history' stated that the book originated out of the recognition that 'the field now needs reordering'. And, in the same year, editorial comments appeared in both the American *Journal of Social History* and British *Social History* admitting to a decline in confidence and optimism regarding the progress of social history. Yet perhaps most revealing of all the doubts expressed was the editorial published in a recent issue of the *Annales*, saying that it was time to 'reshuffle the cards' and calling upon its readers to propose new directions in the sense of both 'new methods and perspectives' and 'new alliances' or 'interdisciplinarities'.[32]

In the meantime, there are other historians, some of whom are themselves involved directly with these journals, who have begun to pursue new paths. Thus, there has been a renewal of interest among social historians in 'politics and the political' (war studies included) referred to in some quarters as 'bringing the State back in'. And there is much research and publication underway drawing on recent 'post-structuralist' and 'post-modernist' developments in cultural anthropology and literary-critical studies which some of its most eager students have given the name 'the new cultural history'. In yet another vein, as we shall soon note, there have been calls to begin the process of bringing together the many studies of the last generation and more into new historical syntheses.[33]

Finding themselves in a quandary – more than twenty years of flourishing historical studies and yet an increasing sense of marginality in schooling and the broader culture – historians have not failed to advance proposals as to how to break out of it. The most obvious strategy, taking advantage of media attention, has been to reassert the supposed essentiality of historical knowledge to general education and/or to seek to formulate and insert the most apparently relevant kinds of historical-studies courses into those academic programmes which have been popular and growing (most often, especially in the United States, these are undergraduate applied and professional programmes such as education, business administration, social services and health sciences).[34]

Others, however, expressing the view that the crisis extends beyond the boundaries of educational institutions – that history and historians have been relegated to the periphery of public culture generally – contend that more extensive action is called for. To these historians the marginalization of the discipline has been due in good part to history's own involutionary tendencies. Acknowledging the advantages of the 'professionalization' and 'academicization' of historical study over the past several generations (developments observed in the earlier-noted comments of J. H. Plumb and C. Vann Woodward and the criticisms made by the founders of History Workshop and MARHO), it is argued that these have also entailed a process of collective self-enclosure. Trained and then encouraged, or obliged, to write merely, if not solely, for others in the discipline, the labours of historians from graduate and doctoral dissertations to articles and monographs have been increasingly orientated solely to professional colleagues or, even worse, those working in a particular subfield or specialization. It is admitted that there are exceptions to this pattern but, it is added, these are just that, exceptions. In other words, historians have failed to attend to ongoing changes and developments in the larger culture and, as a consequence, they have both lost their traditional ('educated') audiences and been out of touch with and unresponsive to the growing popular demands for the past which have been aggressively catered to by other interests. Thus, if the decline of historical study and thought are to be halted and reversed – or, in the language of the day, if history is to regain its 'market share and position' – it must be returned to, or reconnected with, public culture and discourse.[35]

To accomplish this, various strategies and tactics have been urged. These include, in terms of both preparing students and offering scholarly services for such activities: 'public history' – if the demand for the past is so great historians ought not to be ignoring or denigrating it but becoming more involved in the creation of the historical presentations and representations intended to meet it; 'applied history' – if historical study and thought are so valuable they ought to be able to contribute directly to problem-solving and policy-making deliberations; and 'contemporary history' – again, if historical study and thought are so crucial then they ought to be made to address more directly current questions and issues.[36]

All of these are reasonable and probably should be pursued in whatever circumstances. However, these decidedly pragmatic proposals do not sufficiently confront or engage the crisis for, although they do direct historians' efforts beyond the confines of the academy, they tend to be limited to formal 'educational' and 'professional' initiatives and merely call for adaptation to current trends. Unfortunately, what is all too often missing from the deliberations out of which these proposals emerge is an acknowledgement of the *political* origins and character of the crisis. As a consequence, there is also usually a failure to recognize that more is at stake in the response to the crisis than the status of the discipline and, thus, that a grander and more critical conception of history and historical practice is required than those usually afforded in such discussions. There is yet another assessment of the crisis which should be considered here because, advancing a related view of what ought to be done, its problematic arguments reveal in an ironic fashion the limits of much of the 'professional' discussion of the crisis and the challenges confronting historians.

In his book, *Reflections on History and Historians*, Theodore Hamerow, a leading historian of modern Central Europe, has provided one of the most comprehensive discussions of the crisis as he and his colleagues have experienced it in the United States. He looks at the history and nineteenth-century professionalization of the discipline, the contemporary process and rites of 'becoming' a historian and the life it entails, and the persistent concern of historians to validate the study of the past, noting, in the last instance, that recent suggestions to secure a place for history by making it more 'useful' actually have a long and ancient genealogy. Most provocative is the 'historical' perspective which Hamerow brings to bear on the subject of the crisis, arguing that it is actually not a crisis of historical study and thought *as such* but one of the *form* in which they are pursued. What we are witnessing, he contends, referring to the wide and varied development of extra-academic 'historical presentations', is the end of an era in which history has been monopolized by an academic profession. That is, the crisis does not represent the terminus of history but, rather, its metamorphosis. It is not, then, merely a matter of securing or protecting the historical profession by adapting to ongoing changes but, more progressively, of recognizing the opportunities it affords to participate in the breaking down of the walls between the academy and the larger culture. Marvellous! In fact – or, *in any case* – he says that historians need not worry about the permanence of history, need not clamour about its 'usefulness', for an interest in the past is inherent and universal to the human condition. In Hamerow's own words: 'history is of no use; it simply is. It is because the life of the community cannot continue without it'; or, again, more conclusively:

[History] does not have to justify its existence; it simply is, indigenous and instructive, as spontaneous as art, music or literature. It is an essential and distinctive characteristic of all mankind. This argument disposes of the question of the utility of historical learning by declaring it to be irrelevant. We should not ask what is the use of history, any more than we ask what is the use of painting or singing or storytelling. We should rather respond naturally and spontaneously to the deep-seated interest in the past which all of us share.[37]

But there's the rub. In the end Hamerow's prognosis is naïve, a-critical and even, possibly, dangerous. Marc Bloch's words in *The Historian's Craft*, written in 1941 following the defeat of France and its occupation by the Germans, point to the problem in Hamerow's argument when he warns that in spite of our Western civilization's attentiveness 'to its past . . . it is not inconceivable that ours may, one day, turn away from *history*, and historians would do well to reflect upon this possibility'. As Yosef Hayim Yerushalmi observes: 'Western man's discovery of history is not a mere interest in the past, which always existed, but a new awareness, a perception of a fluid temporal dimension from which nothing is exempt.' In other words, looking to the past is *not* the same as *historical* study and thought; or, again, as Yerushalmi poses it, the choice is 'not whether or not to have a past, but rather – what kind of past [and, we might append, *whose*] shall we have'. *That* is not only an intellectual and scholarly question but, equally (at least), a political one, recalling us, students of history most immediately, to the original question of purpose and promise, 'What for, history?'.[38]

As I said above, in an ironic fashion Hamerow's arguments make us aware of the problem characteristic of most of the professional discussions about the crisis. If we turn back from his book to both the social history 'editorials' reviewing the prospects for the field and the pragmatic proposals urging adaptation to current trends, we find that whereas Hamerow proposes but then disposes of the fundamental question of 'purpose and promise' the social history editorials almost consistently fail to raise it and the pragmatists only inadequately speak to it. In the latter cases, both either presume an answer, or possibly (and sadder), avoid or do not even acknowledge the question.[39] Curiously, this would seem to be evidence of 'historical' amnesia – or a process of repressing the profession's memory – for, as we have seen, the original source of the efflorescence of social history and the invigoration of historical scholarship beginning in the 1960s was the political commitment of a generation of young historians and their recognition of the critical possibilities of historical practice. Again, this is unfortunate, because, as I hope the discussions in the chapters which follow will make more evident, an adequate response to the crisis of history will require, first, an understanding of its political origins and character and, second, a *re*commitment to the critical purpose and promise of historical study and thought.

Before that, however, we need to note yet one other, far more ambitious, set of proposals regarding 'What is to be done?' in response to the crisis, proposals also motivated by concern about the professional involution of the discipline but which, although still essentially limited to academic initiatives, call upon historians both to look beyond their own narrow research specializations and to move beyond merely adapting to current trends. In these it is argued that both for purposes of schooling and for communicating to wider audiences, historians should attempt to build a new historical 'synthesis' out of the voluminous studies of a monographic nature which have been accomplished and accumulated during the past two decades. To some, such a synthesis ought to take the form of a *global* or *world* history attuned to the experience of the modern world order within which we live and to the patterns of which we seem to be ever more subject. Yet, there are others, most notably Thomas Bender among American historians (though, as he makes very clear, he is merely rearticulating and elaborating upon ideas originally proffered by the late Herbert Gutman) and David Cannadine among the British, who propose to their respective national colleagues that the new synthesis to be constructed should be a *national* historical narrative for it remains the nation-state which both provides the principal framework of our political and cultural experience and garners our primary commitments of a public nature.[40]

There are, naturally, significant difficulties with such proposals. On the one hand, as evidenced by the two different models, the world-historical and national-historical, there is no consensus among historians on the appropriate focus or framework for such a synthesis; indeed, as the responses to the much more likely-to-be-accepted latter proposal(s) reveal, even among the sympathetic there is little agreement as to what the particular 'national' synthesis ought to be structured around, that is, the thematic which ought to organize such a narrative. Moreover, there is a predictable and reasonable scepticism about the political implications of such an effort at historical synthesis-building in view of the recognized ideological features of previous national syntheses and, especially (as shall be discussed in Chapter 3), because recently the most aggressive calls for historical synthesis have been linked to projects of national 'consensus' and a 'common culture' originating not so much from within the academy or historical profession as from the political forces of the New Right (for which, it must be stressed, neither Bender nor Cannadine appear to have any sympathy). On the other hand, and equally raising the question of the 'politics' of historical synthesis, even allowing for the possibility that there could be something like a general agreement among historians as to the form and content it ought to take, it remains doubtful whether such a synthesis could actually be fashioned at the present time for its achievement depends not only upon the scholarly initiatives of historians but also upon some kind of *public* consensus, or movement towards it (which, as we shall see, appears to be missing at the present time, and fortunately so in view of the politics of the day). Relevant here are the remarks of the historian, Roy Rosenzweig, in response to Bender's call for a new synthesis of American history:

> in considering the problem of history and its public audience, we need to think about both sides of the equation, about both historical production and historical consumption. Who are we trying to reach and why? What are we trying to say to them? In what voice and in what form (e.g., print, film, exhibit) are we trying to speak? Just as there may be no single historical synthesis, there is probably no single means of reaching that multiplicity of historical audiences. Indeed, the problem of creating a historical synthesis is closely tied to identifying a particular historical public for whom that synthesis is to be created.[41]

I shall be returning to this issue in the closing chapter, but I would just add here that I do not cite these difficulties and reservations for the sake of simply rejecting or eschewing such a project for, critically conceived, it warrants serious consideration and, possibly, our enlistment. More immediately, however, the significance of such proposals is that by calling for historians to fashion new syntheses for historical education and public culture, they direct attention to what might be termed the crisis of the *grand-governing* narratives.

CHAPTER 2

———— · ————

THE CRISIS OF THE GRAND-GOVERNING NARRATIVES

Finding the real identity beneath the apparent contradiction and differentiation, and finding the substantial diversity beneath the apparent identity, is the most delicate, misunderstood and yet essential endowment of the critic of ideas and the historian of historical developments.

Antonio Gramsci

POST-WAR SETTLEMENT AND GRAND-GOVERNING NARRATIVES

Neither student rebellion and anxiety at one end of the scale nor the 'advance of modernization' at the other is adequate to explain the making of the crisis of history, its depth and extent and its timing and paradoxical character. If we are to comprehend the crisis we must see it in more 'historical' terms, that is, in relation to the events and developments of those years in which the complex of phenomena composing 'the crisis' actually emerged and began to take shape. It may be difficult to recall in an age of supposed historical amnesia – and, especially now, in the bright light of the apparent collapse of Soviet Communism and its East-European bloc (or empire) – but in the course of the 1970s the Western democratic capitalist world was marked by a pervasive sense of general crisis and, most emphatically in Britain and the United States, *decline*. Writing at the end of that decade Christopher Lasch's words capture the mood which enveloped the North Atlantic states:

Hardly more than a quarter-century after Henry Luce proclaimed

'the American century', American confidence has fallen to a low
ebb. Those who recently dreamed of world power now despair of
governing the city of New York. Defeat in Vietnam, economic
stagnation, and the impending exhaustion of natural resources
have produced a mood of pessimism in higher circles, which
spreads through the rest of society as people lose faith in their
leaders. The same crisis of confidence grips other capitalist
countries as well. In Europe, the growing strength of communist
parties, the revival of fascist movements, and a wave of terrorism
all testify, in different ways to the weakness of established
regimes, and to the exhaustion of established tradition. . . .
Bourgeois society seems everywhere to have used up its store of
constructive ideas. It has lost both the capacity and the will to
confront the difficulties that threaten to overwhelm it. The
political crisis of capitalism reflects a general despair of understanding the course of modern history or of subjecting it to
rational direction.[1]

Here, I would argue, lies the source of the crisis of history.
Beginning in the 1960s but, again, especially in the 1970s, the
United States and Britain experienced a series of political and
economic developments which disrupted and fragmented the
national 'consensus' which had been established in each country
in the years following the Second World War. Perceived as the
discontinuities they were, these disruptions and their reverbera-
tions engendered serious crises in the prevailing progressive and
optimistic American and British national 'grand narratives' or,
what Terrence Des Pres called, our *governing narratives . . .* the
presiding fictions that allow us to behold ourselves and make
sense of the historical world, and by them the status of
knowledge is affected in many ways'.[2] In other words, as this
chapter will seek to demonstrate, the crisis of history has actually
been an expression of an even deeper and more extensive
historical crisis.

Looking back to 1945 one might have expected that in the
wake of two world wars, the Depression of the 1930s, the
Holocaust and the dropping of the atomic bomb, there would
have been little reason for hope, confidence or optimism
regarding the remainder of twentieth-century history. However,
initially inspired by the defeat of Fascism in Europe and Asia and
then reinforced and enhanced by an economic recovery which
became an unprecedented twenty-five year boom in the capitalist

world economy, a confident and, indeed, progressive optimism did come to prevail in the post-war West. Nowhere was this more true than in the United States which, with its national territory virtually unscathed and its industrial and economic strength intact and secure (in contrast to both its enemies and European allies), emerged from the war essentially unrivalled and capable of asserting its political and economic supremacy on an (almost) global scale. With good reason the more than quarter century which followed the Second World War was to be known as *Pax Americana*, for it was a period in which America's 'liberal empire' both replaced the European overseas colonial empires and stood in contrast to the Soviet Union's imposed and direct hold on Eastern Europe and in which the capitalist world economy was effectively built around that of the United States and the American dollar.[3]

Moreover, in these very same years America's domestic order was characterized by the establishment of a post-war 'charter' or 'liberal consensus' reflecting the supersession of the worst economic and social problems of the Depression of the 1930s and the institutionalization of the reforms and compromises of the New Deal. At the heart of this consensus were the State-articulated understandings between capital and labour in which the former acceded to 'the integration of trade unions into the political and economic process, as well as to the guarantee of minimum living standards, relatively full employment, and granting workers a share of productivity gains' and the latter 'accepted capitalist control over production and investment, and acknowledged the criterion of profitability as the fundamental guide to resource allocation – and relatively unencumbered capital mobility and international trade'.[4] Allen Hunter describes this era and the accord which prevailed:

> From the end of World War II until the early 1970s world capitalism experienced the longest period of sustained economic growth in its history. In the United States a new 'social structure of accumulation' – the 'specific institutional environment within which the capitalist accumulation process is organized' – was articulated around several prominent features: the broadly shared goal of sustained economic growth, Keynesianism, elite pluralist democracy, an imperial America prosecuting a cold war,

anticommunism at home and abroad, stability or incremental change in race relations and a stable home life in a buoyant, commodity-driven consumer culture.[5]

This consensus was expressed in a particular *historical* conception of the nation's development and ascent in the world entailing the rearticulation and extension of the classic grand narrative of American 'exceptionalism' with its visions of Manifest Destiny, political freedom and economic and social opportunity. Subject to significant revision in the course of the more than three centuries from its Puritan beginnings through the founding of the Republic to the establishment of American hegemony in the 1940s; informed by or incorporating over time the faiths of Protestantism, Liberalism and Scientism; and proclaimed in various, occasionally contradictory, forms from isolationism to internationalism: America's narrative – its 'Jeremiad' – has been characterized persistently by a fundamental belief in the country's uniqueness and divinely ordained mission. Writing in the early 1970s, the American journalist, Frances Fitzgerald described it thus:

> The nation itself seemed to be less of a vessel than a movement. The closing of the frontier did not mean the end to expansion, but rather the beginning of it in a new form. The development of industry permitted the creation of new resources, new markets, new power over the world that had brought it into being. Americans ignore history, for to them everything has always seemed new under the sun. The national myth is that of creativity and progress, of a steady climbing upward into power and prosperity, both for the individual and the country as a whole. Americans see history as a straight line and themselves standing at the cutting edge of it as representatives for all mankind.

And, returning to this theme several years later, Fitzgerald offered the following recollection (with which I concur) of the history textbooks used in American schools and the grand narrative they rendered at the height of the United States' world position:

> Ideologically speaking, the histories of the fifties were implacable, seamless. Inside their covers, America was perfect: the greatest nation in the world, and the embodiment of democracy, freedom and technological progress. For them, the country never changed

in any important way: its values and its political institutions remained constant from the time of the American Revolution. To my generation – the children of the fifties – these texts appeared permanent just because they were so self-contained. Their orthodoxy, it seemed, left no handholds for attack, no lodging for decay. Who after all would dispute the wonders of technology or the superiority of the English colonists over the Spanish? Who would find fault with the pastorale of the West or the Old South? Who would question the anti-Communist crusade? There was, it seemed, no point in comparing these visions with reality, since they were the public truth and were thus quite irrelevant to what existed and to what anyone privately believed. They were – or so it seemed – the permanent expression of mass culture in America.[6]

In fact, the dominant scholarly historiography of American development in the post-war period came to be called 'consensus history' (which was noted in passing in the last chapter). A sense of this school, both that which it opposed and that which it proposed, is presented by Peter Novick:

> [According to consensus historians] The previous generation had mistakenly thought that the central theme of history had been struggles between haves and have-nots. Postwar historians saw the defense of freedom as the thread which wove American history together. Overall, the progressive emphasis on social conflict was rejected not just as overdrawn but as fundamentally wrongheaded: historians' focus shifted from the conflict of classes to a consensual culture. 'Consensus' became the key word in postwar attempts to produce a new interpretive framework for American history, focussing attention on what united Americans rather than what divided them. In the earliest general statement of the consensus orientation, Richard Hofstadter wrote in 1948 of his growing conviction of the 'need for a reinterpretation of our political traditions which emphasizes the common climate of American opinion'.[7]

Finally, consider the words of William Langer, Harvard Professor and adviser to the Central Intelligence Agency, in *Goals for Americans: The report of the president's commission on national goals* (1960). It is hard to imagine a more confident expression of a nation's status and historical purpose:

> The United States has, throughout its history, cherished ideals of independence, freedom and democracy. The energy and ingenuity of its people as well as the extent and resources of its territory

have enabled it to attain a level of civil liberty, social equality and general prosperity never before achieved. . . . The United States should, at all times, exert its influence and power on behalf of a world order congenial to American ideals, interests and security. It can do this without egoism because of its deep conviction that such a world order will best fulfill the hopes of mankind.[8]

Yet not only in the United States was the post–war mood and perspective increasingly one of optimism and a belief in progress; in Western Europe and Britain, too, these years brought forth great expectations. The British political writer, Peter Jenkins, observes:

In the postwar period Western Europe underwent a remarkable renaissance, literally a rebirth from the ashes of its civilisation. If progress could survive the experiences of the twentieth century then progress was indestructible. This belief was reinforced by the secular faith of the age. God was dead but hope of a heavenly kingdom had been replaced by hopes of an earthly one. Belief in the supreme power of science encouraged belief in the efficacy of social science too. Socialism [sic] became the religion of the age but a broader church grew up around faith in economic management and social engineering. It was complete with a clergy of experts of which the economist was the high priest. John Maynard Keynes provided an Anglican version of the new religion and in the mixed economies and Welfare States of the West a generation grew up which took the advance of prosperity for granted.[9]

Of course, by 1945 Britain, *the* power of the nineteenth century (*Pax Britannica*), had been experiencing for several decades a relative decline in its world position and, now, there were the tremendous social and material costs of having waged a second world war. Nevertheless, there were solid grounds for hopefulness and even optimism. First, Britain had once again emerged victorious and, although it had been badly shaken in the process and was clearly unsettled, the Empire was still intact. Peter Jenkins reminds us:

When the war ended in 1945 nobody predicted decline. To be sure, the country had been greatly enfeebled by the war . . . but the defeated and occupied powers of the continent had suffered far worse devastations. In the euphoria of victory there were few doubts that Britain would recover and hold her position politically as a member of the Big Three [USA, USSR and the UK] and industrially as the world's third greatest power. Policy was based on those assumptions.[10]

And, second, there had been the extremely popular triumph by the Labour Party in the 1945 general elections, promising progressive and democratic reforms and changes. In fact, the six years of Labour government (1945–51) witnessed a series of dramatic developments, including the bringing into public ownership of an array of major industries and economic activities such as 'coal, railways, road transport, civil aviation, gas, electricity, cable and wireless, even the Bank of England' and the equally historic expansion of the State's provisioning of social welfare goods, the most emblematic of which was the creation of the National Health Service in 1948 and the significant increase in the construction and supply of public or council housing. Reinforced by the feelings of national solidarity of the war years and a shared understanding of the need to avoid the social and economic difficulties of the pre-war period (not to mention the already accomplished wartime expansion of the State), these reforms provided the framework for a post-war 'social-democratic consensus' or, perhaps more accurately, 'settlement' accepted by all the major political parties.[11]

Let us be clear about it. Like the United States, Britain – along with the other West European states where the social–democratic consensus was established – remained *capitalist*, but it was, as Joel Krieger explains, a 'politically-regulated capitalism . . . [its] central premise: "full" employment through governmental demand management and increased social welfare expenditure in return for relative social harmony and labour peace. There would be a better-managed capitalism, with considerable limits placed on private prerogative: a capitalism tilted toward a non-ideological social democracy.'[12] The consensus was attested to by the fact that even the conservative parties accepted its parameters: in Britain, following the half-dozen years of Labour Party rule, the Conservatives held power until 1964 and, instead of attempting to reverse the reforms, the Tories opted to maintain and 'manage' them including *most* of the nationalizations of industry – thus, the politics of the settlement came to be known as 'Butskellism', a play on the names of R. A. Butler and Hugh

Gaitskell, Tory and Labour political leaders, respectively. (Something very similar, it should be noted, was also the case in the United States where the Republican Party held presidential office from 1952–60 and yet, operating within the terms of the *much* more circumscribed liberal consensus, did not seek to significantly turn back those developments of the Democrats' New Deal which had survived the immediate post-war years.)

Naturally, social-democratic reforms along with the rise of American hegemony and the loss of, first, India (1947) and, over the next twenty-five years, the remainder of the Empire (except for certain small, though pivotal, territories) necessitated certain crucial amendments to the British grand narrative which had prevailed since at least the Victorian Age of the nineteenth century. Widely referred to as 'the Whig interpretation of history' – though, as many historians point out, with certain variations, it was very much a 'bipartisan', Whig *and* Tory, view of past and present – that narrative moulded not only the teaching and texts of school history and, thereby, the minds of the 'educated classes' at a minimum, but effectively expressed, as well, important aspects of the 'national identity' of the popular classes. In short, the Whig interpretation presented English/British history as a long-evolving process of the growth of freedom and liberal government: commencing in the days of the Saxons, threatened by the Tudors but recovered with the curbing of the Stuart Monarchy in the seventeenth century, and continuing to develop still further ever since. It was decidedly a story of 'improvement' and 'progress' and, as J. W. Burrow observes:

> One thing that we have all learnt from Butterfield is confidence: confidence in the possession of the past . . . even more confidence, perhaps, in understanding the present. The past may be revered; it is not regretted, for there is nothing to regret. Whig history that earns the name is, by definition, a success story; the story of the triumph of constitutional liberty and representative institutions.

Moreover, the Whig view of history was capable of being articulated so as to incorporate not only the creation of a *multinational* 'British' nation-state ('Great Britain') but, also, the making of the British Empire as if these were naturally continuous and extensive features of England's own historical development involving the progressive expansion of English liberties through time *and* space. John Tosh writes: 'the migration of the people overseas, the colonial conquests, and the provision of "civilized" government over inferior races were presented as achievements in which everyone would take pride.' Indeed, as Valerie Chancellor relates in *History for Their Masters*, by the end of the nineteenth century English school-books expressed the imperial assumption that 'all the subject peoples welcomed the peace and order of British rule and that it was the duty rather than the pleasure of the British people to carry out the task of maintaining the Empire'.[13]

Again, post-war developments commanded revisions to this narrative, but they also allowed, or provided for, the persistence of the 'traditional' conception of British experience as a continuing story of 'progress', 'improvement' and the extension and enhancement of the 'rights' of the British people. The new, social-democratic or Welfare-State version of the grand narrative was articulated most succinctly and effectively by the British sociologist, T. H. Marshall, in the late 1940s, in a series of lectures published under the title *Citizenship and Social Class*. Marshall portrayed the modern British state as the product of three stages in the development and expansion of rights: first, following the struggles of the seventeenth century, *civil* and *legal* rights; next, in the course of the nineteenth and early twentieth centuries, *political* rights (culminating in universal adult suffrage); and, finally, in the twentieth century, *social* rights (such as education, health and housing). His 'history' implied that the establishment of these rights, though evidently marked by a certain degree of conflict, was essentially an evolutionary process in which the equality and freedoms of citizenship triumphed over the hierarchy and restrictions of class. It also implied that the development of social rights was irreversible and that there would be further progress.[14]

Undeniably, there were more than sufficient reasons for anxiety in the West: the setting in of the Cold War; the threat of global nuclear destruction; and the far from painless retreat from overseas empire by the Europeans followed by the formation of an antagonistic 'Third World'. Nevertheless, the post-war optimism took hold: 'Whether discussed in terms of the social rights of citizenship, the growth of the integrative capacities of the systems of political representation or the state guaranteed prosperity and political moderation of "modern capitalism" – many influential observers saw in the postwar settlement a promise of economic growth, political stability, and social cohesion.' It took hold so strongly, as Joel Krieger adds, that 'It was, in fact, common to grant an undeserved status of capitalist universality to the atypical arrangements of the long postwar period of relative prosperity and at least moderate labor peace and social harmony'. It seemed to many – and was formulated as such by obliging Cold-War liberal intellectuals – that the West had arrived at the *final* stage of historical development and, furthermore, that it was showing for others to follow *the* way along the path of 'modernization' to a 'future' characterized by the continuous accumulation and expansion of that which had already been achieved. This supposedly historical perspective was well summed up in the phrase 'the end of ideology' which, in the words offered at the time by the American political sociologist, Seymour Martin Lipset, was a product of the 'triumph of the democratic social revolution in the West':

> This change in Western political life reflects the fact that the fundamental political problems of the industrial revolution have been solved: the workers have achieved industrial and political citizenship; the conservatives have accepted the welfare state; and the democratic left has recognized that an increase in over-all state power carries with it more dangers to freedom than solutions for economic problems.[15]

It is crucial to realize that the post-war consensus or settlement was made possible by and depended upon continuing economic *growth*. As Alan Wolfe has explained, speaking of the politics of the American liberal consensus as the 'growth coalition': 'Unlike political choice, economic growth offered a smooth and potentially harmonious future – instead of divisive, possibly ugly, and certainly disruptive struggles over redistributional issues. Rapid economic growth, it was felt, could expand the pie sufficiently so that it would not have to be cut in a different way.' This was equally the case in Britain for both Left and Right. Peter Jenkins remarks, having already accounted for the

Conservatives' need for continued growth: 'for Labour
governments, growth was an even greater imperative than for
Conservative governments living down their reputation of the
1930s. Growth was not only necessary for maintaining full
employment, the cornerstone of the Post-war settlement, but
was indispensable if resources and wealth were to be redistri-
buted in accordance with socialist priorities.'[16]

DISRUPTIONS AND DISCONTINUITIES

Essentially conterminous with the post-war global economic
boom, the liberal/social-democratic consensus survived for about
twenty-five years. There were, of course, stresses and strains
internationally and domestically, and dissent and conflict persisted, for, as we should expect in a class-structured order such as
capitalism, even a 'politically-regulated' capitalism, not all
benefited equally from the settlements and even among those
who benefited more than others, there were good causes for
being antagonistic. Yet, in spite of the many social changes
engendered by the boom, the amount and intensity of the
conflict was truly limited in comparison to previous decades.
However, *contra* the cheerleaders of the 'end of ideology', this
was not to be a permanent state of affairs. Beginning in the
1960s, the consensus was disturbed by a series of challenges
'from below' – of race, ethnicity, generation, class and gender.

The American 'sixties' were defined by major social upheavals,
most notably the struggles for civil rights and racial equality and
the student and antiwar movements. The former included both
the campaigns by black and white citizens against the apartheid-
like regimes of the Southern states and those against the
'unofficial' structures and practices of segregation and discrimination of the North and, also, the black urban insurrections of the
mid-to-late 1960s across the country, expressing exasperation
with the injustices of the post-war social charter. The student and
antiwar movements emanated in great part from America's
colleges and universities, but, like the black struggle, eventually
took their protests to the streets of urban America. Though it
remains debatable what impact student opposition to their

country's pursuit of the war in Southeast Asia actually had, there is no denying, first, that America's campuses became battlegrounds over an array of issues at the centre of which was the Vietnam War and the drafting of young men to fight it and, second, that the antiwar mobilizations fed into and off the even more exuberant youth counterculture of the time contesting the cultural norms and values of the post-war period.[17]

Media attention was transfixed by the action in the streets, but the unrest of the decade was not limited to black and student rebellions. At the same time, contrary to the distortions of television news and entertainments, American workers were also 'in revolt'. As Barbara Ehrenreich recounts: 'The late sixties saw the most severe strike wave since shortly after World War II, and by the early seventies the new militancy had swept up automakers, rubber workers, steelworkers, teamsters, city work-ers, hospital workers, farmworkers, tugboat crewmen, grave-diggers and postal employees.' Moreover, she notes, blue-collar rebellion was not limited to bread-and-butter issues but, often pursued against union directives and through a variety of forms of everyday resistance and struggle, evidenced a growing refusal to accept the dictatorship of industrial work. Indeed, referring as well to the class solidarity of black and white working people against their employers, Ehrenreich contends that the actions and attitudes of American workers showed that they actually shared the concerns of those middle-class student radicals and New Left intellectuals who decried the 'alienation' of industrial society and called for the 'democratization' of America's institutions offering what was to be an unfulfilled – though feared by the powers that be (as we shall see) – potential for the making of a broad, cross-class movement of the American Left.[18]

Also commencing in the 1960s – no doubt inspired by the civil rights and student movements, but very much a product of and further stimulus to the 'feminization' of the labour force – was the resurgence on a massive scale of the struggle for women's equality demanding the abolition of gender-based oppressions and discrimination and, in its more radical versions, projecting the end of all patriarchal social structures and relations.[19] Moreover, following very much in the path opened up by feminism's challenge to the dominant gender structures and identities, there emerged in the 1970s the gay and lesbian liberation movements, the very presence of which provided evidence of the erosion of 'traditional' cultural norms and expectations brought about by both the social changes of the post-war decades and the political and cultural radicalism of the 1960s. And, finally, we should cite the formation of the environmental and consumer ('public interest') movements attesting both to the growing awareness of ecological degradation and devastation resulting from the 'progress' of economic growth and industrialization and to the spreading concern about the motives, priorities and practices of business corporations.

Each of these American developments had its British counterpart. Industrial relations in the 1960s were marked by heightened and intensified shop-floor militancy in most cases involving rank-and-file resistance to management's authority through 'unofficial – i.e. non-union endorsed strikes'. The British student movement with roots in the earlier Campaign for Nuclear Disarmament and, now, catalyzed by opposition to the American war in Vietnam 'challenged the whole range of established attitudes, and helped the development of new left-wing organizations, both reformist and revolutionary'. And, originating in the 1960s but, here too, growing most rapidly in the 1970s was the British women's movement pursuing its own campaigns for gender justice and equality.[20]

Naturally, there were significant differences between the American and British experiences, particularly regarding the issue of 'minorities', both racial and ethnic. There had long been a non-white presence in Britain; however, during the post-war years the 'coloured' or 'black' population grew significantly by way of immigration from the West Indies, South Asia and East Africa (that is, from the Empire and non-white Commonwealth countries). As a result, in the early 1960s there began to arise significant white opposition to further immigration expressing racist hostility to both immigrant and British-born black peoples. Catered to by selected Tory and Labour politicians, such attitudes enabled the formation of various neo-Fascist groups, several of which came together in 1966 to found the National Front whose membership and sympathetic following continued to grow into the mid-to-late 1970s.

Regarding ethnicity or, more appropriately, 'national identity' the 1960s also saw a resurgence of Celtic nationalism. Not only was there the return of the 'Irish question' in the form of both civil rights campaigns by Northern Irish Catholics and the terrorist – or, depending on your sympathies, guerrilla activities – of the revived Irish Republican Army (IRA) but, also, particularly in the course of the 1970s, a renewal of Welsh and Scottish nationalisms expressed most obviously in the growing popularity and support for Plaid Cymru (the Welsh nationalists) and the Scottish Nationalist Party (SNP), respectively. In fact, by the end of the decade these political forces were such that the very cohesion of the United Kingdom appeared to be in jeopardy.[21]

The liberal consensus in America and the social-democratic in Britain held together through most of the 1960s. The labour struggles and 'new' social movements which emerged in those years frayed but did not undo the post-war settlements. Indeed, as various commentators on the period have said, the 1960s may be seen as highpoints for liberalism and social democracy embodied, respectively, in the initiatives of the Democratic Kennedy and Johnson Administrations (1960–8) and the first Wilson Labour Government (1964–70). The Kennedy Administration pursued a truly activist Keynesianism to assure continued economic growth and the ensuing Johnson presidency saw passage of both historic civil rights legislation and the Great Society programmes in pursuit of the War on Poverty in America. Thus, as Joel Krieger recounts: 'To some extent the Great Society programs of the Johnson years worked the integrative miracle of the Keynesian social vision and bought, if not a period of social calm, at least a period of pacification through fragmentation. The urban riots were quelled, student activism contained, the edges of the middle class expanded.' Moreover, reflecting the continuing vigour of labour and the new social movements and the liberal incorporation of their demands and concerns (or, at least, aspects of them), in the next few years Congress approved the creation of the Occupational Safety and Health Administration (OSHA), the Equal Employment Opportunity Commission (EEOC), the Consumer Products Safety Commission (CPSC), and the Environmental

Protection Agency (EPA), and passed the Equal Rights Amendment (1972; though the ERA later failed to secure confirmation in the requisite number of state legislatures). And, in Britain, the Wilson Government promised and initiated a series of economic and social policies and programmes stressing modernization and innovation in both State and economy. These included: the establishment of both a Department of Economic Affairs charged with the task of promoting economic growth through national planning and an Industrial Reorganization Corporation with funds intended to subsidize corporate mergers; the reform of the civil service; the reorganization of secondary education and expansion of higher education through the creation of new universities and polytechnics; and the restoration of Labour priorities in the area of social policy (for example, renewed support for the construction of publicly owned housing). As ever, these reforms and programmes presumed and depended upon economic growth and expansion which were, however, increasingly problematic expectations in the United States and Britain, especially and most immediately, in the latter.[22]

Between 1968 and 1975 the post-war settlements did come undone as a consequence of economic and political developments apparently beyond the control of the American and British governing classes. Walter Russell Mead writes:

> The Kennedy–Johnson years ended in the debacle of 1968, a year of unprecedented trauma for the American empire. The assassination of Dr. Martin Luther King, Jr. [and, we should add, Robert Kennedy], explosive riots in the cities and on college campuses, and the shock of the [Vietnamese communists'] Tet offensive shook the liberal order to its foundations. The most aggressive pursuit of social justice and international security in American history had ended with riots in the streets and the looming probability of America's first unambiguous military defeat in two hundred years. Two ghosts from what liberals had hoped was in the past – Richard Nixon and George Wallace – seemed to be riding the wave of the future, and Hubert Humphrey, one of the great liberals of the century, looked passé and forlorn.[23]

And this was just the start. In the next several years the United States was to be further shaken by its actual withdrawal from and defeat in Vietnam (again, its first), the Nixon–Watergate political scandals resulting in the first-ever resignation of an American President (following the earlier resignation of the Vice-President, Spiro Agnew, for other reasons), the devaluation of the dollar, and the shock of the 1973 Mideast oil crisis which contributed in a most dramatic fashion to what was fast becoming an economic recession bringing to a close the long post-war expansion and threatening a return to the dark days of the 1930s.

In these years Britain, too, experienced a series of national and international economic and political difficulties and setbacks. First, in the later 1960s balance-of-payments crises, devaluation of the pound and declining growth not only disappointed the Wilson Government's economic projections but stymied their modernization projects. Then, from about 1970, both in tandem with the spreading global economic recession and under its own momentum, the long-term decline of the British economy began to accelerate. Moreover, it was becoming all the more evident that the decline involved – in the original 'workshop of the world'! – a process soon to be known as 'deindustrialization', giving rise, in turn, to even greater labour unrest and militancy including politically consequential national miners' strikes. Indeed, these political–economic difficulties made the period 1970–4 one of 'continental-style' governmental instability with parliamentary power slipping from Labour (Wilson) to the Conservatives (Heath) and back again to Labour (Wilson) thereafter followed by the sudden resignation of Wilson in early 1976. Second, on top of these problems, the first Wilson years witnessed significant foreign-policy humiliations. In 1965 white Rhodesians issued their pre-emptive UDI (Unilateral Declaration of Independence) from Britain, to which the Government was seemingly incapable of responding effectively, and this was followed in 1968 by, one, the Government's decision to withdraw all British troops from 'east of Suez' recording in decisive fashion the end of empire and, two, a French veto of Britain's first application for membership in the EEC (European Economic Community). Consider the combination: retreat from empire and exclusion from Europe. And in 1976 all of these were capped off by the Labour Government having to resort to the International Monetary Fund (IMF) for a large loan to stabilize the falling British pound which was granted *on condition that* public expenditures be cut. This, as Peter Jenkins remarks, was 'something which happened to Third World countries'.[24]

Undermined by movements from below and beset by a variety of economic and political problems, the post-war settlements might yet have been salvaged had it not been for the depth and extent of the recession of the 1970s, a *global* economic recession hitting all the advanced capitalist economies and striking especially hard the traditional industrial sectors and regions. So apparently original were the features of this recession – very slow growth, increasing unemployment *and* rising inflation – that a new term, 'stagflation', was coined to describe it and, as the decade wore on, it became ever more clear that the recession was nothing less than a world crisis of the capitalist accumulation process entailing a 'massive restructuring of capital and the international division of labour'.[25]

At the macro level the global recession and its accompanying transformations registered the relative decline of the US economy and the *absolute* decline of the British. And, perhaps most important, it was experienced and sharply felt – though, as one might expect, unequally so – in the everyday lives of American and British citizens in the forms of inflation, unemployment and regional depressions and dislocations. In fact, by the late 1970s, both Americans and Britons had experienced drops in their standards of living.[26]

Predictably, the recession exacerbated the inherent antagonism and already intensifying conflict between capital and labour. Crucial to the persistence of consensus had been that through their organized strengths and the combination of their 'official' and 'unofficial' actions both the American and British working classes (as well as their Western European counterparts) had been able to secure for themselves increases in their real wages and incomes. This continued to be accomplished right into the early 1970s even as capital itself was experiencing what analysts have termed a 'profits squeeze' (which, it should be made clear, was a product not only of labour's victories but, also, of increasing industrial competition resulting from both the successful re-covery and continuing development of the Japanese and West German economies and the industrialization of selected 'Third World' countries).[27] However, in the course of the recession of the 1970s this pattern of working-class advance was to be reversed when capital began to mobilize itself ever more aggressively *and* successfully, in both the workplace and the political arena, against labour (and, too, as we shall see early in the next chapter, against the other forces it perceived as threatening). It is even arguable that it was capital's determination to wage 'class war from above' which finally brought an end to the post-war settlements.

Confronted by apparently original economic and social problems, the absence of growth and, again, the mobilization of capital and its representatives, Western governments were compelled to 'adopt crisis packages'. In their contents we see most clearly the dissolution of the post-war settlements: 'The slowdown in growth and the breakdown of fixed exchange rates undermined the policy regimes that had developed in the period of prosperity. Controlling inflation assumed a higher priority than maintaining full employment; public expenditure programmes no longer seemed affordable and were reigned back; and strict curbs on wages and internal demands were applied.'[28] Stated bluntly, the emphasis given to combating inflation instead of unemployment, and the steps taken to accomplish it, were in deference to the effectively mobilized interests of business–capital. Moreover, further undermining the legitimacy of liberalism and social democracy, these policy priorities – which, we should note, failed to stem the economic and political problems – were first established, respectively, by a Democratic Administration (Carter, 1974–80), and a Labour Government (Callaghan, 1976–9), the original architects of the post-war settlements.

It is hardly surprising after a quarter-century of growth and relative social peace that Americans and Britons perceived discontinuities in the historical development of their respective nation-states and, even more worrisomely, the portents of persistent problems *and* decline: the deepest recession since the 1930s and, since the late 1960s, continuing political and social conflicts along with, in the American case, a severe crisis of its geopolitical hegemony dramatized by defeat in Vietnam and, in 1979, by the fall of the Shah of Iran and the taking of American hostages by the new Islamic-fundamentalist regime of the ayatollahs; and, in the British case, the end of empire and, now, threatening signs of 'the breakup of Britain' plus labour insurgency reaching new heights in the 'winter of discontent' of 1978–9. In the words of the British political scientist, Andrew Gamble:

> What all states faced in the 1970s was a growth in the number of problems that did not seem capable of being solved by ordinary political means. The space for asserting national sovereignty was shrinking; economic management was increasingly unsuccessful; the structures for mobilizing consent for national policies were no longer adequate; and the bases of social order and national identity were under threat.[29]

The perception of discontinuity and decline was registered at all levels of the social order. Among the American and British (and other Western) intelligentsias – Right and Left – talk was increasingly of: 'governmental overload' or 'ungovernability'; a 'crisis of legitimacy' or a 'crisis of democracy'; the 'cultural contradictions of capitalism' or the 'economic contradictions of democracy'; and the 'twilight of authority' or the 'twilight of capitalism'.[30] But not only in intellectual circles were ongoing developments comprehended in the larger terms of a 'crisis'. In his historical survey of America in the 1970s, *It Seemed Like Nothing Happened*, Peter Carroll writes: 'rising unemployment and double-digit inflation contributed to a deepening pessimism about the future'; and, noting the polls and surveys which indicated that in the post-Nixon years Americans had grown extremely suspicious not only of the nation's political leadership but of all the major institutions of American society, he adds:

> The problems of confidence and credibility extended far beyond questions of willful dishonesty, touched the most basic foundations of American culture. The loss of faith in doctors and lawyers, the skepticism about corporate leaders, the omnipresent distrust of politicians – all produced a spreading disillusionment about the competence of the dominant institutions of society. More seriously – and more ominously – these doubts also nurtured a belief that powerful and entrenched groups, in order to perpetuate their positions and values, offered only the most limited visions of the shape and stuff of human existence, of the nature and meaning of ultimate reality.[31]

Even the President, Jimmy Carter, admitted to the extent of the crisis when in a televised speech in the summer of 1979 he addressed the suspicion and alienation which had come to pervade the popular view of government and the growing fear that the future promised merely continuing 'paralysis and stagnation and drift'. Speaking of 'a fundamental threat to American democracy', the President proposed that the problem was neither a military nor a political one but, rather, 'a crisis of confidence . . . that strikes at the very heart and soul and spirit of our national wills'. Yet, offering no new initiatives or directions, Carter in essence wrote the obituary for the liberal consensus.[32]

The recognition of ongoing events as a 'crisis', one involving a process of decline, was all the more evident in Britain. The question of 'the condition of England' – a discourse extending well beyond Britain itself, for the elites of all the Western polities were concerned that the country which in the past had led the way to the modern industrial experience might again be forecasting the future for all of them ('a future that doesn't work', as the title of one volume insisted) – framed and infused British public discussion and debate in all quarters. Articles and editorials in both popular press and academic journals, along with a host of scholarly and not-so-scholarly books, referred to 'the British disease' – slow growth (or even actual decline), deindustrialization, rising unemployment, inflation, fiscal crisis, labour strife and social conflict – and described Britain as 'the sick man of Europe'. James Walvin writes:

> There has grown up a specialised literature concerned solely with the history and process of decline. All major parties pledged themselves to reverse the decline. The topic is discussed regularly on TV, the radio, and in the press. In the form of massive economic contraction, industrial collapse and unemployment, the personal consequences of the decline directly affect millions of people. The British have come to accept that their country has suffered, and continues to suffer, a slide from economic and global power.

As Peter Jenkins tells it, although the nation's decline must long have been a part of the consciousness of the governing class such thoughts were not expressed openly; and yet, by the end of the decade circumstances had so changed that the politics and rhetoric of the 1979 general elections focused on that very issue:

'In 1970 decline was still unmentionable. Now it was official.'[33] (Again, we will return to the perceptions of, and responses to, the 'breakdown' of consensus on the part of the British and American 'ruling classes' early in the next chapter.)

AGAIN, THE CRISIS OF HISTORY

Fomented by severe political and economic difficulties and disintegrating national consensus, the spreading sense that contemporary historical experiences were not only *discontinuous* with previous historical development but that, contrary to the projections and promises of perennial growth and progress, they foreshadowed still further problems and, even worse, *decline*, definitely ran counter to the post-war renditions of the classic American and British national grand-governing narratives. Optimistic and progressive conceptions of history and social change no longer seemed to capture and comprehend the events and happenings which were shaping and determining people's lives and livelihoods. As I said at the outset of the chapter, here, in the crisis of the grand-governing narratives, is the source of 'the crisis of history', the paradox that at the very same time that there has been a devaluation and decline of history in schooling and education (at a minimum) there has been a surge in the popular demand for the past and historical scholarship has been flourishing. In short, lacking confidence in the present and the future – indeed, increasingly anxious and pessimistic about them – Americans and Britons also came to lack confidence in the relationship between past and present.

First, as we might expect, the dissolution of the post-war consensuses and associated grand-governing narratives was reflected in developments in historical education, for it is through the provisioning of the teaching of history in schooling and education that national narratives are articulated most formally and 'officially'. Although it is perhaps arguable that the decline in the number of students pursuing liberal arts majors (history among them) in favour of those degrees, applied and professional, apparently more promising of postgraduate employment was simply a product of the recession and rising unemployment, economic developments cannot explain the turning away from history *in particular* nor the willingness of academic decision-making bodies to allow or to actually approve, as previously discussed: the *reduction* in or, even, complete *removal* of history from the core of university general education programmes (composed of those courses supposed to embody the knowledge required by and defining 'the educated person'!); the continuing, if not accelerating, *displacement* of history by social studies in the schools; and, at all levels, the *fragmentation* of the history curriculum and survey courses themselves. Rather, I would argue, the sudden reversals in the fortunes of the historical discipline, both the decline in the number of history students and the marginalization of the subject in schooling and higher education, were due to the loss of confidence in, and commitment to, the existing form, content and proclaimed utility of historical education on the part of both students and academic authorities – again, brought on by the crisis of the grand narratives. (The perception by students that a degree in history might actually be a liability in the 'job market' was likely due to the hostility towards the 'critical' study of past and present being communicated, as we shall note in the next chapter, by corporate elites, i.e. employers, and their representatives.)

The decrease in confidence in the given relationship between past and present manifested itself not only in the devaluation and decline of historical education. It has been expressed also – and here we comprehend the first paradox of the crisis of history – in the mushrooming efforts by Americans and Britons to renew and to resecure their relations with 'history' which has been most evident in the (also previously discussed) heightened popular demand for presentations and representations of 'the past' and the nostalgia which has characterized so much of it. Peter Carroll relates how already in the early 1970s it appeared to many Americans that 'the only hopeful vision of the American future seemed to exist in the past. . . . The sense of having lost touch with the true America, of having fallen away from history, nourished a new enthusiasm for the American past' – and, thus, in the true capitalist spirit: 'Taking advantage of the wistfulness for better times, the popular culture industries launched "nostalgia" campaigns to merchandise new products. . . .' In Britain, the cultural critic and historian, Robert Hewison has provided a comprehensive analysis of the connection between 'the climate of decline' and the rise of 'the Heritage Industry'. Granting that 'In the face of apparent decline and disintegration, it is not surprising that the past seems a better place', he contends that 'The nostalgia impulse is an important agency in adjustment to crisis, it is a social emollient and reinforces national identity when confidence is weakened or threatened.' Finally, in words even more critical of the commerce than those of Peter Carroll, Hewison argues that the heritage industry 'is an attempt to dispel this climate of decline by exploiting the economic potential of our culture, and it finds a ready market because the perception of decline includes all sorts of insecurities and doubts (which are more than simply economic) that makes its products especially attractive and reassuring.'[34]

I would repeat my statement in the first chapter that we should not too readily equate the popular desire to connect, or re-connect, present and past with all of the commodities and representations produced in response to it, nor should we mistakenly heap all of the recent developments in the creation and re-creation of 'the past' into one pile signposted 'nostalgia'. However, as both Carroll and Hewison describe, nostalgia has dominated the initiatives of the popular culture and heritage industries in the United States and Britain and, thus, it also bears repeating that nostalgia is not history and, against popular aspirations, it has rarely provided for a critical connection of past and present. As Christopher Lasch somewhat sarcastically observes: 'A real knowledge of the past "requires something more than knowing how people used to make candles or what kind of bed they slept in. It requires a sense of the persistence of the past: the manifold ways in which it penetrates our lives" '.[35]

On another, though related, plane of public culture, the appearance of self-proclaimed *post*-modern movements in the arts and intellectual life further attests to the sense of discontinuity and the collapse of confidence in the given relationship between present and past. Sven Birkerts states:

> Briefly, postmodernism espouses the view that a permanent change has taken place in Western culture in the past few decades.

The time line which was the indicator of progress, of directional movement into the future, has shattered. The great eras of growth and innovation are ended. We are postindustrial, post-everything; there are no more terrestrial frontiers. What's more, cultural energies (like our natural resources) are depleted.[36]

Yet, insisting on the discontinuity of present and past, post-modernists do not therefore ignore or eschew the latter but, rather, engage or, better, 'exploit' it in a playful fashion. As the urban geographer, David Harvey, explains:

> Eschewing the idea of progress, postmodernism abandons all sense of historical continuity and memory, while simultaneously developing an incredible ability to plunder history and absorb whatever it finds there as some aspect of the present. Post-modernist architecture, for example, takes bits and pieces from the past quite eclectically and mixes them together at will. . . .
>
> This sort of shift carries over into all other fields with powerful implications. Given the evaporation of any sense of historical continuity and memory, and the rejection of meta-narratives, the only role left for the historian, for example, is to become, as [the French philosopher/historian] Foucault insisted, an archaeologist of the past, digging up its remnants, as Borges does in his fiction, and assembling them, side by side, in the museum of modern knowledge. . . .[37]

Finally, we arrive at the second paradox or contradiction of the crisis of history, that which has made it all the more ironic and galling to historians themselves. To repeat: at the same time that historians have been experiencing a sense of marginalization both in education and the broader cultural 'market-place', historical scholarship has been flourishing. The point is that the same developments which determined both the devaluation and dec-line of historical education and the real growth in the popular demand for the past also provided the conditions for an explosion of social-historical studies. The demise of the post-war liberal and social-democratic settlements and the enervation of the narratives associated with them, freed historians to pursue the kinds of scholarly investigations and innovations previously attempted only by the more radical among them, though admittedly at the increasing expense of coherence in the teaching history and historians' own immediate capacity to communi-cate with extra-academic audiences. It might well be said that the initiatives by younger historians on the Left to revise or radically transform the grand-governing narratives *from the bottom up* which had contributed so much to the growth of social history in the 1960s gave way steadily in the 1970s and 80s to ever more extensive explorations of subject and experiments in method and theory exhibiting an actual indifference not only to those narratives but to the very question of grand narratives.

Thus, we have the makings of the crisis of history. And yet, a key question remains: How is it that the 'makings' of the crisis were actually *made into*, that is, articulated and defined as, *a* crisis and, moreover, a public issue in both the United States and Britain? To address this we must necessarily consider the formation and ascent to political power of those coalitions of forces known as the 'New Right' for, as we shall see – further clarifying its political origins and character *and* posing all the more directly the question of the purpose and promise of historical study and thought – the actual making of the crisis, its definition and placement on the American and British public agendas, has been bound up with their respective, but essentially identical, political projects, the refashioning of late twentieth-century capitalist hegemony through the creation of post-liberal/post-social-democratic, more specifically, *conservative* national consensuses and governing narratives.

CHAPTER 3

———— · ————

THE USE AND ABUSE OF THE PAST

A crisis occurs, sometimes lasting for decades. This exceptional duration means that incurable structural contradictions have revealed themselves, and that, despite this, the political forces which are struggling to conserve and defend the existing structure are making every effort to cure them within certain limits, and to overcome them.

Antonio Gramsci

HEGEMONY AND HISTORY

Expressing in particular the crises of the grand-governing narratives in the face of spreading perceptions of discontinuity and decline, we have seen that the conditions characterizing the crisis of history in Britain and the United States arose in the 1970s out of the ongoing dissolution of their social-democratic and liberal national consensuses. Yet we still have not explained how it is that the crisis of history, specifically the devaluation and decline of historical education, came to be defined *as* a crisis, that is, as a public concern and issue. To do so we must look even more closely at the relationship between history and politics in these years, for the actual making of the crisis into a subject of public debate and deliberation was intimately connected to the formation and rise to political power in both Britain and the United States of new conservative political coalitions. Known on both sides of the Atlantic as the New Right, their ascendance was symbolized (most spectacularly) by the parliamentary and presidential election victories of 1979 and 1980, respectively, of Margaret Thatcher and Ronald Reagan and embodied in their ensuing decade-long Conservative and Republican regimes.

This is not merely an 'academic' or 'historical' problem. As I argued at the outset of this work, and will now address in this and the following chapter, what makes it all the more crucial that we fully recognize and appreciate not only the political origins but, also, the political making of the crisis of history is that what is at stake is not simply the 'status' of the historical discipline, but the very purpose and promise of historical study and thought and, ultimately, the visions of past, present and possible futures to prevail in our public cultures. As this chapter will indicate, it is not only that the use *and* abuse of the past were critical to the coalescence of both the British and American New Rights, to their successful electoral campaigns and, thereafter, to the efforts by the Thatcher Government and Reagan Administration to advance and mobilize support for their domestic and foreign policy initiatives, thereby making both the past and its relation to the present into public issues. It is, moreover, that the persistent use and abuse of the past by Thatcher, Reagan and their New Right associates, *along with* their formulation and placement of the crisis onto the British and American political agendas *and* the proposals which they have advanced and pursued to address it, have all been tied to their political projects of creating new, post-social-democratic and post-liberal, conservative consensuses and governing narratives. The question of success aside (to be addressed in the next chapter), the British and American New Rights' attempts to mobilize the past and history have represented concerted efforts not only to ideologically legitimize their policy and programme initiatives but to refashion late twentieth-century capitalist *hegemony*.

In setting limits to the determinations of the market, the postwar social-democratic and liberal consensuses represented real victories for working people. They were not, however, the transcendent transformations of politics and society proclaimed by the Cold War liberal ideologists. However reformed, Britain and the United States (and the rest of the West) remained *capitalist*, that is, still structured (to varying degrees) by inequalities, oppressions and conflicts of class, race and ethnicity, and gender at the heart of which is the inherently antagonistic exploitation and domination of labour by capital. To recognize this necessarily proposes the problem of order and power expressed so finely by the American economist, F. Stirton Weaver: 'Class societies are not a product of Nature. It takes great human effort and struggle to create and maintain a system in which some people do the work from which others derive the benefits.' Viewed in this light, the post-war consensuses are best comprehended as (remarkably successful) experiences of 'hegemonic' rule and, at least to some extent, their fragmentation and dissolution in the course of the 1960s and, especially, the 1970s can be considered 'crises of hegemony'.[1]

Derived in particular from the thought of Antonio Gramsci, 'hegemony' refers to a relationship between classes in which the dominant class secures the conformity and consent or, at least, the acceptance and accommodation of the lower classes to the given social order through an array of political, economic and cultural/ideological activities pursued via both the State and the institutions of civil society. As Ralph Miliband explains:

> In any class society those who control the main means of domination and exploitation naturally seek to reduce as much as possible the manifestations of struggle and pressure emanating from below. It may be possible to achieve this by relying almost exclusively on rule by force; but such rule is bound to be very difficult, uncertain and liable to sudden termination. . . Far better, clearly, to 'win the hearts and minds' of as many people in the subordinate population as possible.

In other words, hegemony is a process of ruling not simply through force and coercion (or the immediate threat of such) but, as much as possible, by persuading the ruled that *the way things are is the way they ought to be* or at a minimum – and a far more realistic ambition it is, considering that the differential experience of rulers and ruled will necessarily tend to undermine the coherence of their respective understandings of the world – that 'whatever may be wrong with [the existing social order] it is remediable without any need for any major structural change, and that any radical alternative that may be proposed – meaning in effect a socialist alternative – is in any case bound to be worse, indeed catastrophically worse.'[2]

The pursuit, achievement and maintenance of hegemonic order is no simple task. It is not merely a matter of a class – in this case, capital or, more likely, a particular fraction or sector of capital – developing a coherent sense of identity, a conception of its interests which transcends the imperatives of any specific enterprise, and aspiring to extend or translate its dominant position into hegemonic rule. Beyond this, according to Gramsci, a 'potential hegemon' must accomplish four further developments which, it is arguable, are all the more challenging in the context of liberal–democratic polities. First, in addition to becoming conscious of its collective interests, engendered in the course of social conflicts, the dominant class must be 'organized'. This is realized, Gramsci contends, in the formation of an 'intellectual elite' whose tasks are to articulate the interests of, and to lead and represent, the class or group:

> Critical self-consciousness means, historically and politically, the creation of an *elite* of intellectuals. A human mass does not distinguish itself, does not become independent in its own right without, in the widest sense, organizing itself; and there is no organization without intellectuals, that is without organizers and leaders, in other words, without the theoretical aspect of the theory–practice nexus being distinguished concretely by the existence of a group of people 'specialized' in conceptual and philosophical elaboration of ideas.[3]

Second, since a dominant class is a 'minority', if it is to succeed in realizing hegemonic rule it must (that is, its political and intellectual leaders and representatives must) make alliances with other classes, class fractions and/or social groups. And, of course, the participants in such an alliance or bloc must be inclined to support – or, at least, defer to – its politico-economic position and priorities. At the same time, to secure the alliance may well entail the dominant class having to give up or suspend its immediate demands in favour of its longer-term goals, that is, the establishment of hegemony does not necessarily transpire on the original and preferred terms of the dominant class. As Gramsci himself observed: '[within "essential" limits] the fact of hegemony presupposes that account be taken of the interests and the tendencies of the groups over which hegemony is to be exercised, and that a certain compromise equilibrium should be formed – in other words, *that the leading group should make sacrifices* of an economic-corporate kind.'[4]

Third, in addition to the requirements of organization and the formation of alliances the aspirant hegemon must, to paraphrase Marx, make 'the ideas of the dominant class, the dominant ideas'. Obviously, the labours of the intellectuals are critical to this endeavour. Again, to be clear about it, this does not mean – however much the dominant class might desire and seek it – the creation of a one-dimensional culture either in terms of ideology or consciousness. Basically, what is essential is that the dominant class, through its command and/or (unevenly) 'privileged access' to the idea and culture-producing institutions (for example, religion, education, communications media, leisure enterprises), be able to '*define* the parameters of legitimate discussion and debate over alternative beliefs, values and world views' – at the upper limit determining and informing social consciousness and identities and, at the lower, public discourse and the public agenda. Pivotal here is how effective the dominant class's intellectuals are in presenting that class's own imperatives, interests and aspirations as universal, as being those of society as a whole.[5]

Turning more directly to the subject of the present work, it is a question of how successful the dominant class's intellectuals are in shaping and informing collective historical memory, consciousness and imagination by advancing a vision (or visions) of past, present and possible future which ratifies and legitimizes the contemporary social order and pattern of development and, in effect, the dominance of the dominant class. Here, as well, it is not simply a matter of producing and marketing presentations and representations of history which celebrate capitalism and the 'leadership' of the powers that be (though that is definitely very much a part of it), but, beyond that, of articulating and cultivating renditions of the past and its relation to the present *and* the future which are perceived by the subaltern and lower classes as reflecting and expressing not solely the experiences, concerns and aspirations of the dominant class, but those of 'the people', 'the nation', as a whole.

Presented in these briefest of terms, the ideological dimension of the struggle for hegemony and, even more specifically, the effort to shape and inform 'historical' thinking and the national grand narrative – or what the British cultural historian and theorist, Raymond Williams, called the 'selective tradition' or 'significant past' – can seem far more simple and singular a process than it is. It should be remembered that historical memory, consciousness and imagination originate out of the entire welter of public and private experiences making it a most complex and plural development. For a start, the 'pasts' rendered by, or in, different institutional settings – for example, corporations, the media, schools, churches, families – will likely vary, each stressing a somewhat different, and even possibly antagonistic, set of values and beliefs. Moreover, making it all the more arduous to determine historical thinking and sensibilities in liberal-democratic societies, is that the capacity of the dominant class and its intellectuals to actually control the form and content of the 'pasts' rendered by, or in, even the most 'public' of these institutions varies considerably from one to another (consider, for example, the different degrees of 'control' which can be exercised by capital in the corporately owned media, the democratically selected government, and the professionally ruled historical discipline). All of which is not to deny the possibility of hegemonic rule fortified by 'the past' and 'history', but to insist that we appreciate all the more the nature of the struggle and respect the craft and tenacity of those who prevail in it.[6]

In fact, much work has been carried out in recent years in both Britain and the United States into the 'social construction of the past' and many of these investigations have explored in particular the ways in which presentations and representations of the past and its relation to the present are elaborated and propagated such that they underwrite and enhance the contemporary social order and power structure. They include analyses of an extensive array of public productions and reproductions of 'history': film and television productions (fictional, documentary and docudrama); historical fiction and romances; popular history and 'nostalgia' magazines; corporate advertising and public relations; entertainments and tourist attractions; museums and restorations; the rituals and symbols of public holidays and commemorations; and history curricula and textbooks.[7] For example, in a pioneering essay, 'Visiting the past', American historian Michael Wallace has examined the creation and evolution of Henry Ford's Greenfield Village, John D. Rockefeller, Jr's Colonial Williamsburg, and a selection of related developments, and shown how these premier history museums, and the many others modelled after them, were a means by which the dominant classes, consciously or otherwise, 'appropriated the past'. He offers the following summary observations:

> All history is a production – a deliberate selection, ordering, and evaluation of past events, experiences, and processes. The objection is rather that the museums incorporated selections and silences on such an order that they falsified reality and became instruments of class hegemony. The museums generated conventional ways of seeing history that justified the historic mission of capitalists and lent a naturalism and inevitability to their authority. Perhaps more important, they generated ways of not seeing. By obscuring the origins and development of capitalist society, by eradicating exploitation, racism, sexism, and class struggle, from the historical record, by covering up the existence of broad-based oppositional traditions and popular cultures, and by rendering the majority of the population invisible as shapers of history, the museums inhibited the capacity of visitors to imagine alternative social orders – past or future.

Wallace goes on to propose that these museums have served the existing order in yet another fashion. Beyond what they have included and excluded, he says, the museums convey the idea, through their form and content, that the past is 'something sharply separated from the present'. Referring here to the 'antiquarianism' which he finds persistently characteristic of the museums' collections and modes of exposition, Wallace contends that such practices essentially have contributed to a sense of history as being 'pleasant but irrelevant to present concerns'.[8]

Once again, studies such as these reveal that the struggle for hegemony entails not simply the elaboration of visions of past and present crudely and blatantly celebrating the powers that be (though, as I said above, it is clearly a part of it), but a manifold process of suppression, derogation, trivialization, marginalization, and, if necessary (*or* commercially desirable!), *incorporation* of *aspects* of the experiences and aspirations of the subaltern and lower classes. In this vein, as was noted in the first chapter, the many responses to the heightened demand for the past since the 1970s have included an expansion in the number and variety of history museums both in the United States and in Britain. This has regularly involved the creation of exhibitions and representations of the experience of the 'common people'. Nevertheless, this process of incorporation has been a highly selective one. Almost consistently such developments have focused on 'everyday' material, social and cultural life and where a story or narrative is 'provided' it has been that of 'modernization', of progress, improvement and, in those terms, a movement from the simpler to the more complex. Strategically absent from such historical presentations are social and class antagonisms and conflicts and an acknowledgement that there were serious *alternative* political and economic possibilities to that which has transpired. The question, in other words, is not only that of inclusion, of integration, but on what – or *whose* – terms it takes place.[9] (This is a most critical question, not only with reference to museums and similar representations of the past, but *especially*, as we shall see later, in the construction and reconstruction of historical education and curricula currently underway in both the United States and Britain.)

Finally, the fourth requirement of hegemonic rule, according to Gramsci, is that the dominant class promote and 'ensure economic development' which is crucial in industrial–capitalist economies not only to further bind the coalition or bloc, but to attain and maintain the consent of working people. In Gramsci's words: 'Political consensus is regained (hegemony is retained) by broadening and deepening the economic base with individual and commercial development'.[10]

To conclude, it should be reiterated that hegemony does not mean a cessation of social antagonisms and conflicts; such a social order remains an *order of struggle*, one subject to constant dispute and negotiation. As Raymond Williams put it: '[Hegemony] has continually to be renewed, recreated, defended and modified [because] It is also continually resisted, limited, altered, challenged by pressures not all its own.'[11] Ultimately, what is crucial to successful hegemonic rule is that the disputes, and the aspirations informing and motivating them, be contained by way of neutralization, incorporation, marginalization and/or suppression in order to avoid, inhibit and/or prevent the development of widescale dissent and rebellion inspired by 'radical' or 'revolutionary' aspirations and dreams of alternatives. Indeed, the maintenance of the hegemonic order would appear to be all the more problematic and challenging in the midst of an increasingly global economy and particularly in societies such as the United States and Britain where the grand-governing narratives actually proclaim and celebrate the progress of democratic rights and social and economic improvement, apparently affirming of aspirations and movements that challenge the prevailing structures and relations of class, race and gender which contradict them. Thus, there are perhaps no better examples of hegemonic order than the formation of the post-war liberal and social-democratic settlements for it is arguable that even the movements of the 1960s sought and pursued changes to a great extent within their terms and it was not until the economic difficulties of the mid-1970s that they really broke down. In fact, as I proposed in the last chapter, that this happened was not so much signified by the emergence of struggles for change from below as by the determination of capital, in the face of the pressures and imperatives imposed by the recession and the ongoing changes in the global economy and accumulation process, to wage 'class war from above' in response to them.

CLASS WAR FROM ABOVE

Gramsci defined a 'crisis of hegemony' in this way:

> In every country the process is different, although the content is the same. And the consent is the crisis of the ruling class's hegemony, which occurs either because the ruling class has failed in some major political undertaking for which it has requested, or forcibly extracted, the content of the broad masses (war, for example), or because huge masses . . . have passed suddenly from a state of political passivity to a certain activity, and put forward

demands which taken together, albeit not organically formulated, add up to a revolution. A 'crisis of authority' is spoken of; this is precisely the crisis of hegemony, or general crisis of the State.[12]

Following more than a decade of Reaganism and Thatcherism, it is hard to conceive of the circumstances prevailing in the 1970s as having been 'revolutionary', that is, threatening (or promising?) of radical democratic and even (in Britain) socialist developments – especially since we are so often taught or informed that the 'radical' years were those of the decade earlier![13] Yet that was very much how American and British economic and political elites did perceive the situation, particularly, it would appear, corporate capital.

As we have seen, squeezed from below by labour struggles and from 'above' by international competition, American capital in the early 1970s was also increasingly subject to government regulation and controls brought about by democratic movements for the protection of the environment, the consumer and the worker. Moreover, in the shadows cast by a series of corporate scandals, the 1973–4 energy crisis, and a deepening recession, surveys revealed a declining confidence in, and a growing hostility towards (among other things), American business and its leadership. Basically unfamiliar with such conditions, American executives imagined themselves to be under siege and, compared to the preceding years, they certainly were. David Vogel, a professor of business studies, writes:

> not since the New Deal had the American business community felt so politically vulnerable. A survey of 1,844 *Harvard Business Review* readers conducted in 1975 revealed that nearly three-quarters were extremely pessimistic about the ability of the American commitment to private property and limited government to survive the next decade. In a survey of Fortune 500 CEOs contacted by *Fortune* in 1976, 28 percent responded that 'government' was the most serious problem faced by their companies and 35 percent stated that 'government' was the most serious problem faced by business in general. At a series of private conferences of corporate chief executive officers sponsored by the Conference Board in 1974 and 1975, the vast majority indicated that they thought the future of the American free enterprise system was extremely problematic. As one executive put it: 'At

this rate business can soon expect support from the environment-alists. We can get them to put the corporation on the endangered species list'; another suggested that 'the American capitalist system is confronting its darkest hour'.

Along with 'regulation', executives bemoaned the 'rising tide of entitlement' and identified the increased taxes to cover the growing array of State activities as another major impediment and threat to 'capital formation' and economic growth.[14]

British managers also perceived themselves as surrounded and, indeed, if American businessmen had reason to feel besieged then their British counterparts had even more right to feel so. In their case it was not merely a matter of increasing State regulation of market activities which, though marked by a series of policy shifts in recent years, had become a regular feature of post-war economic life; it was now a question of how much further public, i.e. State, *ownership* of industrial and commercial enterprise would be extended. Emerging from a Labour Party pushed leftwards by an increasingly militant union movement were a series of 'socialist' proposals entailing not only the expansion of State economic planning but the rapid nationaliza-tion of the 'commanding heights of the economy', that is, selected manufacturing industries and insurance and banking activities (in other words, the City, Britain's Wall Street), and also the development of 'industrial democracy' in the form of worker-representation on company boards equal to that of shareholders. Moreover, as part of the 'social contract' which the Labour Government (Wilson) negotiated with the unions in 1974 it was agreed that the 'social wage – collectively consumed services and security benefits' would be increased in exchange for union acceptance of an 'incomes policy'. And this implied even higher taxes.[15] Thus, as we might expect, interviews and surveys of company directors and managers registered their rising fears about the future of British capitalism. As Colin Leys found: 'In the mid-1970s a majority of manufacturing executives had come to feel that the survival of capitalism was at stake. They judged that unless trade union power was drastically reduced, control of capital would pass out of owners' hands and profits from manufacturing would progressively disappear.'[16]

Again, we might debate the existence of a crisis of hegemony, but to those who led American and British capital there was little doubt. The developments of the late 1960s and early 1970s were understood by them to be not simply discontinuous with earlier experience and portending of further decline (relative or absolute) but directly threatening to their prerogatives and priorities if not (at least in Britain) their social being. Compelled all the more by the 'profits squeeze' (the problem of 'capital formation'), it did not take long for them to respond. First of all, in both the United States and Britain there was a dramatic resurgence of workplace and industrial campaigns against union organizations and their members both in order to drive down the cost of labour and to actually break the organized power of the working class. Bennett Harrison and Barry Bluestone have written of the withdrawal by corporations from the American 'social contract' and the strategies pursued to restore profits and corporate authority:

> the globalization of production, the hollowing of the firm, outright union-busting, and revised labor-management relations that included demands for the lowering of wages, the proliferation of part-time work schedules . . . and the increased subcontracting of work. Together, these developments added up to a realization of the objective – publicly enunciated by a conservative government [the Nixon Administration] back at the very beginning of the 1970s – of 'zapping labor'.[17]

Similar things occurred in Britain including the sponsorship and utilization of 'Espionage and "union-busting" organizations . . . the Economic League, Common Cause, and British United Industrialists. These specialized in blacklisting union activists, infiltrating unions, financing court proceedings against unions and the like.' (However, better organized and more politicized than their American brothers and sisters, British unionists were better equipped to deal with such tactics.)[18]

Not only in the workplace, but just as aggressively in the political and wider public arenas, capital mobilized to 'zap' labour and its other antagonists. American business had long been organized but the 1970s saw a major revitalization of large- and small-business organizations all of which intensified their political and lobbying campaigns against the ambitions of labour, environmental and consumer groups. Most notable, however, was the founding of the Business Roundtable in 1972. What was special about this group was that its 'membership was restricted to the CEOs of major corporations' and within a short time it 'consisted of 180 chief executive officers, representing 180 of the nation's largest firms'. Moreover, to belong was not simply to subscribe to the Roundtable's lobbying efforts in Washington but to participate *directly* as a corporate leader in that process. The 'politicization' of American business also involved: variably successful attempts at coalition-building among the different sectors of capital; grassroots organizing through employees and shareholders; the establishment of PACs (political action committees) to coordinate financial contributions to candidates sympathetic to their interests; *and* 'advocacy advertising' campaigns marketing not products, not commodities, but the views of corporate America on contemporary issues.[19]

Historically, British capital had been less organized than American. In the 1960s, however, this began to change with the founding of the Confederation of British Industries (CBI) which has been described as 'the U.S. Chamber of Commerce, the National Association of Manufacturers and the Business Roundtable all rolled into one'. Although its heterogeneity was both a strength and a liability, with the 'political crisis of capital' the CBI not only increased its membership but that membership was all the more prepared to join in a coordinated effort to halt the 'forward march of labour'. It should be added that as well as becoming more actively engaged in asserting their influence and power, British companies and their executives also substantially increased their contributions to the Conservative Party (which, as we shall see, was moving steadily to the right).[20]

Capital was, in fact, extremely successful in addressing the immediate questions on the political agenda. In the United States business mobilizations secured the defeat of the major legislative initiatives of organized labour and the consumer movement and contributed to seriously watering down the environmental bills which passed through Congress. In Britain capital 'prevented' the enactment of a series of socialist proposals and impeded or blocked the implementation of others; thus, nationalizations were limited and did not include any elements of 'the City', and 'industrial democracy' went nowhere. Also, as was noted in the last chapter, the interests of capital prevailed in the 'debate' over the priority to be given to combating 'inflation or unemployment?' which in the years of a Democratic Administration (1976–80) and a Labour Government (1976–9), made the liberal and social-democratic consensuses appear all the more terminal and their respective 'policy regimes' all the more bankrupt.[21]

These workplace, industrial and political campaigns in effect represented the withdrawal of capital from the post-war settlements – though, of course, they were in response to struggles which, however much pursued within their terms, were seeking their extension and/or revision. Moreover, capital did not merely seek to win industrial and legislative battles. American and British executives realized that it was important to proceed to redefine the political agenda and, beyond that, to attempt to establish a new consensus, a new 'hegemonic' order, more conducive to persistent and evolving capitalist priorities and prerogatives. They were not oblivious to all that this would require (a problem would be that different sections of capital had different ideas as to what exactly ought to be done).

The first and most original initiative in this direction was that of the Trilateral Commission which was launched in 1973 by David Rockefeller, the head of Chase Manhattan Bank, for the purpose of developing consensus and cooperation among the economic and governmental elites of Western Europe, Japan and the United States (i.e. *tri*lateral). In other words, it was to serve as a vehicle for capitalist class formation on an international scale. Of course there were precedents upon which to build, but this was a new endeavour intended to enhance capital's capacity to meet domestic and international challenges in a coherent fashion *and* to prevent the intensifying competition among the industrial-capitalist states from deteriorating into really disruptive conflicts. The membership of the Commission was to be limited to individuals from particular elements of the respective national elites: those from the economic elites were the 'heads or deputy heads of giant *transnational* firms and banks' (my italics), and those from the political elites were 'centrists' (extending no further than the right wing of the social-democratic parties and the left wing of the conservative parties). Thus, the Commission was composed of figures basically associated with the liberal and social-democratic policy regimes and, in this respect, there was a notable absence of representatives from labour (except for a *very* few individuals).[22]

At the same time, the Commission's operations were designed to involve a cadre of 'intellectuals', established 'liberal' economists and social scientists recruited from the elite universities and research institutes (the founding Director of the Commission was Zbigniew Brzezinski, Professor of International Relations at Columbia University), whose task was to prepare papers to be discussed at its gatherings. In this way, members were to be educated to the issues and intellectuals to the views and needs of the members, and out of the engagement 'understandings' and a vision were to be developed and elaborated.

In this regard, the 1975 'Report on the governability of democracies' prepared for and issued by the Trilateral Commission under the title *The Crisis of Democracy* is most interesting and revealing. In the papers which comprise the Report the 'crisis' was formulated as one of 'governability': 'The demands on democratic government grow, while the capacity of democratic government stagnates. This, it would appear, is the central dilemma of the governability of democracy which has manifested itself in Europe, North America and Japan in the 1970s.' There were references to the changing 'global' economic and political 'contexts' challenging democratic governance, but the entire Report stressed the shared 'domestic' challenges. Although the papers treating each 'region' of the Trilateral world are characterized by the same concerns and tone, that on the United States is most illuminating. Referring to the heightened political consciousness, participation and activism of 'public-interest groups, minorities, students and women' along with the growth of 'white-collar unionism', all of which are seen as assaults on existing patterns of authority, the American contribution by political scientist Samuel Huntington speaks of how these movements were challenging, nay, threatening, democracy itself! Indeed, Huntington writes that 'some of the problems of governance in the United States today stem from an "excess of democracy". . . .' Informing us that 'democracy is only one way of constituting authority' and that in the 1960s it was implemented in institutional settings where it ought not to have been, he proceeds to restate the Cold War, essentially anti-working-class, proposition that 'the effective operation of a democratic political system usually requires some measure of apathy and noninvolvement on the part of some individuals and groups.'[23]

Having identified the problem – from the perspective of the 'governing class'[24] – the Report also targeted the most significant social group endangering democratic government. Offering a brief historical sociology of class hostilities to democracy which cites practically every group – the aristocracy, the lower middle classes, the military, the working class – *except* the bourgeoisie itself, the Report declares that:

> At the present time, a significant challenge comes from the intellectuals and related groups who assert their disgust with the corruption, materialism, and inefficiency of democracy and with the subservience of democratic government to 'monopoly capitalism'. The development of an 'adversary culture' among intellectuals has affected students, scholars and the media. . . . In some measure, the advanced industrial societies have spawned a stratum of value-oriented intellectuals who often devote themselves to the derogation of leadership, the challenging of authority, and the unmasking and delegitimation of established institutions, their behavior contrasting with that of the also increasing numbers of technocrats and policy-oriented intellectuals [i.e. the 'good guys' of the Trilateral Commission!]. In an age of widespread secondary-school and university education, the pervasiveness of the mass media, and the displacement of manual labor by clerical and professional employees, this development constitutes a challenge to democratic government which is, potentially at least, as serious as those posed in the past by the aristocratic cliques, fascist movements and communist parties.[25]

Is it too obvious to state that such declared antipathy towards 'value-oriented intellectuals' had potentially serious implications for historians, especially those of a critical persuasion?

The Report goes on to propose that certain steps be taken to address the crisis, a few of which – such as more effective economic planning to encourage growth, development and social improvement and efforts to reduce workplace 'alienation' (but *not* including industrial democracy) – clearly reflected the

Trilateralists' roots in the liberal and social-democratic consen-suses. However, there were two proposals which broke with 'traditional' rhetoric and registered their desire to *counter* the supposedly subversive influence of the 'intellectuals' of the media and academe. One actually recommended limiting the freedom or, in the Report's words, the 'power of the media': 'significant measures are required to restore an appropriate balance between the press, the government and other institutions.' The measures were not specified but it was added that should they fail to be enacted through self-regulation, an alternative 'could well be regulation by the government'. The other proposal was directed at higher education, calling for its modernization in Europe and, in addition to 'retrenchment', its *rationalization* in the United States:

> What seems needed . . . is to relate educational planning to economic and political goals. Should a college education be provided generally because of its contribution to the overall cultural level of the populace and its possible relation to the constructive discharge of the responsibilities of citizenship? If this question is answered in the affirmative, a program is then needed to lower the job expectations of those who receive a college education. If the question is answered in the negative, then higher educational institutions should be induced to redesign their programs so as to be geared to the patterns of economic development and future job opportunities.[26]

What makes the Trilateral project so notable here is not just the crew of elite figures it gathered together and that it further reveals the pronounced anxiety on the part of the economic and political elites about the dissolution of the post-war settlements, but that – equating the social orders of the Trilateral states with the culmination of democratic development *and* assigning to themselves the role of guardian – it publicly testifies to their hostile disposition towards democratic movements and aspira-tions from below, their particular enmity towards those intellectuals who aspired to foment public debate and/or contribute to those struggles, and, moreover, their intention to confront and contain them. Finally, let us not forget that these were supposed to be the 'liberal' elements among the political and economic elites.[27]

Not surprisingly, in view of the 'status' of the individuals who have been involved with it, the Commission was and remains extremely influential and it has been well represented in the cabinets of Western governments.[28] However, on its own the Commission (and the forces it represented) could not possibly have refashioned capitalist hegemony. It was recognizably too elitist, indeed, antipopulist a 'movement'; too closely associated with the 'failing' policy regimes; and much too easily targeted (especially in the United States) for its 'internationalism'.[29] Yet in these same years there was another, more 'radical' political movement in the United States and Britain which also aspired to refashion capitalist hegemony and was potentially more capable of doing so. It was not, as the powers that be had feared, a coalition of the Left, unifying labour, the new social movements, minorities and women but, rather, of the Right, a 'New Right'.

THE NEW RIGHT AND THE PAST

Even more, far more, than the Trilateral Commission, the formation and rise of the New Right in both Britain and the United States expressed the dissolution of the post-war settlements and the intensification of class war from above. These new conservative movements were in crucial ways different from the Trilateralists. They were 'populist' in orientation and, although they too saw themselves as part of an international movement (by no means limited to Britain and the United States), they were constructed as national, indeed, *nationalist* coalitions of forces. Also, in contrast to the Trilateralists, the British and American New Rights were vehemently opposed to the persistence of the liberal and social-democratic consensuses and policy regimes (though, as I shall note, especially in the American case this position was variably understood within the coalition). However, what they did share with the Trilateralists and were, in fact, all the more intent upon, was the recognition of the need to repel the struggles of labour, the new social movements, minorities and women, to counter what both referred to as the 'adversarial nature' of the 'intellectuals' and, beyond that, to redefine the prevailing political agendas and refashion capitalist hegemony.[30]

At the centre of the British and American New Right coalitions, respectively, was a cohort of political figures who, having captured the Conservative and Republican Parties in the wake of the dismal Heath and Nixon experiences of the early 1970s, proceeded to wage successful campaigns against the feeble Labour and Democratic governments of the latter half of the decade, culminating in the 1979 and 1980 election victories of Margaret Thatcher and Ronald Reagan. These struggles entailed persistent assaults on the remnants of the post-war settlements *and* the articulation of visions of renewal and restoration of economic growth, social stability and political authority intended to speak to both capitalist and popular concerns and anxieties – thereby enabling the formation of the new conservative 'coalitions' or, at least, providing for a perceived mutuality of interest, between capital and more popular social groups. This is not the place to take up a comprehensive examination of the emergence and ascendance of the New Right, but recalling the ingredients essential to the establishment of hegemonic rule – the creation of an intellectual elite, the formation of alliances, the articulation of ideas appealing to 'national' and 'popular' understandings and aspirations, and the promise of economic vitality – one would have to conclude that their leaders had read their Gramsci![31] Our particular interest, however, is in how their ascents to power made the crisis of history into a public issue with significant implications for historical study and thought. As I said at the outset, it is not only that the use and abuse of the past has been a central feature of the politics of the New Right in both countries, but that this practice along with the New Rights' formulations of the crisis and the steps proposed to address it have all been tied to their pursuit of hegemony.

To the extent that hegemonic reform and transformation depend, for a start, on intellectual leadership, the emergence and triumphs of 'Thatcherism' and 'Reaganism' (as the British and American New Right 'programmes' came to be called) were, indeed, bound up with what political observers termed 'intellectual revolutions'. This refers to the formation in the early and mid-1970s of intellectual elites who, by virtue of their being both well-placed in party, cultural and/or economic establishments and extremely well-financed by corporate endowments, effectively captured the attention of the (supposedly 'adversarial') media and through the course of the decade succeeded in reconstructing political discourse along 'New Right' lines. Peter Riddell describes this period in Britain:

> From the mid-1970s onward the views of what became known as the New Right assumed prominence in intellectual debate and were associated with Mrs. Thatcher and her allies. It was the heyday of the counter-attack against collectivism. Economists such as Hayek and Friedman were the new prophets. In the contest of ideas the Conservative Party appeared to be making the running and could no longer be called the stupid party, as was highlighted by the enthusiastic involvement of converts from the centre/left such as [historians] Hugh Thomas and Max Beloff . . . and Paul Johnson.[32]

The term 'New Right', referring to the intellectual and ideological developments of the 1970s in Britain (but also the political and social groups from which they emanated) comprehends two quite distinct currents which were nevertheless united in Thatcherism. These two are 'neo-liberalism' and 'neo-conservatism', the former more prominent in political-economy terms and the latter in social policy formation. Derived from the works of Friedrich Hayek and Milton Friedman, neo-liberal economic thought in Britain took the special form of 'monetarism' (though the 'supply-side' rendition of neo-liberalism favoured by Reaganism was also important). Andrew Gamble has summed up such thinking: 'New Right economists argue for market solutions to economic problems and reject governmental ones. Their general catechism – markets good, governments bad – unites all strands of economic liberalism.' Moreover, following Hayek and Friedman they insist that the economic freedom of the capitalist market economy is a prerequisite to political freedom.[33] These ideas had been actively propagated in opposition to both the Keynesianism and social-democratic welfare programmes of the post-war settlements by such organizations as the Economic League, AIMS (of Freedom and Enterprise), the Institute of Economic Affairs and the Freedom Association – plus the Adam Smith Institute (1981). But most significant in the development and advance of right-wing Toryism, or Thatcherism, was the establishment in 1974 of the Centre for Policy Studies with Sir Keith Joseph as Chairman and Margaret Thatcher as President. The Centre was rightly called the 'think tank for monetarist policies in Britain' and, as Peter Riddell states: 'Sir Keith's role was to interpret the New Right and to set the intellectual tone.'[34]

The son of a highly successful businessman, Keith Joseph had long been an assertive and ambitious political figure, but it was in 1974 that he was, in his words, truly 'converted to Conservatism'. The Conservatism he had in mind, however, was not then dominant in the party and thus his first task was to present forcefully the views and ideas which were to become identified with Thatcherism. He directly addressed the question of the 1970s: What's wrong with Britain? His repeated answer was that: 1. 'the economy is overburdened with government' and 'state expenditure is greater than the economy can bear'; 2. the trade unions are resisting the changes necessary to increase productivity but expecting and demanding more and more from the economy; and 3. there has been a 'running vendetta conducted by the Socialists against our free enterprise system and those who manage it'.[35]

We do not have the space to treat the political economy of Thatcherism, but what is important here is that Sir Keith regularly stated that the reasons for the problems of the British economy 'go back deep into social history'. And he and his colleagues proceeded to offer their own historical interpretations of Britain's political, economic and cultural development. For example, targeting Keynesianism and the welfare state, Sir Keith contended that the wrong lessons had been drawn from the experience of the Depression and the Second World War regarding State intervention in the economy and social affairs. In short, he insisted that when examined closely economic growth and development *and* social welfare progressed furthest in the 1920s and 30s when government actually abstained from significant action and – compounding the illusions about the 1930s and 40s – that people too readily equated the growth of State activities during the war years with the eventual victory over the Germans in 1945 giving State 'direction' of economic and social activity a favourable image.[36]

Even more significant for the way in which it connected with Margaret Thatcher's own 'historical' campaigns, was Sir Keith's reinterpretation of the making of modern Britain:

> Britain never internalised capitalist values, if the truth be known. For four centuries, since wealthy commercial classes with political standing began to be thrown up following the supersession of feudalism and the selling off of monastic property, the rich man's aim was to get away from the background of trade – later industry – in which he had made his wealth and power. Rich and powerful people founded landed-gentry families; the capitalist's son was educated not in capitalist values but against them, in favour of the older values of army, church, upper civil service, professions, and landowning. This avoided the class struggles between middle and upper strata familiar from European history – but at what a cost.[37]

Sir Keith continually argued that it was necessary for *radical* action to be taken, which meant that Conservatives had to reject the search for the 'middle ground' in relation to what he saw as the leftward movement of British politics and instead seek out the 'common ground with the people and their aspirations'.[38] The *historic* project he proposed for the Conservatives was 'to recreate the conditions which will again permit the forward march of *embourgeoisement*, which went so far in Victorian times and even in the much maligned "thirties" '. By 'bourgeois values' he meant 'a further time-horizon, a willingness to defer gratification, to work hard for years, study, save and look after the family future'. Again, this was not associated with the wealthy commercial classes who had been incorporated into the landed gentry but with 'the peasant, small shopkeeper, independent craftsmen, and practitioners of the free professions'. *Embourgeoisement* was not only necessary for the upper classes but for the social order as a whole. Indeed, referring again to the Victorian era he said: 'The artisan of Victorian days who read literature, supported radical causes, was sober and self-improving, gave hope that the workers could become bourgeois.' However, he explained, recent developments had undermined such a possibility. He blamed the reversal of the process through which everyone was becoming 'bourgeois' on the socialists and those Conservatives who had been willing to govern in terms of the social-democratic consensus. As the party of opposition, Sir Keith called upon Conservatives to prepare for government by aggressively engaging the socialists in 'the battle of ideas', confident that 'We share more values and aspirations with the people, however they vote. . . . Our task is to articulate them.'[39]

Sir Keith's own campaign in the battle of ideas included co-authoring the book *Equality*, the objective of which was 'to challenge one of the central prejudices of modern British politics, the belief that it is a proper function of the State to influence the distribution of wealth for its own sake'. Through the work, Sir Keith and his co-author, Jonathan Sumption, set out to show – by way of theoretical logic, historical reference and certain presumptions about human nature – that the 'demand for equality of results' is misguided and dangerous. Suffice it to say that the crux of the argument is that egalitarianism is a threat to liberty: 'Levying war on humanity is not too harsh an expression for the kind of society which is actually being constructed in the name of equality in many parts of the world.' Moreover, in an approach characteristic of the New Right as much as the Old, the Soviet polity (à la Stalin), and the social-democratic project are presented as merely variations on a theme: egalitarianism = concentration of power in the State = coercion sooner or later.[40]

Less prominent than the neo-liberals, but still very significant in the British New Right's intellectual struggles (and ideological campaigns, too, through a variety of highly public figures such as Margaret Thatcher herself), were the neo-conservatives who gathered together in the Conservative Philosophy Group (1975) and the Salisbury Group (originally housed at Peterhouse College, Cambridge). Among the leading neo-conservatives have been the historian, Hugh Thomas, and the philosopher, prolific author and editor of *The Salisbury Review*, Roger Scruton.[41] In contrast to the neo-liberal call for a return to an unrestricted, or less-restricted, market economy, the neo-conservatives urged the return to another nineteenth-century vision of the social order, emphasizing not freedom but 'hierarchy, authority and nation' (truly more 'traditional' Tory values!). Yet another neo-conservative of some importance, but whose views have been quite different than Scruton's, is Ferdinand Mount, a former editor of *The Spectator* (a popular independent Conservative weekly), who was to become adviser to Prime Minister Thatcher and her semi-secret Family Policy Group which was convened in 1982 to formulate plans to 'establish clearer family responsibilities'. In a book titled *The Subversive Family* he attacked not only feminist demands for radical social change, but also liberals and social democrats who insist that State welfare support is essential for the family's survival as an institution, contending that the family is a 'natural' unit and, therefore, should not, must not, be subjected to State aids and regulations.[42]

These neo-conservative intellectuals intersected with more popular groups and 'moral campaigns' (for example, Festival of Light and the National Viewers and Listeners Association) which were opposed to the social and cultural liberalizations of the post-war decades, especially those seen as associated with the movements and changes of the 'sixties'. These groups were to be mobilized to Thatcherism by a Conservative rhetoric of 'moral decline' paralleling that of economic decline and by the fashioning of images of the 'good' society supposed to have existed *before* the social–democratic age and its 1960s offspring. Though limited in comparison to the role of the Moral Majority forces in the American New Right, it is through the neo-conservative intellectuals and the more popular groups for whom they claimed to speak that morality and the family were formulated as political issues.[43]

It would seem that the neo-liberals and neo-conservatives could not possibly have been accommodated in a single New Right, for the neo-liberals' assertion of the imperative to limit the role of the State in favour of expanded freedom of choice and individual initiative and responsibility runs directly counter to (at least) the Scruton variety of neo-conservatism which contends that 'the concept of freedom . . . cannot occupy a central place in conservative thinking' and must always be subordinated to 'another and higher value, the authority of established government'. But perhaps what brought them together in Thatcherism was, as David Edgar has suggested, that both neo-liberals and neo-conservatives saw an urgent need for 'social discipline' to begin to reverse the developments of the past few decades and this was to be achieved through a combination of the rigours of the market and the authority of the State.[44] Thus, not surprisingly we have found both neo-liberals and neo-conservatives revering, and harking back to, the Victorian era (at least, that is, a particular reading of it). In other words, their differences were resolved and the 'coalition' was accomplished by way of 'the past', by way of a 'historical' narrative offering a distinctly alternative rendition of British 'progress' and development to that engendered by the social-democratic consensus.

A conservative 'intellectual revolution' was also pivotal to the coalescence and rise of the American New Right 'coalition'. We might begin by noting the many public statements by leading conservative business and political figures (contemporary with the development of the Trilateral Commission) urging campaigns against the 'adversarial culture' of intellectuals. Among the most notable of such calls for action was that of William E. Simon, Secretary of the Treasury (1974–7) and, thereafter, a corporate consultant and head of the Olin Foundation (a premier benefactor of conservative and neo-conservative 'think-tanks' and academic centres and programmes). In his 1978 book, *A Time for Truth*, Simon wrote that America was 'careening with frightening speed towards collectivism . . . a statist-dictatorial system' and he implored American corporate executives to fight the advance of the 'New Despotism'. In particular he directed American capital to contribute to the 'building up' of a 'counterintelligentsia' to combat the 'dominant socialist-statist-collectivist orthodoxy which prevails in much of the media, in most of our large universities'. Specifically, in regard to higher education, he commanded that 'Business leaders cease the mindless subsidizing of colleges and universities whose departments of economics, government, politics and history are hostile to capitalism' and to transfer their foundation dollars away from their 'philosophical enemies' and to those who 'endorse capitalism'.[45] However blunt and extreme the language, Simon was apparently speaking for many of the corporate elite, for they had already begun to enthusiastically contribute to an array of conservative and neo-conservative think-tanks and pro-capitalist research and 'public education' endeavours.[46]

As my use of the terms 'conservative' and 'neo-conservative' imply, the New Right 'intellectual revolution' in the United States, as in Britain, involved quite varied elements. First, there were the academic and establishment intellectuals who, in many cases, had begun their careers on the left in the 1930s and 40s, but in the course of the Cold War 1950s and the political and social turmoil and changes of the 1960s had moved steadily rightward and by the 1970s were clearly identifiable as a new breed of conservatives, *neo*-conservatives. Addressing questions and subjects ranging from domestic to foreign policy and international affairs, their ranks have included such luminary figures as Irving Kristol (*the* leading voice of neo-conservatism who has been directly involved, in many instances with William Simon, in instigating and setting up a variety of their enterprises and undertakings), Daniel Bell, Robert Nisbet, Daniel Patrick Moynihan, Michael Novak, Peter Berger, Seymour Martin Lipset, Nathan Glazer, Norman Podhoretz, Midge Dector and Jeane Kirkpatrick.[47] Their labours and activities through the 1970s (and beyond) were not only to be well-funded, but well-recorded and well-noted by the media (and, in certain cases, by the aspiring presidential candidate, Ronald Reagan, and his election team). The centre for neo-conservative thought, and its promotion, was (and remains) the American Enterprise Institute (AEI) in Washington. Established in 1943 to promote free-market ideas in opposition to New Deal politics and policies, in the late 1960s and early 1970s AEI began to recruit the formerly liberal and now 'neo-con' social scientists to its enterprise and activities. This led to something of a revision of its priorities but, remaining ardently pro-capitalist, greatly enhanced its intellectual credibilty and enabled it to become, with significantly increased funding from Fortune 500 companies, one of America's foremost social science and policy-orientated think-tanks, providing an impressive array of research, publishing and educational activities in support of business and conservative agendas.[48]

The neo-conservatives' publications were not simply monographic. Arguably, far more important has been their command – by 'capture' or initiation – of a remarkable variety of periodicals. The two most significant of these have been *Public Interest*, a journal of social and public policy (founded by Irving

Kristol and Daniel Bell in 1965), and *Commentary* (sponsored by the American Jewish Committee – but far from representative of American Jewish public opinion! – and edited by Norman Podhoretz), a magazine of culture and politics which also regularly has attended to questions of American foreign policy.[49]

Though by no means committed as a group to the Republican Party (for example, Daniel Patrick Moynihan remained a prominent and active Democrat, gaining election as a Democratic Senator for New York State in 1976),[50] the neo-conservatives were nevertheless quite influential in shaping the 'climate of opinion' in which the Reagan Republicans could achieve victory. They contributed to the cause of the Right in a major way by conducting persistent attacks on the policies and programmes associated with the 'Great Society' of the Johnson Administration which fed into the broader campaign against liberalism. Just as important, however, were the arguments on American foreign policy presented in the pages of *Commentary*. These were specifically intended to 'move' public thought and discourse beyond the so-called 'Vietnam syndrome' which supposedly was inhibiting the US government's capacity to respond effectively to Soviet aggression and expansion (presumed by *Commentary* editors and contributors to be *the* cause of all the upheavals and struggles in the Third World). In fact, as part of this, two campaigns of 'historical revisionism' were undertaken in the magazine. The first was an effort, in the words of historian Walter LaFeber, to 'rewrite the record of failed military interventionism in the 1950 to 1975 era in order to build support for interventionism in the 1980s. More specifically, the new revisionists are attempting to shift historical guilt from those who instigated and ran the war to those who opposed it.' The second, conducted several years into the Reagan Administration, involved the rewriting of the making of the Cold War by resurrecting the 1950s McCarthyite accusation that Franklin Roosevelt had been 'duped' by Stalin at Yalta and, thus, had 'sold out' the East European states to the Soviet Union. In both cases the United States, it was claimed, had failed to stand up to Soviet expansion: in Vietnam because of liberal and Left dissent at home, and in the pre-Cold War period due to liberal Democrats failing to see the truth about the Soviets. In each case, the neo-conservatives' arguments were shown to be historically suspect – if not worse – and clearly more the product of 'political extremism' than scholarship.[51]

At a more general level, neo-conservative writers accused liberals and Leftists of using a 'double standard' in their analyses and evaluations of US policies in the Third World. Here one thinks immediately of Jeane Kirkpatrick's articles in *Commentary*. In fact, Kirkpatrick's writings are prime examples of the use and abuse of the past. She herself was most insistent about the importance of 'history' to political thought and action. Repeatedly in her speeches and articles Kirkpatrick demanded that we learn from 'experience', that we 'take the cure of history'. And yet, her own attentions to the past were crudely ideological and selective. This can be seen especially well in 'Dictatorships and double standards' (the essay which brought her to the attention of candidate Reagan and led to her appointment as his Ambassador to the United Nations and foreign policy adviser on Latin America), where she provided an 'historical' interpretation of the Shah's rule in Iran and the Somoza dynasty in Nicaragua and argued that the United States had to stand by allies such as these to prevent Communist takeovers. The article basically ignored the US role in establishing and maintaining those regimes and reduced the nature of those dictatorships to 'authoritarianism', which she contrasted with the much more oppressive and harsh 'totalitarianism'. She used the former concept to describe Third World dictatorships of the 'Right' and the latter those of the 'Left'. In such a manner, she minimized the brutality of the Shah's and Somoza's governments and, even more shockingly, the nightmares of the Brazilian, Chilean, Argentinian and Uruguayan military dictatorships in which thousands were tortured and 'disappeared' (i.e. murdered). Kirkpatrick explained that her call for American support of its 'authoritarian' allies was not so pessimistic: 'Although there is no instance of a revolutionary "socialist" or Communist society being democratized [1989, *sic*!] right-wing autocracies do sometimes evolve into democracies.' But naturally, she added, such things take time, having already referred to the British development of democracy: 'the road from Magna Carta to the Act of Settlement, to the Great Reform Bills of 1832, 1867, and

1885, took seven centuries to traverse.' One might also note how on another occasion she stated quite bluntly that 'The United States was never a colonial power.'[52]

Alongside the neo-conservatives was a cluster of conservative groups specifically termed the 'New Right' and operating as a 'coalition' of movements throughout the 1970s. At its core was the Conservative Caucus, the National Conservative Political Action Committee, and the Committee for the Survival of a Free Congress, led by Howard Phillips, Terry Dolan and Paul Weyrich, respectively. Like the neo-conservatives, the New Right has had its own think-tanks, the most important of which has been the Heritage Foundation established in 1973 with principal funding from Richard Scaife (of the Mellon Family) and Joseph Coors, the Colorado beer millionaire.[53] Less involved in public education than AEI, but even more committed to policy formulation, in 1980 the Heritage Foundation prepared a massive volume, *Mandate for Leadership*, to guide the Reagan 'transition team' as it moved into the White House. Among its many proposals for change were recommendations to cut back and 'reform' the National Endowments for Humanities and the Arts, which its authors asserted had become 'politicized'. It was pretty evident that what they had in mind was the fact that the Endowments had funded projects which critically addressed questions of class, race and gender.[54]

It should be noted that this 'New Right' was said to be 'new' more because of its aggressive populist fund-raising and organizing style than its ideas. Actually there were direct and strong ties to the Old Right coterie around William F. Buckley, Jr and the *National Review* by way of the New Right's leaders having been activists in their youth movement, Young Americans for Freedom, which avidly fought for Barry Goldwater in the 1964 presidential campaign. Indeed, it was Goldwater's defeat which instigated these young right-wing Republicans to develop new political strategies and tactics. Thus, again, the New Right was intentionally much more populist in its orientation and appeal. Its actual 'structure' was that of a 'coalition' built upon 'single-interest'-based movements. That is, fund-raising and mobilization were carried out by, and depended upon, such single-issue campaigns as anti-abortion, anti-pornography and pro-'decency', law and order, and anti-gun control. And it was this stress on 'conservative', 'traditional', 'Christian morality' in social policy matters which brought the New Right politicos into league with Protestant 'fundamentalism' and provided for the creation of the Moral Majority organization under the leadership of the Rev. Jerry Falwell and the apparent shift of Southern fundamentalists from the Democratic to the Republican camp.[55]

New Right political economy in the United States was also based on the antistatist, free-market and monetarist ideas of Hayek and Friedman, but the Reagan presidential campaign of the late 1970s proclaimed itself for the related theory of 'supply-side' economics. Supply-siders contended that economic growth depended on lowering middle- and (especially!) upper-income tax rates to inspire saving and investment. It was to be popularized in the highly promoted and best-selling book by George Gilder, *Wealth and Poverty*, in which he presented a, to say the least, curious historical argument linking 'entrepreneurial individualism' and 'traditional culture', indeed creating a 'past' in which capitalist activity and Christian morality and spirituality are seen as co-equal. This type of argument served as a major intellectual/ideological contribution to the New Right alliance between free-marketeers and Protestant fundamentalists.[56]

Thus, it is arguable that what provided for the coalition of the American New Right around Reagan Republicanism was not unlike that which enabled the coalescence of the forces of the British New Right around Thatcherism, that is, 'history', for what these apparently disparate groups did share was a yearning for 'the past'. For many of them it was a past imagined to have existed prior to the developments and changes wrought by the New Deal; for all of them it was a past prior to the 1960s. There are numerous other examples which might be cited of the use and abuse of the past by figures of the British and American New Rights, but we should turn in particular to Margaret Thatcher and Ronald Reagan around whom – and by whom – the New Rights were organized to take political power and refashion capitalist hegemony.

THATCHER'S AND REAGAN'S RAIDS ON THE PAST

As the emergent leaders of the New Right Conservatives and Republicans in the 1970s and, then, their victorious political candidates and heads of government in the 1980s, Thatcher and Reagan magnificently articulated the ideas and aspirations of those movements. For the sake of welding together the disparate elements of the Right, confronting and undermining the post-war settlements and, beyond these, creating new post-liberal and post-social-democratic consensuses, Thatcher and Reagan forcefully mobilized particular renditions of Britain's and America's pasts. To address the sense of and anxiety about discontinuity and decline, Thatcher and Reagan conjured up inspiring portraits of the British and American pasts, respectively, and promised to overcome the prevailing malaise and renew and restore the 'good society' and the progress which they claimed had been foresworn and undermined by socialists and liberals in the post-war settlements. In other words, each spoke of a present and future reconnected with the past, the 'historic' Britain, the 'historic' America.

Naturally, as conservatives both Thatcher and Reagan were to be expected to 'speak from the past' as if it really mattered. For example, when asked in 1983 what her 'vision' for Britain at the end of the decade was, Thatcher replied: 'First, we are more than a one-generation society. As Edmund Burke put it, people who never look backward to their ancestors will not look forward to posterity. We are interested in keeping the best of the past, because we believe in *continuity*. . . . Second, we are *conserving* the best of the past. . . .' This was not to be so simple, however, because according to her own arguments in the 1970s, the Left had waged a persistent campaign against British culture past and present:

> We are witnessing a deliberate attack on our values, a deliberate attack on those who wish to promote merit and excellence, a deliberate attack on our heritage and our past. And there are those who gnaw away at our national self-respect, rewriting British history as centuries of unrelieved doom, oppression and failure – as days of hopelessness, not days of hope.[57]

Thatcher was in accord with her co-founder of the Centre for Policy Studies, Sir Keith Joseph, that it was essential for Conservatives to be engaged in the battle of ideas and, moreover, that this necessarily entailed the reinterpretation and re-presentation of the past. Thus, she joined him in the historical project of recovering and redeeming the Victorian period for the present. For example, in a 1977 lecture we find assertions which were to be increasingly characteristic of her rhetoric:

> The Victorian age, which saw the burgeoning of free enterprise, also saw the greatest expansion of voluntary philanthropic activity of all kinds, and new hospitals, new schools, technical colleges, universities, new foundations for orphans, non-profit-making housing trusts, missionary societies. . . The Victorian age has been very badly treated in socialist propaganda. It was an age of constant and constructive endeavour in which the desire to improve the lot of the ordinary person was a powerful factor. We, who are largely living off the Victorians' moral and physical capital, can hardly afford to denigrate them.[58]

Thatcher's Victorian age was offered as a repository of the values and social practices which she could reassert and restore in the late twentieth century. In 1983 she said:

> I was brought up by a Victorian grandmother. We were taught to work jolly hard. We were taught to prove yourself; we were taught self-reliance; we were taught to live within our income. You were taught that cleanliness is next to godliness. You were taught self-respect. You were taught always to give a hand to your neighbour. You were taught tremendous pride in your country. All of these things are Victorian values. They are also perennial values.[59]

Strangely merging somehow with her recollections of the Depression years of the 1930s, the Victorian age Thatcher revealed in her speeches was a time of independent initiative and self-discipline, family care and responsibility, and neighbourly support and cooperation – in contrast to post-war dependence on and control by the State, and anomic social and cultural patterns emanating from the 1960s. In this way she 'historically' articulated – or at least held together – the ideas and aspirations of the neo-liberals, who wanted to expand the domain of the market, and the neo-conservatives, who wanted to restore authority and deference. She did so by proposing that the 'best of the past' was the initiative = entrepreneurialism and discipline = work ethic imposed by the 'free market', and the social controls = paternal authority and hierarchy enforced by the Victorian family and workplace, all guaranteed in the last instance by a strong, though limited, State. Thus, freedom *and* control are harnessed together in Thatcher's Victorian portrait for the present. Socialist and feminist historians rightly responded that her picture of the Victorian age was one-sided, mythological, absurd, and/or plainly inaccurate – at the same time, acknowledging the power of her myth-making and how it exploited the nostalgia and sense of loss apparently characteristic of 1970s Britain.[60]

In a similar fashion, Reagan, too, stressed the importance of holding onto, and the necessity of learning from, the past – or, as his 1967 speech at his undergraduate Alma Mater, Eureka College in Illinois, was titled, 'The value of understanding the past'.[61] In his study of Reagan's rhetoric, Paul Erickson has observed: 'The past matters. We need to rely on it for our guidance as we approach the future. This position, the most basic premise of Anglo-American conservatism, underlies all of Reagan's politics.' Thus he quotes from Reagan's 1981 commencement address at Notre Dame University to illustrate Reagan's declared concern for remembrance:

> My hope today is that in the years to come and come it shall – when it's your turn to explain to another generation the meaning of the past and thereby hold out to them the promise of their future, that you'll recall the truths and traditions of which we've spoken. It is these truths and traditions that define our civilization and make up our national heritage. And now, they're yours to protect and pass on.

Erickson does not, however, suggest that Reagan's seeming reverence for 'the past' was necessarily respectful of it. That is, his analysis shows how Reagan 'moves rhetorically back and forth between fiction and the real world'. In the end, he says, Reagan's representation of the past 'is not history, but consciously crafted mythology'.[62]

Also like Thatcher – indeed, for many years prior to the 1970s

– Reagan saw himself as engaged in the battle of ideas against 'collectivism', foreign and domestic. In fact, more so perhaps than for Thatcher, Reagan's war against the Left has involved both sounding the alarm on 'the Communist' threat at home and abroad and, in turn, making the cause of capitalism a national and international campaign theme of his presidency. He himself identified the source of these views in his experience as a Hollywood actor (while still a New Deal Democrat). It was in the 1940s and early 50s as a leader of the Screen Actors Guild that he says he confronted at first-hand the dangers of government interference in the workings of the market (namely, the movie industry) and, also, Communist efforts to take over Hollywood through the unions.[63] On the latter he said in 1981:

> I know that it sounds kind of foolish maybe to link Hollywood, an experience there, to the world situation, and yet, the tactics seemed to be pretty much the same. But that much rewritten history of Hollywood and distorted history has hidden from many people what actually took place back there in the late forties after World War II. It was a Communist attempt to gain control of the motion picture industry, because at that time the Hollywood motion picture industry provided the film for 75 percent of the playing time in all the theatres of the world. It was the greatest propaganda device, if someone wanted to use it for that, that's ever been known.[64]

During the late 1950s and early 60s, Reagan served as a corporate spokesperson for the General Electric Corporation, which had him travelling cross-country preaching the virtues of 'free-enterprise' and warning of the ever-present threat from abroad of Soviet Communism and, at home, from the 'encroaching control' of socialism represented by the expansion of the welfare state. On one such occasion in 1961 he sought to put it all in perspective. Repeating the prediction of, in his words, 'one of the foremost authorities on communism', that 'by 1970 the world will be all slave or all free', he then declared that the American Revolution (1776) was 'the only true revolution in man's history. All other revolutions simply exchanged one set of rulers for another.'[65]

Though very much like Thatcher in his appeal to supposedly pre-New Deal ideals, Reagan did not nominate a specific period for resurrection or emulation. Rather, as Robert Dallek has described it, Reagan offered 'small-town America', that is, 'traditional sense of place with traditional values' – recommending character-building experiences to develop self-control and self-reliance, along with 'pride in country and the work ethic'.[66] Speaking in October 1964 on nation-wide television in support of Goldwater's presidential campaign, Reagan reached back to Plutarch to oppose the welfare state: 'The real destroyer of the liberties of the people is he who spreads among them bounties, donations and benefits.' He persisted in this theme for more than twenty years, returning full force to it in his 1986 State of the Union Address to Congress. Insisting that 'family and community remain the moral core of our society', he argued that the welfare state has fostered a 'welfare culture' within which the 'breakdown of the family [has] reached crisis proportions'. Then, quoting from none other than Franklin D. Roosevelt himself – completely out of context and spirit – he said: 'Welfare is a "narcotic, a subtle destroyer of the human spirit". And we must now escape the spider's web of dependency.' Thereupon he called for a thorough review (questioning?) of the welfare system. He had told the Conservative Political Action Conference annual dinner in 1981: 'We can restore to their rightful place in our national consciousness the values of family, work, neighborhood, and religion.'[67] (One is compelled to ask if it really required a Marxist to explain that social being shapes social consciousness and that industrial unemployment, urban poverty and decay, and the demise of the American family farm were hardly supportive of such values!)

Since he did not tie his past-to-be-recovered to any particular period in American history, Reagan was not temporally limited in his staking of claims on the past. While Thatcher conjured up nineteenth-century allusions and illusions, Reagan mobilized all of US history to his purposes. From his acceptance speech at the 1980 Republican National Convention through his second term in office, he instructed us in the making of America, marching out the Pilgrims at Plymouth, Tom Paine, the Founders of the Republic, Abraham Lincoln, Franklin Roosevelt and John Kennedy (amongst so many others), to express the continuity of his vision with those of the past whom Americans hold in high esteem. (Even considering the narrowed range of 'legitimate' politics in the United States compared to those of Western Europe, it remains unclear as to whether it was the audacity of the speaker or the oft-cited historical amnesia of the American people which enabled Reagan to quote or cite the examples of Roosevelt the New Deal Democrat and Kennedy the liberal in support of his own policies, which were so obviously hostile to the domestic policies of either earlier administration.) Nor did Reagan restrict his resurrections to elite personages. He often included stories in his speeches which related the past experiences of 'ordinary' Americans caught up in moments of national and international crises, especially, for example, 'incidents' from the Second World War. In fact, Reagan regularly spoke of history itself. On the occasion of his second inauguration, he said: 'history is a ribbon unfurling; history is a journey. And as we continue on our journey we think of those who traveled before us . . . standing inside this symbol of our democracy [the Capitol Building] . . . we see and hear again the echoes of our past'; and on another occasion: 'History's not a static thing. History moves; it never stops. And the American Revolution continues as we continue to push back the barriers to freedom.'[68]

Yet perhaps the crudest uses and abuses of history by Thatcher and Reagan were those linked to international affairs: Thatcher's rhetoric on the 1982 Falklands War with Argentina and Reagan's on Central America and Germany.

Anthony Barnett, in *Iron Britannia*, has examined the nationalistic and patriotic fervour which swept Parliament and the press following the Argentine invasion of the Falklands. Noting that the war 'was pressed upon [Thatcher] by Parliament itself', Barnett's survey shows that Thatcher was, nevertheless, most capable of exploiting 'the opportunity' – as the elections the following year confirmed (though admittedly it was not the only determining factor).[69] Most remarkable among her pronouncements – as Barnett himself clearly indicated by reprinting it as an appendix to his book – was Thatcher's speech at Cheltenham Racecourse following the war. Therein Thatcher pursued her characteristic ways by commencing with an attack on those who might have dissented or hesitated from the battle and then drawing upon the nineteenth century as a political weapon. In this case she offered the Victorian age not as one of self-reliance or family-based morality, but as the Age of Empire:

> When we started out, there were the waverers and the fainthearts . . . the people who thought we could no longer do the great things we once did. Those who believed that our decline was irreversible – that we could never again be what we were . . . that Britain was no longer the nation that had built an Empire and ruled a quarter of the world. Well they were wrong. The lesson of the Falklands is that Britain has not changed and that this nation has those sterling qualities which shine through our history.[70]

Invoking what she termed 'the spirit of the South Atlantic – the real spirit of Britain', Thatcher offered direct and indirect comparison between the Falklands War and her leadership of the nation, and the Second World War and Churchill's leadership: 'British people had to be threatened by foreign soldiers and British territory invaded and then – why then – the response was incomparable.' As the speech continued, however, it became evident that Thatcher was not merely celebrating victory in the Falklands, or even the 'spirit of Britain', but rather she was performing a massive resurrection of past and contemporary history for the purposes of 'class war Conservatism' waged from above against the organized working class.[71] Thus she turned the Falklands experience against the labour movement: 'Just look at the Task Force as an object lesson. Every man had his own task to do and did it superbly. Officers and men, senior NCO and newest recruit – everyone realised that his contribution was essential for the success of the whole. All were equally valuable – each was differently qualified.' There was also a lesson for management, she explained: the leadership of the officers in the Falklands was a model of what was possible and 'Now is the time for management to lift its sights and to lead with the professionalism and effectiveness it knows is possible.' Yet the real lesson was for the working class, the particular target at that moment being the National Union of Railwaymen, though eventually (1984–5), as we know, it was to be the mineworkers: 'What has indeed happened is that now once again Britain is not prepared to be pushed around.' (For 'Britain' read 'capitalist state'.)[72]

Again, Reagan's use and abuse of the past was not limited to any particular period of American history. Neither did his historical imagination stop at America's borders. This can be seen especially well in his propaganda campaign against the Sandinistas and his many attempts to secure funds for the *contras*. In its first term the Reagan Administration repeatedly made false or exaggerated assertions regarding the Nicaraguan government's domestic and foreign policies at the same time that the Central Intelligence Agency (CIA) was covertly setting up, training and supporting exiled Somozista–National Guardsmen in guerrilla *and* terrorist tactics. In early 1985, following the 1984 elections, the Reagan Administration revised its rhetorical campaign to secure congressional and popular support for supplying the *contras* with aid and equipment (made necessary by an earlier ban established by Congress). Not only were the Sandinistas viciously portrayed as 'puppets of the Cubans and Soviets' and purveyors of 'drugs, terrorism and communism', but now the *contras* came to be defined as 'freedom fighters' – and were thereby elevated to a status previously reserved for the Hungarians who had risen against the Soviets in 1956. Moreover, the entire campaign was framed in historical terms. A prime example of this is found in Reagan's weekly national radio address of 16 February 1985. Grossly misrepresenting past and present, Reagan described the *contras* as 'democratic resistance fighters' whose revolution was betrayed by the Sandinistas and he called upon the American people not to forsake their internationalist tradition: 'Time and again in the course of our history, we've aided those around the world struggling for freedom, democracy, independence, and liberation from tyranny.' In the lines which followed he raised up the images of the two world wars and the American Revolution of 1776. Attending to the last he invoked the names to which ethnic-conscious Americans could not help but be drawn: 'America may never have been born without the help and support of the freedom-loving people of Europe, of Lafayette and Von Steuben and Kosciusko. And America did not forget.' Three weeks later, once again speaking at a Conservative Political Action Conference annual dinner, Reagan referred to the 'freedom fighters' in Afghanistan, Angola, Kampuchea and Central America, saying specifically of the *contras*: 'They are the moral equal of our Founding Fathers and the brave men and women of the French Resistance.' (The observation offered by the Editors of *In These Times*, the independent American socialist weekly, is worth recording. They suggested that Reagan had his history upside down, for if anything, Reagan himself would be better cast as George III than Lafayette.)[73]

In the same period, Reagan was capable of misrepresenting and denigrating one of the finer examples of American 'internationalism', the volunteering for the Abraham Lincoln Brigade by young Americans, Communists and others, to fight in the Spanish Civil War (1936–9). Committed to defending the Republican government against Franco's ultimately successful rebellion of right-wing and Fascist forces (which was directly aided by Hitler's Nazi Germany and Mussolini's Fascist Italy), the Lincoln Brigade was nastily and wrongly described by Reagan as having been viewed by 'most Americans' as 'fighting on the wrong side'. And yet, this did not keep him, while on an official visit to Spain several months later, from citing the Lincoln Brigade as a precedent for Americans to send 'aid' to the Nicaraguan *contras*![74]

There is so much which might be detailed in any accounting of Reagan's use and abuse of the past. But surely the crudest and most vulgar of his 'historical' assessments was his remark explaining his 1985 visit to a German military cemetery in Bitburg where soldiers of the infamous Waffen SS are buried. Responding to a reporter's question regarding why he did not drop the visit to the cemetery, as requested by fifty-three US Senators and numerous veterans' and American Jewish organizations, Reagan bluntly stated that those Nazis 'were victims, just as surely as the victims in the concentration camps'. This remark was seemingly removed from Reagan's New Right agenda and thus – though still outrageously inexcusable – might easily have been attributed to a lapse of thought (not uncharacteristic of Reagan in his second term). Such statements, however, were made by Reagan through the entire course of the controversy surrounding the itinerary of his visit to West Germany as part of his West European tour in commemoration of the fortieth anniversary of the end of the Second World War in Europe. But, indeed, the past did matter – in the United States and in Germany – for Reagan's attempt to reconstrue history was very much a part of his effort to support the German Right and thereby secure the West German government's continued cooperation on the stationing of nuclear armaments and eventually 'Star Wars'. Moreover, at the very same time there was beginning the campaign by 'neo-conservative' German historians – with the encouragement of a variety of New Right political and public figures – to rewrite the German war experience and the Holocaust in order to historically 'relativize' (in effect, 'justify') the latter and remove the German 'nation' from the 'shadows' of Hitler's Third Reich.[75]

Writing in 1985 in the twentieth anniversary issue of *The Public Interest*, sociologist Robert Nisbet presented 'The conservative renaissance in perspective'. Though his historical analysis focused on the resurgence of the conservative political tradition in the United States during the 1960s and 70s, his conclusion spoke in more universal terms. He observed that:

> A brilliant French critic, Emile Faguet, called the first generation of conservatives in Europe 'prophets of the past'. That is very good. They speak by design from the past and often about the past. Churchill said he loved the past, was uneasy about the present, and feared the future. Clement Atlee once said Churchill['s] mind was like a layer cake with each layer a different century, including one 'which may have been the twenty-first'. But for all that Churchill was considerably ahead of his partners, including FDR, in his grasp of the present and its imperatives.
>
> Prophets the conservatives may be, but they have also been, and will doubtless continue to be, guerrillas of the past. Their sorties in politics, economics, education, and a great deal of the whole cultural area have been among the high water levels of history the last 200 years in both America and Britain, and indeed other parts of the West. I suspect that traditional conservatives will remain prophets and guerrillas of the past.[76]

In the light of Thatcher's and Reagan's pronouncements on the past, we must register our dissent when Nisbet refers to conservatives as 'guerrillas of the past'. Surely, at least Thatcher and Reagan would be more appropriately defined as having been 'terrorists', for their raids on history are well captured by a definition of 'terror' found in the *American Heritage Dictionary*: 'A policy of violence aiming to achieve or maintain supremacy.'[77] Though we have not descended to an Orwellian scenario, Thatcher's and Reagan's rhetoric and initatives demand that we do not soon forget O'Brien's ominous words in the novel *1984*: 'Those who control the present control the past . . . those who control the past control the present.'[78]

THE NEW RIGHTS' HISTORICAL EDUCATION PROJECTS

We have seen that 'the past' was crucial to both the coalescence of the forces of the British and American New Rights, respectively, and to their waging of the battle of ideas both against the surviving post-war settlements and in favour of new, conservative consensuses. In essence, they contested not only the present and the future but the past as well and in so doing they effectively made it and its relation to the present into a public issue. But this was not the only way in which the New Rights advanced 'history' to the forefront of public debate and discourse. They also formulated the decline of historical education as an issue, as a 'crisis' warranting public attention and political action. Of course, it is only natural that the New Rights, intent upon refashioning capitalist hegemony, should be concerned about educational questions, especially those of historical education. As the *Annales* historian, Marc Ferro, writes in his international survey of historical education and the myths propagated in each instance: 'Our image of other peoples, or of ourselves for that matter, reflects the history we are taught as children. This history marks us for life. Its representation, which is for each one of us a discovery of the world, of the past of societies, embraces all our passing or permanent opinions, so that traces of our first questioning, our first emotions, remain indelible.'[79]

The historical curriculum of public education is the most official, the most authoritative, articulation of a nation-state's 'selective tradition', its grand-governing narrative. Thus, it is an essential target – arguably, *the* essential target – of a hegemonic project.

It has been noted repeatedly in this chapter that a declared intention of the ideological campaigns of the New Right (with the eager support of corporate interests) was the ambition to counter the 'value-oriented intellectuals', humanists and social scientists, historians included if not especially. In fact, the questions of history, historical practice, and historical memory, consciousness and imagination were fundamental to the New Right. Friedrich (F. A.) von Hayek, one of the intellectual 'fathers' of New Right political economy and philosophy is well remembered for his definition of state intervention in economic and social affairs *as*, in the title of his best-known book, *The Road to Serfdom*. Less often referred to, but not forgotten by his followers and admirers, were his admonitions about historical thought and historians as public intellectuals. Just after the Second World War (April 1947) Hayek organized the Mont Pélérin Society (after the place in Switzerland where its first meetings were held).[80] Recognized as the foundation of the free-market, (neo-)liberal movement of what was to become the New Right, the Society's original European and American member-ship consisted of historians, economists, political scientists, jurists and social philosophers concerned about what they perceived to be the declining belief in and commitment to 'private property and the competitive market'. Notable is that their 'Statement of aims' not only called for examining and addressing the 'present crisis' but, also, for the development of 'methods of combating the misuse of history for the furtherance of creeds hostile to liberty':

> The central values of civilisation are in danger. Over large stretches of the earth's surface the essential conditions of human dignity and freedom have disappeared. . . . The position of the individual and the voluntary are progressively undermined by the extensions of arbitrary power. . . The group holds that *these developments have been fostered by the growth of a view of history which denies all absolute moral standards* and by the growth of theories which question the desirability of the rule of law.[81]

A few years later, at a Mont Pélérin Society Conference on the 'treatment of capitalism by historians', Hayek himself spoke directly to the problem of the 'power' and 'influence' of historians:

Political opinion and views about historical events ever have been and always must be closely connected. Past experience is the foundation on which our beliefs about the desirability of different policies and institutions are mainly based, and our present political views inevitably affect and color our interpretation of the past. . . . There is scarcely a political ideal or concept which does not involve opinions about a whole series of past events, and there are few historical memories which do not serve as a symbol of some political aim. . . . The influence which the writers of history thus exercise on public opinion is probably more immediate and extensive than that of the political theorists who launch new ideas. It seems as though even such new ideas reach wider circles usually not in their abstract form but as the interpretation of particular events. The historian is in this respect at least one step nearer to direct power over public opinion than is the theorist.

What concerned him most was that contemporary political thought had (supposedly) come to be 'governed' by a 'socialist interpretation of history', a 'particular view of economic history' antipathetic to capitalism. As a consequence, he contended, public discourse was characterized by a variety of historical 'myths', one of which apparently vexed him beyond all others:

There is . . . one supreme myth which more than any other has seemed to discredit the economic system to which we owe our present-day civilization and to which the present volume [stemming from the conference at which he spoke] is devoted. It is the legend of the deterioration of the position of the working classes in consequence of the rise of capitalism.[82]

Hayek insisted that the supposed 'facts' supporting the decline of the living standards of working people in the Industrial Revolution 'have long been proved not to have been facts at all'. (We should note, however, that his own assertions were hardly unanimously subscribed to by 'professional economic historians' and the question has remained a contentious one.)[83]

Nevertheless, if Hayek and his associates were anxious about historical thought and historiography in the 1940s and 50s, then, in the light of the development of 'radical' and 'critical' history in the 1960s and the ascendance of social history and history from the bottom up in the years following, it is hardly surprising that conservatives and neo-conservatives were to be so troubled and, moreover, motivated to do something about the 'new' Left historians. Never failing to ascribe the fault to the Left, the spokespersons of the British and American New Rights proceeded to link the difficulties of their respective nation-states to the decline of historical education. That is, they formulated the 'crisis of history' in Britain and the United States as being the product of the rise of the adversarial culture, specifically radical history and historians, and as contributing to their national economic, political and moral problems and 'impending' decline. Thus, among the steps they declared necessary to reverse the latter process was the renewal of historical education. This would require, they claimed, redressing not only the marginalization of history in schooling but, also, its content *and* confronting those who, they claimed, were responsible for it.

In 1975, at a North American meeting of the Mont Pélérin Society honouring Hayek and his work, the British historian, R. M. Hartwell, who had himself been actively engaged in attempting to combat the 'myths' about the Industrial Revolution, returned to the problem of 'capitalism and the historians'. Speaking of the power of 'intellectuals' to shape public opinion he stated: 'Unfortunately, for the health of a free society . . . the intellectuals since the Enlightenment have had "progressive" views; in the eighteenth and nineteenth centuries, democratic and egalitarian views; and in the twentieth century, interventionist and socialist views.' And, bemoaning the persistently intimate connection between socialist intellectuals and historians of modern capitalism, he proposed a means by which the Right might pursue the battle of ideas in favour of capitalism: 'History, universally taught at all levels of education and widely read by the general public, should be seen for its potential as an important weapon in ideological conflict.'[84] His was to be one of many voices of the Right urging action on historical education, though his political comrades more often talked *not* in the blunt terms of 'capitalism' but in those of 'the nation' and 'nationalism'.

As the Opposition in the later 1970s, the Conservatives made it a theme of their rhetoric on education. Dr Rhodes Boyson, Tory shadow spokesperson and, later, Under-Secretary of State for Education, declaimed that: 'society will be destroyed unless our children are again taught the unique qualities of British history and institutions. They are now increasingly fed on a diet of watered-down, vague world history, with parts of the media using every opportunity to provide platforms for sad and ill-mannered young men to decry our past.'[85] Margaret Thatcher herself has already been quoted above regarding 'those who gnaw away at our national self-respect, rewriting British history as centuries of unrelieved doom, oppression and failure'. In 1979 she attuned this point to the specific problem of education: 'a whole generation has been brought up to misunderstand and denigrate our national history. Far the blackest picture is drawn by our socialist academics and writers of precisely those periods of our history when greatest progress was achieved.'[86]

Similar words were being voiced by leaders of the New Right in the United States. Irving Kristol (as noted above, the top figure of neo-conservatism and partner with William Simon in a series of New Right ventures) repeatedly argued in the 1970s in his *Wall Street Journal* column that American college students were becoming 'anti-business' because of what they learned from 'value-forming humanities professors' in such disciplines as 'history'. Engaged during the bicentennial of American independence in a campaign to 'deradicalize' the American Revolution which was described by Sidney Blumenthal as 'historical revision' for the purpose of 'bolster[ing] his own political position', Kristol nevertheless insisted that 'The average college professor of history, sociology, literature . . . is just as inclined to prefer fantasy over reality.'[87]

Ronald Reagan, too, had occasion to speak against (Left) academics, first as a candidate and then as Governor of California (1967–71; public higher education is organized and funded by the respective states). In 1970, in a speech titled 'What is academic freedom?', Reagan levelled an accusation at faculty who refused to assert that 'there are any absolutes' when he added: 'Strangely and illogically this is very often the same educator who interprets his academic freedom as the right to indoctrinate students with his view of things', and 'The student generation is being wooed by many who charge that this way we have known is inadequate to meet the challenges of our times.' He had stated a few years earlier what he would have:

> If scholars are to be recognized as having a right to press their particular value judgements, perhaps the time has come also for institutions of higher learning to assert themselves as positive forces in the battles for men's minds . . . and [we] might even call on them to be proponents of those ethical and moral standards demanded by the great majority of our society.[88]

As Prime Minister and President, respectively, Thatcher and Reagan were able to act on their 'anxieties', and their appointments to head their governments' departments of education made historical pedagogy and appreciation central concerns of their offices (if not fiscally, at least rhetorically).

In 1981 Thatcher reshuffled her Cabinet and Sir Keith Joseph moved from Industry to the post once held by Thatcher herself a decade earlier in the Heath Government, Secretary of State for Education. In 1983 Sir Keith announced a set of initiatives which involved reform of the school curricula in several subjects including physics, English *and* history. An important aspect of the changes to be carried out was the 'nationalization' of the curriculum in these fields. As part of his campaign to garner support for the scheme, Sir Keith presented the keynote address to the Historical Association Conference in February 1984. Speaking of the crisis of the historical discipline he stressed the political, economic and cultural significance of historical education, and in classically Conservative terms he stated that 'one of the aims of studying history is to understand the development of the *shared values* which are a distinctive feature of British society and culture and which continue to shape private attitudes and public policy.' We should also note his statement – to which I believe any good soul of the Left would subscribe – that

> It is particularly salutary that pupils are brought to realize that the ideas and values as well as the material conditions which they take for granted were acquired through processes which are often painful and difficult and that the institutions we most value were won at a price in human endeavour: a price that continues to be asked of each succeeding generation.[89]

Of course, the real question was *how* this was to be realized – *whose* vision of British experience would define this 'national curriculum'?

In the months which followed, Sir Keith energetically pursued his campaign for reform. In response to criticism, he denied that his plans included making the teaching of history more 'nationalistic', though he did command that it should 'foster a sense of pride in one's country and its achievements'.[90] In one sense this is quite reasonable, for as the English Marxist historian, Christopher Hill, declared in reaction to Sir Keith's call: 'We have much to be proud of in our past . . . one of the great literatures of the world, much of it on the side of freedom . . . [also] the creative achievements of the British people . . . [e.g.] traditions of popular resistance to tyranny.' (At the same time, however, Hill did not fail to add that 'We have a great deal to be ashamed of in our history', citing the slave trade, the plundering of India and Africa, the opium trade, etc.)[91] But Sir Keith's project entailed more than an appreciation of the British past. The nationalization of the history curriculum arose not simply out of an intention to arrest the decline in young Britons' historical education and knowledge, but, also, out of Thatcher's and Joseph's desire to turn the teaching of history to Conservative purposes in the 'battle of ideas'. As *The Times* reported it, the Thatcher Government was concerned about what they considered to be leftist 'bias in the classroom'.[92]

Related to all this, we should recall an episode of ten years earlier during the Heath Government in which Margaret Thatcher was Secretary of State for Education. In January 1973 the story broke that the Conservative Party was providing so-called 'political education' conferences for sixth-formers which were being organized through the schools, apparently taking advantage of there being a Tory government in power. Noting the location chosen for these conferences, and the continuing dramatic decline in the number of Young Conservatives, *The Times* reported that the conferences 'were the first stage of a nationwide plan to make the party's presence felt among new voters in marginal constituencies'. Speaking as Secretary of State for Education, Mrs Thatcher rejected a demand by Labour for an enquiry on the grounds that 'curriculum was subject to the control of the local education authority in a primary school and of the governors in a secondary school.' A few weeks later, once again confronted on the issue in the House of Commons, she stated: 'This House has given me no specific powers over secular education. The history of British education is to keep ministers out of control of curriculum matters.'[93] Nevertheless, a decade later she would have her own education minister break, radically, with that 'tradition'.

It should be noted that Sir Keith was by no means alone in publicly pushing for a national history curriculum to instil pride in Britain's achievements. So, too, did Lord Hugh Thomas, retired Professor of History at Reading University and a close personal adviser to Margaret Thatcher. Even more significant in the historical profession, Geoffrey Elton was making use of his new status as Regius Professor of History at Cambridge University to call for a renewed commitment to the teaching of *English* history. For almost twenty years he had been preaching against innovation in historical studies – against, that is, as was briefly noted in Chapter 1, *social* history and *international* studies – and decrying what he interpreted to be the increasingly critical perspective which historians were taking on England's past. On at least one occasion he proposed that 'the historian's task consists among other things, if I may so put it, in a crude re-kindling of a certain respect for a country whose past justifies that respect.' Returning to this theme in 1984 (after the Falklands War and the Tories' second election victory) Elton said in the inaugural lecture of his Regius professorship: 'A *New Statesman* era like ours, full of self-deprecation and envy, can do with the corrective of a past that demonstrates virtue and achievement.' Suggesting certain themes to be pursued he urged that English history be taught emphasizing its length and 'continuity'.[94] To be clear about it, when Conservatives – whether Sir Keith Joseph or Geoffrey Elton – demand that history emphasize 'shared values' and 'continuity' they are essentially dismissing the study of social divisions, exploitation and oppression, and the struggles from below to overcome them and proposing a view of British history as essentially already 'achieved'.

Sir Keith Joseph's counterpart in the United States was William J. Bennett, who ascended from the directorship of the corporately endowed National Center for the Humanities in

North Carolina to the head of the National Endowment for the Humanities (the NEH is a federal agency), a position he held until early 1985 when Reagan appointed him Secretary of Education.[95] Prior to his government posts, Bennett, an academic philosopher, had been a regular contributor to neo-conservative journals, a co-author of an anti-affirmative action text, *Counting by Race: Equality from the founding fathers to 'Bakke' and 'Weber'*,[96] and a consultant and contributing author to the aforementioned Heritage Foundation volume prepared for the Reagan presidential 'transition team'.

While heading the NEH, Bennett authored *To Reclaim A Legacy*, a report on the state of the humanities in higher education which was extremely critical of how these subjects had been allowed to decline in university curricula over the previous two decades. Specific recommendations were offered towards their 'revitalization' and 'restoration', and history was assigned a leading role in the crusade. The study of 'at least one non-Western culture' was cited as essential, but primary emphasis was given to 'Western Civilization. . . . Because our society is the product and we the inheritors of it'. Admittedly, this sounds marvellous! Very much akin to Sir Keith's call for restoring historical education in Britain, Bennett's arguments could be perceived as high-minded in spirit and tone:

> the humanities can contribute to an informed sense of community by enabling us to learn about and become participants in a common culture, shareholders in our civilization. But our goal should be more than just a common culture . . . we should instead want all students to know a common culture rooted in civilization's lasting visions, its highest shared ideals and aspirations, and its heritage.

Who would not, at first, be inspired by such language?

> We are a part and a product of Western civilization. That our society was founded upon such principles as justice, liberty, government with the consent of the governed, and equality under the law is the result of ideas descended from great epochs of Western civilization – Enlightenment England and France, Renaissance Florence and Periclean Athens. These ideas, so revolutionary in their time yet so taken for granted now, are the

glue that binds together our pluralistic nation. The fact that we as
Americans − whether black or white, Asian or Hispanic, rich or
poor − share these beliefs aligns us with other cultures of the
Western tradition.[97]

To Reclaim A Legacy received a highly favourable response in
the media. Nevertheless, the politics of the NEH report were
scarcely hidden. First, unlike Sir Keith's speech, which at least
implied attention to human 'endeavour' in historical education,
the Bennett paper did not propose that history convey a sense of
the *conflicts* between social and political groups over the
supposedly 'shared' ideas and values, the 'common culture', *and*
the social order and relations which determined their lives. Nor
did it posit the necessity of examining the distance between
'ideal' and 'experience' in Western civilization *and* in the world
history which had been 'made' by the 'West'. In fact, *To Reclaim
A Legacy* is characterized by the virtual absence of any
recognition that the constitution of the humanities includes social
history.

The absence of any reference − more precisely, the *exclusion* −
of social history from the humanities was not merely a reflection
of the new intellectual 'elitism' prevailing at the NEH. It was
also a deliberate attempt to delegitimize the field for its
association with the labours of historians of the Left (who were
themselves working to revitalize history and the humanities *but*
in a democratic direction by approaching the past from the
bottom up!). Declaring that the decline of the humanities was
traceable to events of twenty years ago − that is, *not* to the 1970s
but to the 'sixties' − it all but stated as much. Even more to the
point, the report sounded especial alarm at 'the tendency of some
humanities professors to present their subjects in a tendentious,
ideological manner' and attacked what it viewed as the
'subordination' of the humanities to the status of 'handmaiden to
ideology . . . and contemporary prejudices'.[98]

To be fair, the NEH report was not an undemocratic
document. It might even be read as 'populist' for it did not
postulate any limits to the audience for the humanities, and the
texts accorded a place in the 'core curriculum', the 'tradition', the
'canon of Great Books' to be studied, include what might be
termed 'radical' works from the classical to the contemporary,

for example, writings by Rousseau, Marx and Martin Luther King, Jr. However, the neglect of social history and related developments in historiography since the 1960s was a notable and polemical omission.[99]

Writing in *The Nation*, Leonard Kriegel offered a series of appreciative but, also, critical reflections on *To Reclaim A Legacy*. There was one aspect of the report, however, which perturbed him in particular: '[Bennett] apparently believes we should educate everyone who can be educated, but he carefully avoids – and avoids so cleverly that I cannot believe it is accidental – the question of the *purpose* for which students should be educated.'[100] Kriegel's comments, both the favourable and the hostile, were mostly on the mark, yet on this specific point he read the report a bit too innocently (or so it seemed). Examined critically and in connection with the larger project of the New Right, the report communicates that the purpose of humanities and historical education for Bennett and his colleagues is not just the stated aim of 'transmitting a tradition' (which itself we might well argue about!) but, also, the cultivation of a one-dimensional view of Western and world-historical development in which the United States is seen to be both the heir of Western civilization and the final fruition of its development.

Joining the Cabinet as Secretary of Education in 1985, Bennett continued to write and speak on this subject, emphasizing the crisis of history in particular. In a 1986 Department of Education report, *What Works: Research about teaching and learning*, Bennett and his assistant secretary, Chester Finn (later to return to 'civilian' academic life and commence his own campaign, in the fashion of the British Tories, for *national* educational standards and curricula), wrote of the necessity for teaching 'cultural literacy', one of the foremost goals being that: 'A shared knowledge of these elements of our past [history, literature, and political institutions] helps foster social cohesion and a sense of national community and pride.'[101]

In his talks and speeches as Secretary, Bennett regularly framed the crisis as a political one. The decline of history, he argued, represented a failure by the schools to 'transmit [the nation's] social and political values', and thereby 'help legitimize the political system'. Proposing an 'intellectual initiative' – which he

referred to as a kind of 'defense initiative' (thereby linking it to
the ongoing revival of the Cold War) – Bennett urged a renewed
commitment to history teaching separate from the teaching of
social studies. In language reaffirming the practice of comprehending US history in exceptional terms and as the
culmination of Western civilization he confidently said that

> If taught honestly and truthfully, the study of history will give
> our students a grasp of their nation, a nation that the study of
> history and current events will reveal is still, indeed, [in Abraham
> Lincoln's words] 'the last best hope on earth'. Our students
> should know that. They *must* know that, because nations can be
> destroyed from without, but they can also be destroyed from
> within.[102]

An important aspect of Bennett's campaign for historical
education as political education was the persistent critique of
'cultural relativism' (which was, in general, a dominant theme of
New Right and Moral Majority attacks on the contemporary
public school system). In this vein, Bennett's Under Secretary of
Education, Gary Bauer, spoke to the Association of American
Publishers about the relativism he found to be characteristic of so
many of the social studies books used in schools. It was his
assessment that the 'textbooks . . . are quick to be hyper-critical
of American institutions while glossing over the . . . character of
totalitarian governments'. Essentially, Bauer was complaining
that the textbooks were too neutral, and while he did not
propose that government get involved, he did say: 'If no
government agency can tell you what to publish – and clearly in
this country none must ever do so – then it falls on your
shoulders to act responsibly in helping decide what our children
learn.'[103]

Bennett's successor at the NEH, Lynne Cheney, continued his
drive to 'revitalize' humanities and historical education. She also
continued to pursue his ideological and political campaign. For
example, in 1987 in her first major broadside, *American Memory:
A report on the humanities in our nation's schools*, she spoke at
several points of the threat of national 'decline' and connected the
crisis of history to it:

> A system of education that fails to nurture memory of the past

denies its students a great deal. . . . Indeed, we put our sense of nationhood at risk by failing to familiarize our young people with the story of how the society in which they live came to be. Knowledge of the ideas that have molded us and the ideals that have mattered to us functions as a kind of civic glue. Our history and literature give us symbols to share; they help us all . . . feel part of a common undertaking. . . . By allowing the erosion of historical consciousness, we do to ourselves what an unfriendly nation bent on our destruction might.[104]

A year later, Cheney sustained her offensive by way of yet another NEH report, *Humanities in America*. This time she stressed the 'populist' theme of the need for university academics to become more concerned with addressing their work to extra-campus and extra-curricular audiences. However, even as she acknowledged that the 'Western tradition *is* a debate', she continued effectively to banish social history from the domain of the humanities. In fact, her attacks on critical scholars, those who contend that a social and political reading of 'the tradition' is essential, were all the more pointed: 'Some scholars reduce the study of the humanities to the study of politics, arguing that truth – and beauty and excellence – are not timeless matters, but transitory notions, devices used by some groups to perpetuate "hegemony" over others.' (Actually, it is arguable that Cheney not only exiles *social* history from the humanities but all truly *historical* questions!) Again, allowing for 'some sense of estrangement from society' on the part of academics, she nevertheless highlights 'the extreme alienation of some faculty members', who are clearly made out to be those who emphasize social and political issues in their teaching and scholarship. Celebrating the apparent popular desire for public and extra-curricular humanities activities and education, she berates these 'alienated' intellectuals for their (supposed) disaffection from 1980s American cultural life:

Indeed, it is hard to feel alienated from a society that seems increasingly to understand the importance of a standard Matthew Arnold once held up. 'Again and again I have insisted', he wrote, 'how those are the happy moments of humanity, how those are the marking epochs of a people's life, how those are the flowering times for literature and art and all the creative power of genius, when there is a *national* glow of life and thought, when the whole of society is in the fullest measure permeated by thought, sensible to beauty, intelligent and alive.'[105]

Thus, the humanities are to be served up for popular and pleasant consumption, the goal of which is the development of a national consensus around already-established 'shared values'.

It should also be noted, though it fell outside the activities of the Reagan Administration and, in fact, Bennett himself disavowed its tactics, that the New Right spawned an organization called Accuracy in Academia (AIA) which took upon itself the task of classroom surveillance against liberal and Left 'bias'. Its founder, Reed Irvine, who was also responsible for Accuracy in Media (AIM), claimed that there were 10,000 Marxist professors in American higher education. AIA's plan was to recruit students and retired persons (the latter of whom often receive free tuition at their local colleges) to confront social science and history professors who, in their view, spread 'disinformation or misinformation'. The group met with little success but not without doing some damage and generating in several places an environment hostile to intellectual and academic freedom.[106] (One of the problems with AIA, it was noted by sympathizers, was that the initiative came from 'outside the university'; what was needed, it was said, was a campaign by conservative professors against the Left. In 1988 such a group, the National Association of Scholars, was organized, sponsoring its first conference in the autumn of that year under the title 'Reclaiming the academy: responses to the radicalization of the university'.[107])

As in the case of the Thatcher Government, there is far more which might be recounted of the Reagan Administration and its New Right allies' use and abuse of the past and history (for example, the renditions of US constitutional history offered by Attorney General Edwin Meese, III, in his attempts to undermine aspects of the affirmative action programme and civil rights legislation.[108]) But what has been discussed should be adequate to attest to the practice.

Conservatives, as Robert Nisbet claims, have traditionally spoken 'by design from the past and often about the past' (though clearly a past to which many of us would not too often assent). As a result, it is the Right which 'traditionally' has most been able to assert claims to speak *for* the past. In this sense, Thatcher, Reagan and their colleagues were to be expected to speak often in terms of 'days gone by'. However, the British and American New Right coalitions have done more than this. They have sought to harness and manipulate the past for their immediate and long-term requirements and goals. And, by reducing and subordinating it to their present ambitions, they actually have denigrated the past. They have not mastered history – for an effective relationship between past and present, a meaningful *historical* dialogue, entails respect – but they have used and abused it. And for this reason alone historians and others, not only of the Left, must confront and continue to confront them.

Yet, in a certain sense the initiatives of the New Right were to be welcomed, for (still holding off on the question of their success) in their efforts to further the break-up of the post-war settlements and develop new, conservative consensuses and national grand-governing narratives in support of them, they did accomplish the *making* of the crisis of history into a public issue. And, lest there be any doubt about it, there really was, and is, a crisis – at least, that is, for those of us who believe that history should be a central ingredient of schooling and education. Here too, however, the New Right must be confronted, for their use and abuse of the past and their particular formulations of the crisis and programmes to address it, place on the political agenda not just the question of the status of the discipline but, as I have stated before, the more critical ones of the purpose and promise of historical study and thought and, ultimately, the visions of past, present and possible futures to prevail in our public cultures.

CHAPTER 4

———————— · ————————

THE END OF HISTORY?

The 'critique' of political economy starts from the concept of the
historical character of the 'determined market' and of its
'automatism', whereas pure economists conceive of these elements
as 'eternal' and 'natural'. . . .

Antonio Gramsci

A POST-LIBERAL AND POST-SOCIAL DEMOCRATIC CONSENSUS?

It should now be evident that both the origins and the making of
the crisis of history were political in character. Ensuing from the
dissolution of the post-war liberal and social-democratic settlements and the national grand-governing narratives associated
with them, the developments constituting the crisis were
articulated as such and situated on the public agenda by the
American and British New Rights in the course of their
campaigns for and ascendance to governmental office in the
1970s and 80s. Revealed to a great extent in the persistent use and
abuse of the past on the part of their leaders and spokespersons,
these initiatives were instigated not simply by a concern about
historical study and thought, specifically, the ongoing decline
and marginalization of historical education, but, all the more, by
the New Rights' shared ambitions to further the break-up of the
post-war accords, to counter both the struggles from below and,
what they perceived as, the growing presence and influence of
the intellectual Left, *and* to recondition and revivify their
respective national grand-governing narratives in support of the

creation of new, *conservative* consensuses. That is, recognizing the fundamental role of schooling in the determination of collective historical memory, consciousness and imagination, the 'making' of the crisis of history, as evidenced by the New Rights' particular constructions of both the problem and the strategies and programmes advanced to address it, was actually intended to provide for the revision and reinvigoration of historical education and curricula in such a manner that they would contribute to their projects of rescuing and refashioning late twentieth-century capitalist hegemony. Thus, the crisis is not merely about the position of the discipline in schooling and higher education or, even, in the wider culture and society. Rather, it is about the far more crucial question raised at the outset of this work: 'What for, history?' And what is at risk in our response is not just the future direction of historical practice, scholarship and pedagogy, but the visions of past, present and possible futures emanating from them.

Clearly, the New Right Republican Administrations and Conservative Governments which have held political power for, now, over a decade have been *extremely* consequential. Although the basic structures of the 'welfare state' have survived in both the United States and Britain, the New Right regimes have instituted major shifts and changes in public and social policy priorities and programmes. In the United States in the 1980s there was a massive military and defence build-up entailing huge expenditures at the same time that drastic cuts were pursued in a vast array of social programmes. The spending on arms was recognized as having contributed to the, admittedly, remarkable economic growth of the mid- and late 1980s, following a very deep national and global economic recession in the early years of the decade; however, since the Reagan Administration cut taxes, especially for the rich, the *increased* total spending by the government led to record-setting federal deficits which have been referred to as 'military Keynesianism', and are now seen as threatening further debilitation of the US economy. Moreover, from the outset the Reagan Administration engaged in executive actions and legislative initiatives on questions of labour and industrial relations, the environment, the civil rights of minorities, education and the family, and relations between

Church and State reflecting the demands and aspirations of those classes and social groups composing its New Right coalition. And in international affairs the Reagan Administration engaged in a decidedly imperial and cold war foreign policy which included the aforementioned covert *and* illegal support of the Nicaraguan *contras* and the invasion of the Caribbean island-state of Grenada, along with a series of other overt and covert operations in Asia and Africa in support of right-wing dictators, guerrillas, and terrorists (the consequences of which are now being confronted).[1]

Concurrently, like their American comrades, the British New Right has endeavoured while in power to enact a variety of policies and programmes called for by the constituents of their political alliance and, given the 'constitutional' differences between the American and British systems of government, the Thatcher Government was able to legislate and/or undertake a series of schemes even more radical in character across the entire terrain of public life. Most spectacular among them have been, first, the extensive privatizations or *de*nationalizations of public enterprises including not only manufacturing and service establishments but, also, public utilities and, second, the centralization or 'nationalization' of public authority signified, for example, not only by the *nationalization* of educational curricula but, all the more significantly, by the abolition of metropolitan city governments (e.g. the Greater London Council/GLC).[2]

It must be added that these brief summary paragraphs do not begin to take in the disarray, confusion and hardship resulting from the politico-economic, public and social policies followed by the American and British New Rights in the cause of the so-called 'free' market *versus* the State – for example, the regional dislocations linked not simply to world-economic developments but furthered and exacerbated by the Reagan and Thatcher regimes.

Nevertheless, in spite of these 'accomplishments' we might well ask to what extent the American and British New Rights actually have succeeded in establishing post-liberal and post-social-democratic, conservative consensuses and articulating new renditions of their respective national grand-governing narratives. The most immediate answer – at least for now – must be *no, not exactly*, for neither in the United States nor in Britain has the Right been able to create the kind of social and cultural order, or movement towards it, which would truly warm the hearts of the diverse groups and forces which they had so effectively mobilized in the 1970s and arduously held together through the 1980s. In fact, it (presently) seems that the New Right coalitions on both sides of the Atlantic are falling apart in the wake of the departures from high office of their political champions, Ronald Reagan and Margaret Thatcher – though not necessarily as a direct consequence of their retirements.[3]

Of course, more important than the cohesion of the New Right coalitions is the degree to which those movements have actually effected a change in the views, values and ideals of Americans and Britons such that they would express increasing commitment to, and identification with, conservative politics, ideals and visions. Here too, however, the efforts and campaigns of the Right must be accounted as 'disappointing' for, although they have repeatedly countered and undermined their liberal and social-democratic political oppositions, studies, polls and surveys record continuing popular affirmation of those principles and policy priorities historically associated with the post-war settlements, that is, with the liberal and social-democratic Keynesian-welfare state regimes![4] Although this should not lead us to discount the significance of the New Rights' political victories and what they have wrought *or*, as I will discuss shortly, their political and ideological struggles to re-establish capitalist hegemony, it does imply that their electoral victories have been due more to their adeptness at mobilizing and harnessing popular anxieties, fears and hopes than their having accomplished a transformation of the political and cultural views and values of the American and British peoples. Unfortunately, it also registers the fact that the American and British Lefts have yet to develop the politics and visions capable of engaging the persistent liberal and social-democratic orientations of their fellow citizens.

It is arguable that not only have the New Rights failed to create or inspire a new consensus in either the United States or Britain, but that the sense of discontinuity and decline which arose in the 1970s, providing them with the opportunities to achieve political power, has resurfaced in a pronounced way (if it ever actually dissipated). It is not just that national and global recession once again threatens to disrupt and undermine economic and social life following the growth of the mid–to–late 1980s (the benefits of which were most unevenly distributed). Indeed, however much it may be due to the continuing processes of de–industrialization in both countries and the actual decline, respectively, of the American and British economies relative to those of Germany and Japan (about which public anxiety is well symbolized in the US case by the achievement of best–seller status by Professor Paul Kennedy's 1987 book, *The Rise and Fall of the Great Powers*), the roots of the resurgent perceptions of historical discontinuity and decline are not merely economic, either conjunctual or structural. Whatever the election–style rhetoric of New Right politicians defending their times in office, public discourse and debate emanating from Left, Centre *and* Right are characterized by serious concern and worry regarding the progress of and prospects for economic *and* political, social and cultural development. Along with those being sounded about industry, investment, trade and fiscal policy, there are increasing alarms about popular disaffection from civic and public life, the enervation of citizenship and the malaise which seems to have overtaken democratic politics.[5]

Not surprisingly, therefore, in neither country has the New Right accomplished the articulation of a new, confident and optimistic, national grand–governing narrative or, for that matter, the reinvigoration of an earlier version of such. Nor, for all their efforts to shape their nations' 'selective traditions', have the Republicans and Tories been able to enforce or secure conservative renditions of the American and British pasts, respectively, within historical education and curricula. In the United States – where, it must be noted, school curricula are determined at the state and local levels – the arrival of the crisis of history on the public agenda has instigated the formation of several major public and private commissions to explore and report on the value and imperatives of historical education. However, composed of school officials, teachers, university academics and private citizens, these bodies have not readily supported the kinds of historical pedagogy or particular goals which have been pushed by Republican Departments of

Education. They do, as we might expect, assert the 'importance' of the teaching of history and the dangers of its further dilution and marginalization; but their reports do not appear to express or reflect a deep consensus on what the actual focus or framework of such historical study ought to involve which is where the real debates about form and content are occurring. In fact, even as historical pedagogy is being revalued and, possibly, returned to the centre of educational curricula at all levels of schooling, it has become the subject of heated battles. An example of this, related to the question noted at the end of Chapter 1 regarding the appropriate framework for the new historical synthesis to be crafted by historians favouring such an initiative, is *where* the greatest attention ought to be placed in historical curriculum: American history *or* world history – and, in the latter case, is it to be 'Western' or a more 'global' history? Another, intersecting, but far more dramatic, issue has been that of 'pluralism' and 'multiculturalism' and how they are to be secured in the teaching of past and present; that is, how should the diverse experiences and traditions of America's racial and ethnic minorities – most especially, but not alone, African and Hispanic-Americans – be rendered in historical, social-studies and humanities education? (I shall be returning to the question of historical education in the final chapter.)[6]

As we have seen, in contrast to the American case, the British New Right was able 'constitutionally' to institute *national* educational curricula – though it should be remembered that this entailed a significant shift in public policy and practice. In early 1989, six years after Sir Keith Joseph's original call for national curricula in several subjects, the Thatcher Government organized a National Curriculum History Working Group whose task was to 'make recommendations on attainment targets and programmes of study for history . . .'.[7] Appointed to membership were a selection of school administrators, teachers and inspectors, university faculty from history and education studies, and a retired naval commander who served as chairman. Almost all the public expectations were that the Working Group would produce a report, a curriculum structure and contents, pleasing, above all, to the New Right politicians who commissioned it. Yet, as the Group deliberated, mixed signals appeared. Not unexpectedly, in view of both her determination and her use and abuse of the past, it came out that Mrs Thatcher herself had been displeased by the directions they were taking and, moreover, that she had directly intervened in the process. It was reported in the press that the Prime Minister was perturbed in particular by what she considered to be the Working Group's failure in their interim report to give adequate emphasis to 'British' over 'world history' and 'chronology and facts' over 'skills and understanding' and that she had proceeded to instruct the Group through her newly appointed Secretary of State for Education, John MacGregor, to revise their recommendations accordingly. Again, in view of Thatcher's declared preferences and 'historical' rhetoric, her instructions to the members of the Working Group can be read as directing them to the development of a curriculum built around not just a more national but a more national*ist* narrative of 'British' historical development. And it should be noted that the Working Group did respond to her request by making certain limited changes along the lines she 'suggested' even though its members apparently felt that they had sufficiently stressed British history, chronology and facts.[8]

There was, of course, a brief controversy over Thatcher's interventions, but the disapprovals voiced seemed to be of little consequence and, thus, expectations persisted that the Working Group would generate a history curriculum appealing to Conservative sensibilities. And yet, lo and behold!, the Final Report issued in April 1990 was decidedly *not* the document presumed to be forthcoming, that is, it did not propose a curriculum for historical education expressive of New Right convictions and ambitions. Yes, the programme proposed was structured around British history and chronology and facts were emphasized. However, more important than these, arguably, 'generic' issues is that the curriculum outlined in the Final Report clearly indicated that the Group was responsive to the questions and substantive scholarship advanced by critical social historians during the past twenty years and more, to the varied political and social struggles which have shaped modern Britain past and present and to the complex and changing place of British experience in the wider world. Notably, the introductory and explanatory remarks of the Report record that the Group was very conscious of the political implications of their labours and the potential for the abuse of what they would produce. For example, regarding the problem of specifying 'historical information' in the respective 'attainment targets', the text warns of the 'very real danger' that doing so could be perceived as imposing an 'official history' which would have the effect of 'freezing historical scholarship'. Also, the Group was sensitive about the concept of 'heritage' apparently due to both its reverential – and, possibly, commercial – air and its singularity. Thus, it is stated that every effort was made to work in terms of 'inheritance':

> For historical purposes the word 'inheritance' may be more precise in its meaning, implying 'that which the past has bequeathed to us' – and which it is for individual people to interpret, employing the knowledge and skills of history. While all people in Britain partake to a greater or lesser extent of a shared 'inheritance', they also have their own individual, group, family, etc. 'inheritances' which are inter-related. The study of history should respect and make clear this pattern of inheritances.[9]

We will return to the question of history curricula in the final chapter, but I cannot help but note at length the entertaining (and, for the Left, consoling) observation of R. W. Johnson. In introductory remarks (1990) to an earlier-written essay on the former socialist and now right-wing historian and ideologue, Paul Johnson, he writes of the conservatives' 'intellectual' campaigns and their inability to redirect academic and scholarly life and thought:

> Despite all the talk about the new conservatism, when intellectual authority is wanted it is sought in writers of a generation and more ago. . . . But on the whole, the Reagan–Thatcher conservatives have distrusted their intelligentsias too much to want to appeal to intellectual authority. There was, indeed, no real prospect of dislodging or converting the liberal-left intelligentsia from the commanding heights it occupied. Instead, the new conservatives simply abandoned the intellectual high ground to these, their ancient foes, and swept around them at a lower level, making use of a ragtag and bobtail collection of polemicists, popular journalists, ambitious young hopefuls, born-again economics professors and whatever came to hand – sometimes even

ex-lefties, foaming at the mouth in their eagerness to purge their own past sins. This little army, thanks to the patronage of government, a following wind in the media and the sheer energy and aggression of their polemic achieved not inconsiderable success. Intellectually they were not good enough to win a war of ideas – to change the way the Academy thought – but they were wise enough to know this . . . and to avoid open debate. But their job was merely to throw the Academy off balance . . . to keep it at bay, to surprise it with abuse. This they did. . . .[10]

It might well be contended that *in any case* the American and British New Rights never could have succeeded in their goals of cobbling together new national consensuses and grand-governing narratives to accompany them. It is not only that their coalitions were inherently unstable – that is, there were contradictions which necessarily imperilled the long or, perhaps, as we see, even medium-term survival of the New Right alliances (as discussed in Chapter 3). It is, moreover, that the very *politics* of the American and British New Rights, contrary to their rhetorical pretensions have been a radical politics of division and divisiveness – indeed, even their talk of 'shared values' was a mode of partition and exclusion (that is, those who shared those values *versus* those who did not). The leading figures of the New Right forces presented themselves as crusaders and 'conviction politicians' unwilling to be deterred from their missions of terminating the liberal and social-democratic consensuses and driving from public life those who had allowed or, better, been responsible for the onset of processes of political and economic decline. Reagan and Thatcher, we should not forget, promised nothing less than 'revolutions' against the prevailing orders. In words equally applicable to the Reagan Administration, Andrew Gamble has stated of Thatcher and her Government:

From the outset the Thatcher Government intended to be different. 'Our country's decline is not inevitable', proclaimed the 1979 manifesto. 'We in the Conservative party think we can reverse it.' The Thatcherites wanted their government to be different, not merely from the social democracy of the 1970s but from postwar conservatism as well. There was a crusading mood and a belief that old ways and old values had to be challenged.
Margaret Thatcher herself scorned consensus. She called for a return

to a politics of principle and urged her party to occupy the moral high ground and abandon compromise and retreat.[11]

The conservative American columnist, George Will, an ardent fan of Mrs Thatcher, enthusiastically wrote:

> She has shaped Britain's public conversation as decisively as de Gaulle shaped France's precisely because consensus is not her aim. She asks, 'Do you think you would ever have heard of Christianity if the Apostles had gone out and said, "I believe in consensus"?' [Fellow Tory, Norman] Tebbit says that Thatcher's goal of 'killing socialism' is achievable. . . .[12]

As we know, New Right aggression and antagonisms were not directed at liberal and socialist politicians alone, but were characterized by a larger sociology of class, race and gender exploiting and challenging the anxieties and fears of the day in hostile fashion against trades union leaders and members, the poor and unemployed, racial and ethnic minorities (and, in Britain, immigrants), feminists and women's rights activists, and gays and lesbians.[13]

The divisiveness of the Reagan and Thatcher regimes can be seen most *materially* in their political economies of class. This is so not only at the 'margins', that is, in the unemployment and public neglect of the poor and homeless at one end and, at the other, the extravagance and celebration of the 'lifestyles of the rich and famous' exemplified (at least in the United States) by the likes of Donald Trump – the combination of which led many an American commentator to describe the 1980s as the 'decade of greed' and their British counterparts to conjure up the Disraelian imagery of 'Two Nations'. A 'politics of inequality' was a principal and dynamic feature of the Reagan–Thatcher years (persisting, thus far, into the 1990s). As social and statistical studies are now making plain, the old adage about 'the rich getting richer and the poor getting poorer' is not merely proverbial but, with reference to the experiences of Reaganism and Thatcherism, scientifically accurate! The point is that the further concentration of wealth among the wealthiest and concurrent loss of economic standing and/or wherewithal for the middle and lower strata are hardly the economic and social ingredients called for in the making of a new consensus.[14]

Admittedly, a problem with the analysis offered here is that in an increasingly *global* capitalist economy it seems to assume a degree of nation–state autonomy and a capacity on the part of national governments and those who wield their powers to control events and developments which may no longer exist. By no means do I intend by this to discount the centrality of the State or the responsibility of those who command it, but it is a serious reservation. And recognition of it brings us to a most ironic aspect of the New Rights' seeming *success* in refashioning capitalist hegemony and, potentially, supporting grand-governing narratives.

REFASHIONING HEGEMONY

The American and British New Rights have failed to establish the new orders and consensuses projected by their political coalitions. *But*, depending on the definition one uses, it is arguable that their regimes have been successful in achieving their shared goal – and, most importantly, that of the corporate elite – of refashioning and resecuring capitalist hegemony. However much social researchers may find that the core structures of, and popular commitments to, the welfare state and its priorities and ideals have survived Reaganism and Thatcherism, there is no denying that the New Right Republicans and Conservatives have effectively redefined the public agenda; they have torn asunder the post-war settlements and accords and all but routed their political oppositions. Although the Democratic Party continues to be the majority party in both Houses of the US Congress (having briefly lost control of the Senate in the mid-1980s), it is the Republican Administrations which have set the course and the pace of political debate and developments. The Democrats neither offer, nor appear to represent, an alternative challenging to the Republicans except to the extent that elements in the party continue to assert 'traditional' liberal politics and even here the Republicans have been able to counter it by equating and stigmatizing such liberalism (the 'L' word) with the images of the bankrupt politics and programmes of the

1970s. Similarly, in Britain the Labour Party continues to be the Loyal Opposition and there are even occasional promises of future election victories; however, the progress of Labour has been determined more often by the political initiatives, miscalculations and mistakes of the Tories than by their own collective imagination and initiatives. Moreover, as all are aware, the Labour Party itself has moved to the political centre in response to Thatcherism, eschewing as much as possible the politics of 'socialism' and accepting the reformation of the politico-economic terrain carried out by the Tories.[15]

Outside the party political arena the New Right Republicans and Conservatives also have undermined, if not actually vanquished, both the American and British labour movements and the 'new social movements' (perhaps less so the environmental movement, though it has been asserted that the reason for this is that the corporate elite has learned to accommodate, incorporate and, even, commercialize environmentalism!). In direct confrontations with government and corporation both 'on the line' and in the legislative process the American and British labour movements have repeatedly suffered defeat – an apparent result of which has been a further decline in union rolls. Like the 'class struggles' of the labour unions, those for racial and gender justice persist but they are seriously weakened and fragmented, more often fighting limited defensive actions than engaging in any advances. And, most crucially, in terms of the possible emergence or formation of a coherent Left politics capable of threatening or seriously challenging the predominance of the Right (which, as was noted earlier, is now actually in some disarray) there is little evidence of the coalescence of these movements.[16]

As various American and British critics have contended, among the most consequential of the New Right regimes' accomplishments has been the *depoliticization* of public life.[17] Again, this is not to say that a new consensus is emerging – at least not in the manner of those of the post-war decades. The absence of significant political movement from below and in opposition does imply, however, a pervasive popular sense of impotence in the face of contemporary history. Indeed, the same studies and surveys which reveal a continuing commitment to

policies and programmes characteristic of the liberal and social-
democratic consensuses also indicate a widespread cynicism
about the ability of the 'common people' to do anything to bring
about such a 'project'. In other words, what we find is *not*
consensus but resignation and accommodation, that is, a
widespread belief that there is no hope for, or in, popular
political action, in the agency of the common or working people
to instigate and create real change. Speaking of the American
scene but, perhaps, capturing the situation in Britain as well,
Philip Mattera has written:

> These days there is not much collective dreaming in America. The
> erosion of living standards and the increase in economic insecurity
> have brought about a climate of quiet frustration and cynicism.
> People have been caught between official pronouncements that
> these are the best of times and their personal realization that life is
> getting tougher every day. The contradictory evidence is having
> an immobilizing effect: most Americans do not see a way out of
> this dilemma and consequently have grown wary of any change at
> all. While people in other parts of the world, notably Eastern
> Europe, are boldly confronting their oppression, the U.S. feels
> like a political backwater.[18]

This depoliticization of American and British public life is
quite an achievement and we should not fail to 'appreciate' the
agency of the New Right in concert with, and in favour of, the
'class war from above' pursued by capital in bringing it about. It
is fundamental to the restoration of capitalist hegemony. Yet,
without at all depreciating their efforts in this, we must recognize
that it also reflects the *limits* or, better, the *contradictions* and *ironic*
consequences of the New Rights' own politics and regimes.
Promising to reverse the perceived processes of national decline
and to restore their respective nations' historic 'continuities' and
'progress' (there is general agreement that whatever the actual
implications of their ambitions and actions, the New Right in
both countries did effectively monopolize the language of
'nation' and 'nationalism'), Reagan and Thatcher and their
associates called for the 'liberation' of American and British
economic life from both the taxation, regulation and control of
the liberal and social-democratic governments and the demands

of labour and the new social movements. And, having secured political power, they did pursue radical antidemocratic, anti-labour and pro-capital policies in the proclaimed cause of *national* renewal. The contradiction of their campaigns is not only that they have made all the more intense the tensions and antagonisms between the 'freedoms' of the market and the stability and values of family and community (thereby jeopardizing their own coalitions), but that in the context of the ongoing restructuring of the world economy their policies also have had the effect of furthering the interests of *transnational* capital. As Stephen Gill explains (in the American case):

> Reaganomics, whilst being in some ways a nationalist strategy, . . . acknowledged and harnessed the higher degree of integration of the United States into the global political economy . . . whereas Nixon's apparently defensive tactics [in the early 1970s] partly sought to protect American national capital, and to an extent American workers, from the effects of international competition, Reagan's policies were more offensive, more market-based, and involved an attack on organized labour. Reagan's policies also facilitated a growth in concentration within certain sectors of the American economy, so that its bigger corporations were better able to compete internationally. Thus, although perhaps not consciously intended, Reagan's policies none the less reinforced the tendency towards *transnational hegemony*.[19]

The globalization of corporate operations (investment, trade *and* production – captured in the image of 'the global factory') has entailed – to the extent that they were ever really coterminous – the further decoupling and dissociation of the multinational corporations' priorities from those of the respective nation-states out of whose histories and territories they grew. In the process, the working classes of the United States and Britain (etc.) have become ever more subject to the international competition for capitalist investment in their locales, regions and nation-states which the peoples of the Third World have experienced for some years. Devastated by the politics of the New Right regimes and confronted by the powers and imperatives of capital, the 'powers' and possibilities of local and, even, national movements of labour and other popular groups to shape contemporary history appear reduced and limited (if not, as some have started to argue, historically redundant); indeed, even the powers of national governments begin to appear so in the context of the real *and* reified contemporary world economy. Nigel Harris has succinctly described the developing world order of capital–labour relations:

> Although capital can go international, this is much more difficult for labour. . . . Yet without measures to curb competition, the power of employers is enormously increased. They can play off groups of workers in many different countries against each other. . . . The penalty for those who fail to work for the lowest world price of labour is unemployment. It is here that the fears in the more developed countries are most justified. After more than a century and a half in the long, slow struggle to establish order in the national labour markets, suddenly it seems world capital can escape and, furthermore, can force the reversal of all those gains. Capital has stolen a march, and labour is still far from understanding the implications of that, let alone beginning to create the appropriate institutions to counter it.[20]

In the fashion of English urban working-class graffiti: 'Capital rules, OK!' Again, real and reified, the laws of the market, the laws of capital accumulation, prevail. Enfeebled and fragmented, the forces of the American and British Left, 'liberal' to 'socialist', continue to be seen as bankrupt. Their 'traditional' policies and programmes are considered too 'costly' in view of the imperatives of capital and, unable to foment *national* political coalitions, they are nowhere near establishing the necessary multinational/international understandings and efforts (which is not to say that existing bodies such as the Socialist International could not).[21] Thus, global capital's political economy is apparently transcending the politics of nation-states – the market effectively envelops and subordinates democracy. Put bluntly, the decline of democratic politics in favour of corporate imperatives and decision-making would seem to represent – to quote the phrase heard so often these days – the 'triumph of capital'.

The refashioning of capitalist hegemony is, then, underway and the New Rights can be said to have at least laid the groundwork for one of their foremost goals. Ironically, however, contrary to their pronounced *nationalist* ambitions, promises and aspirations, the triumph of capital has entailed and appears to portend continuing difficulties *and* national decline (at least on a relative scale). Beyond the termination of the post-war settlements and the depoliticization of public life, the major achievement of the Reagan and Thatcher regimes has been *not* the manifold projects of their respective coalitions but that they have advanced the cause of *transnational* capital – in other words, the socially more limited but politico-economically grander project associated with the Trilateral Commission (discussed above in Chapter 3). This has not (yet) provided the foundations, material or ideological, for a new national consensus in either the United States or Britain, but it has endowed the powers that be with an ideological theme and 'weapon' which, in the long tradition of ruling classes, is being formulated in *historical* terms with powerful and problematic implications for collective historical memory, consciousness and imagination.[22] To be more precise, we continue to witness the making of – or, at least, the attempt to make – a new grand-governing narrative, a narrative proclaiming that the contemporary order (or disorder!) of things actually represents the culmination of world-historical development, the *end of history*. This is splendidly exemplified by the manner in which the Western elites have sought to comprehend and incorporate into public thought the dramatic events and developments of '1989'.

THE PRESENT AS FUTURE

From Beijing Spring to the overthrow of the Communist governments of East-Central Europe, it need hardly be said that 1989 was a truly *historic* year, filled with revolutionary moments and changes. And yet, as it began, the only thing which promised to be *historical* about it was that it would bring the 200th anniversary celebrations of the 'fall of the Bastille' and start of the French Revolution, which were themselves assured to be anything but rebellious or, even, memorable in character. Indeed, as the time approached, it became ever more apparent that the Bicentennial would serve less as an occasion for celebration or commemoration of the ideals of 'liberty, equality and fraternity' than as an opportunity to entomb the Revolution and with it the very concept of radical-democratic action and political, economic and social change. Looking at the French plans and preparations, Daniel Singer, European editor of *The Nation* magazine, penned:

> Long live the Revolution – as long as it is dead and buried with no prospect of resurrection. That thought springs to mind as the French begin to celebrate the bicentennial of their great Revolution. The program is most impressive. Books . . . conferences . . . exhibits and . . . plays. . . . But the climax will come naturally, on July 14, when French President Mitterrand will be accompanied by such iconoclastic sans-culottes as George Bush, Margaret Thatcher and Helmut Kohl – a party that appears more suited to honor Marie Antoinette than commemorate the storming of the Bastille.[23]

It was not simply that the centrepiece to it all was, in 'traditional' late twentieth-century fashion, a made-for-TV spectacle completely *ahistorical* in conception and design,[24] but that there was already underway a multifarious (and not completely unconcerted) campaign to 'dance on the grave of the Revolution' in France and, all the more, in the United States and Britain.

As was noted earlier in this work, a central dimension of the post-war settlements (especially in the United States) was Cold War anti-Communism expressed in the constant reference to the clearly oppressive, if not totalitarian, regimes of the Soviet bloc as providing absolute proof of the political darkness and economic bleakness which is 'socialism' and the *political* imperatives of a 'free-enterprise' economy. It was near-impossible to gain a hearing for either a critical reading of Soviet history or the argument that such states were not really socialist, given the absence of democratic freedoms and the suppression of struggles for human rights (not to mention the fact that the liberties and freedoms supposedly associated with capitalism historically had been nowhere to be found as recently as the *capitalist* states of Nazi Germany and Fascist Italy!). Yet, in the late 1980s, with the inauguration of the undeniably profound and (almost) universally welcomed processes of *glasnost* and *perestroika* in the Soviet Union and certain of the East European states, Western leaders, with the assistance of an all-too-often a-critical media, took up the cries of 'the death of socialism' and 'the triumph of capitalism' – regularly adding the assertion that these developments attested to the ultimate futility of revolutionary and radical struggles (*except*, it would seem, for the kind being pursued as Reaganism and Thatcherism). These propositions appeared to be confirmed, as well, by the failure of the French socialists to secure their democratic-socialist agenda while in power (1981–6) – an effort that ran counter to the contemporary New Right regimes of the United States, Britain and West Germany. The 200th anniversary of the Revolution of 1789 afforded a chance for the powers that be to publicly acclaim – if not 'officially proclaim' – the mortality of socialism as revealed by the evidently distinct but, if properly rendered, connectable developments transpiring in the Soviet Union and France. Moreover, the return of the French socialists to parliamentary power later in the decade was widely cited as evidence of the 'maturity' of French public and political life since the party had disavowed its 'socialist' platform in favour of a more centrist one.[25]

Enhancing the credibility of the political and economic elites' pronouncements and their particular efforts to 'bury the Revolution' was the support they received from a host of intellectual and academic luminaries who themselves were given a warm helping hand (and most lucrative commercial boost) by the managers of the electronic and print media. There was no single line advanced on the history and legacy of '1789'. Its gravediggers and pallbearers included not just those 'traditional' conservatives who never would have found any redeeming value in the upheavals. Far more important a presence was that of historians and writers who could still find value in at least aspects of the Revolution and its contributions to the making of modern France and the world but who, at the same time, could assure everyone that they had run their course and, therefore, anxiety was no longer necessary. The pre-eminent figure in this camp has been the former French Communist and now neo-conservative historian, François Furet, who was crowned the 'King of the Bicentennial' by French television. Furet's writings have been the most respected and 'fashionable' among the current wave of 'revisionist' historians engaged in beheading, or completing the decapitation of, the classical Republican and, later, Marxist interpretation of the Revolution as a 'class', specifically 'bourgeois', revolution. (Notable here is that Furet's recent scholarship was strongly supported with grants from the aforementioned Olin Foundation headed by William Simon.)[26]

Even more important in setting the tone for the Anglo-American public reception and perception of the bicentennial was the book, *Citizens*, by historian Simon Schama. Widely and highly promoted and praised in the press for its literary style and eloquence, Schama's narrative is so taken up with the 'blood' and the 'violence' perpetrated by the revolutionaries that the picture of the Revolution delivered reduces it to having been a process and experience of, in the words of Eric Hobsbawm, 'gratuitous horror and suffering' which 'achieved nothing commensurate with its costs'. Though one is tempted to state sarcastically that the book's achievement of best-seller status is merely a reflection of the Anglo-American sense of superiority when it comes to civil affairs and political stability, it is arguable that the promotion of *Citizens* reflected and exemplified the eagerness on the part of the cultural and intellectual elites to denigrate the Revolution and those who 'made' it from above *and* below and, its reception, the readiness on the part of the upper- and middle-class 'reading public' to subscribe to antiradical political and historical images.[27] (Without denying the violence and horror of the revolutionary experience or, for a moment, proposing it as a model for radical-democratic action today, I would just ask for the sake of critical historical thinking that we not forget the admonition of E. P. Thompson that 'stability, no less than revolution, may have its own kind of Terror'.)[28]

Reflecting on the arguments of the most *au courant* intellectuals and historians, Daniel Singer correctly observed (in February 1989) that:

> the historians who dismiss revolution as the curse of the Third World or merely a historical feature are not maintaining that the next social upheaval will inevitably be different from the storming of the Bastille or the seizure of the Winter Palace [in the Russian Revolution of 1917]. They are really arguing that there will be no such upheaval at all. Clearly they are too clever, and too keen on their profession, to proclaim openly the end of history. Yet like all faithful servants of an established order, they treat that order as something fixed in perpetuity. By denying its class nature, by

dismissing the possibility of radically altering property and other social relations, they allow for quantitative but not qualitative change. Precluding an alternative, they limit their own vision, and that of their readers, to the capitalist horizon.[29]

A legacy of the French Revolution (though, to be clear and honest about it, not its only one, nor its alone), the radical-democratic ideals of liberty, equality and fraternity were not, however, to be so easily retired or buried. In May–June 1989, even before the bicentennial of 14 July 1789, Chinese students· and workers staged massive and heroic demonstrations in Beijing and other cities. Recalling the American, French, Russian and their own Chinese Revolution, the demonstrators both erected models of the 'goddess of liberty'/Statue of Liberty and sang 'the Internationale'. In their tens of thousands and, at certain moments, millions, they called for 'democratic reforms' of the Chinese State and its political economy. Tragically, the demonstrations were crushed by the government and a process of repression and Orwellian control of information and history was reinstituted all the more aggressively.[30]

Suppressed in China, liberty, equality and fraternity were not so effectively put down in Eastern Europe, where struggles from below suddenly emerged or, given the respective histories of the East European countries, *re*-emerged. However much laden with the weight of ethnic and national animosities and rivalries and persistent anti-Semitism, and motivated by imperatives of material survival and/or envy of Western European affluence, the popular movements of liberation in Poland, Czechoslovakia, Hungary, East Germany, Romania and Bulgaria asserted the most basic of *democratic* aspirations, that 'people should govern themselves'.[31] Admittedly, catalyzed and 'permitted' to grow by a Soviet imperial state itself apparently overwhelmed by serious problems 'at home' and publicly committed by its leader, Mikhail Gorbachev, to *glasnost* and *perestroika* in the hope of transforming polity and economy 'from above', the peoples of Eastern Europe were, nevertheless, fully and genuinely responsible for their own risings – the climactic moment of which for Western 'viewers' was the breaching of the Berlin Wall.[32]

Immediately recognized and celebrated for what they were – struggles for freedom and democratic rights (though, I grant, not these alone) *and* the closing moments of the Cold War – it was not long before the East European revolutions were being incorporated into the prevailing discourse, that is, reduced to the simple formula of 'the death of socialism and the triumph of capitalism'. Among the crudest instances of this was the Mobil Corporation's advertisement headed 'And the walls came tumbling down' on the Op-ed page of *The New York Times*. Its text declared:

> We snap on the TV and find thousands of people in some foreign squares shouting for free markets.
>   *Free markets?* Even American voters are said to have trouble with the concept. How can it cause the world so to quake? Yet it has and it does.[33]

There was some recognition in the 'serious' media that in Poland, Hungary, Czechoslovakia and East Germany leading elements in the risings were of the democratic Left and there were aspirations and commitments to try to chart a 'third way' between 'capitalism' and 'Communism' by drawing on aspects of both along with a great deal of inspiration and direction from Swedish social-democratic politics. It became ever more plain, however, that the reconstruction of East European industrial and commercial life would be subjected directly to the imperatives of the capitalist world economy and the only alternatives which seemed to present themselves were economic stagnation (if not collapse), *or* privatization, foreign investment and integration by way of the global corporation (with no guarantees of economic growth and development) while trying to transform their welfare systems from Communism to social democracy.[34] (Without intending to trivialize what has happened, I cannot help but note that a most curious, yet symbolic, example of the 'incorporation' of these revolutions and the end of the Cold War was the commercial retailing of the Berlin Wall, the sale of 'authentic' chunks and pieces in American discount department stores.)

The discourse of the triumph of capitalism predominated at the outset of 1989 and became all the more amplified in the course of the year. Indeed, it was not limited to the gloatings of the political and economic elites. The pages of newspapers, magazines, intellectual journals, reports and rapidly-produced books and monographs repeated, in various tones, the *historic* implications of what was happening: 'The collapse of communism . . . The death of socialism . . . The triumph of capitalism . . . Capitalism: the wave of the future'. The international management theorist, Peter Drucker, in a book titled *The New Realities* wrote that we had entered a new epoch in which 'socialism [from American liberalism and European social democracy to Soviet Communism] has become the anachronism. Instead of capitalism being a transition stage on the socialist road, it now increasingly appears that socialism is a detour on the capitalist road.' Edward Yardeni, in-house intellectual for Prudential-Bache Securities, announced in a much-touted pamphlet: 'The big picture shows that people around the world share a desire to prosper. And increasingly they believe that capitalism is the means to that end – not communism, socialism. . . .'. The American economist and prominent intellectual figure of the Left, Robert Heilbroner, who had previously predicted the demise of 'business civilization', now offered a new view of capitalism's state in the world. In *The New Yorker* magazine, in an article actually titled 'The triumph of capitalism' which had ripple effects in several intellectual quarters, he said: 'Less than seventy-five years after it officially began, the contest between capitalism and socialism is over: capitalism has won.' And liberal sociologist, former West German parliamentarian (and Trilateralist), and British academic figure, Sir Ralf Dahrendorf, in a book written in the wake of 1989, *Reflections on the Revolution in Europe* (titled à la Edmund Burke's response to the French Revolution of 1789), commanded that 'the point has to be made unequivocally that socialism is dead, and that *none of its variants* can be revived.'[35]

American sociologist and socialist, Stanley Aronowitz may overstate the commitment of the 'masses' to triumphant capital but his thoughts capture the spirit of the times:

> While world capitalism continues to wallow in one of the longer global economic crises of its 400-year history, it has never been ideologically more powerful; or, to put it more precisely, its key tenets – market, entrepreneurship, private ownership of the means of production, and possessive individualism, which is no longer merely an Anglo-American belief – have gripped significant portions of the masses in the East as well as the West. The

emergence of these ideas conjoins with the increasingly powerful argument that freedom presupposes a relatively free market, especially for consumer goods.[36]

Also speaking from the Left, the words of economic historian Joyce Kolko further register, in a warning-like fashion, the implications of such a discourse for collective historical memory, consciousness and imagination: 'The orthodox ideology is now so pervasive that few people any longer *even conceive of other than a capitalist future.*'[37]

How all of this relates to the question of 'What for, history?' should be increasingly clear, but we ought, perhaps, to note one more instance of the articulation of the triumph of capital as emergent grand-governing narrative, the publication and reception of the article, 'The end of history?', authored by Francis Fukuyama prior to his appointment by the (post-Reagan) Bush Administration as deputy director of the US State Department's policy planning staff. Originally published, in the summer of 1989, in the American neo-conservative journal, *The National Interest*,[38] the piece was to be widely promoted, excerpted and debated not only in the American media but, both in English and translation, internationally; indeed, the article and the response it garnered were phenomenal.[39]

Clearly inspired by the remarkable events beginning to unfold in the Soviet bloc, Fukuyama argued that what we are seeing is neither simply the 'end of ideology' as proposed in the 1950s by Cold War liberal writers and social scientists nor 'a convergence between capitalism and socialism' as once insisted upon by yet other political analysts, but, rather, the 'unabashed victory of economic and political liberalism'. Declaratively invoking the theories of the German philosopher, Georg Friedrich Hegel, Fukuyama stated that 'What we may be witnessing is not just the end of the Cold War, or the passing of a period of postwar history, but the end of history as such: that is, the end point of mankind's ideological evolution and the universalization of Western liberal democracy as the final form of government.' He granted that at least in the short run there will still be issues with which to concern ourselves, because at present the victory of liberalism has only been accomplished at the level of 'ideas and consciousness'; nevertheless, he insisted, the spirit of liberalism has prevailed and, in time, the material world will be transformed in its image.[40]

Columnists and students of contemporary affairs subjected both the theoretical and historical details of Fukuyama's argument to rigorous criticism. However, along with contesting the particulars of the end of history thesis, we should realize and keep in mind what the article actually represented: yet another initiative by the intellectual Right in favour of the changing but persistent efforts of the powers that be to secure capitalist hegemony and to create a new consensus. Whatever its intellectual merit (or otherwise), the end of history thesis emanates from the very same project as that motivating the American and British New Rights' respective but similar endeavours to determine the selective traditions, the significant pasts, to be cultivated in the reinvigorated historical–education curricula. As we have seen, that project has been the fashioning of a new *governing* narrative – one specifically intended to sanctify the present order of things by portraying it as the *culmination* of history, the finest and final fruition of Western and world development, the best of all possible worlds – beyond which the choice is either *more* of the same or economic and political retrogression. Moreover, we should also note that the end of history thesis expresses the continuing development of that project in that it reflects the imperative, the necessity, of attuning the sought-after hegemonic and 'consensual' order to the 'freedoms' and priorities of an increasingly global corporate economy. In short, the present *becomes* future, or, as Daniel Singer ironically put it: 'There was history but it has no future. The age of capital is eternal.'[41]

Thus, we return once again to the problematic of the crisis of history and repeat that in such terms it is not simply about the status of the discipline, but, even more importantly and fundamentally, about the very purpose and promise of historical study and thought. And what is ultimately at stake in our response to the crisis is the vision of the past, present and possible futures that will prevail in our public cultures and discourse. We must ask ourselves both as students of history *and* as citizens (and here, too, I guess we should extend our appreciation to the New Right for reminding us of the intimacy of history and political life): Is the study of the past and its relations with the present to be pursued for the sake of creating a consensus in favour of the world as it is? *Or* is it to be pursued for the contributions it might render to the making of new – perhaps, *a* new – history?

CHAPTER 5

———————— · ————————

BREAKING THE TYRANNY OF THE PRESENT

The French Revolution has abolished many privileges, has raised up many oppressed: but it has only replaced one class with another. Yet it has left a great teaching: that privileges and social differences, as products of society and not of nature, can be overcome.

Antonio Gramsci

THE CHALLENGE

The situation we confront is not that of the 1950s and 60s. The New Right and the powers that be in the United States and Britain have not established the kinds of consensuses characteristic of the post-war liberal and social-democratic settlements and reflected in confident, optimistic and progressive national grand-governing narratives. Nor have they succeeded in establishing new hegemonic orders in the sense of securing popular *affirmations* of the priorities, policies and programmes (or lack thereof) which they have instituted during the last decade and more. That is, they have not (yet) accomplished the refashioning of late twentieth-century capitalist hegemony in the simple sense of ideological domination: 'when a certain way of life and thought is dominant. In which one concept of reality is diffused throughout society. . . .'[1]

Yet, if we understand hegemony as an 'order of struggle' (as outlined above in Chapter 3), then the New Rights can be said to have succeeded for, as we have seen, although there persists a degree of popular commitment to liberal and social-democratic principles and priorities, they have revised and continue to set the political agenda and there is little evidence of dynamic and challenging opposition from below. Again, there *is* struggle, but it is limited, dispersed and essentially defensive. In other words, capitalist hegemony does prevail in that the popular stance is apparently one of pragmatic acceptance and accommodation and there is little hope expressed that collective action and agency on the part of 'the common' or working people can be effective in changing the political and social order. As the British critic, Patrick Wright, sadly reflects: 'Thus dawns the era of anxious irresponsibility in which everyone seems both helpless and innocent – not just of what happens to themselves, but of the fate of others both near and also at the farthest reaches of an increasingly instantaneous world system.'[2]

Making it all the more problematic is that such a state of affairs, a widespread presumption of the futility of human and social agency, has come to characterize popular thinking in the face of an energetic and aggressive – however unevenly successful – New Right politics, class war from above and, most recently, the history-making risings of the East European peoples. To be sure, the prevailing discourse is not that *all* action is hopeless but, rather, that human energies are only worth venturing in private and economic pursuits – *not* politically. There is a strong similarity here to the view of history to be found in the writings of the post-1945 American 'consensus, or counterprogressive intellectuals'. David W. Noble has described the content of their arguments: 'the attempt to achieve political virtue must end in tragedy because it symbolized an effort to control history, the pursuit of economic self-interest, in contrast, represented a humble acceptance of the fallen nature of humanity. Their conservative jeremiad could warn against political pride, but not against ambition in the marketplace.' However foolish it may sound, it is no joke that the ideologues of the dominant class broadcast the triumph of capital as the end of history and, moreover, that it is being marketed as the grand-governing narrative, portending serious consequences for historical memory, consciousness and imagination. Norman Birnbaum observes: 'Modern authoritarianism is not subtle, but it is omnipresent. Its new form is not obeisance to human authority alone, but a reification of the present, a refusal to believe that human institutions could be different.'[3]

Curiously, a similar tale to that proffered by the New Right and the elites of corporate capitalism is being told by others, many of whom claim a more critical posture towards the world and even ties with the Left. As noted above (in Chapter 2), 'post-modernists' not only portray contemporary experience as discontinuous with the past but contend that 'a permanent change has taken place' in Western and world culture and history. In essence they, too, assert that the present, our contemporary experience, represents an *ending* or, actually, an *afterwards*. The philosopher, Agnes Heller, writes in *The Postmodern Political Condition* that:

> the primary concern of those living the present as postmodern is that they live in the present while at the same time, both temporally, as well as spatially, they are *being after*.
> Politically speaking, those who have chosen to understand themselves as postmodern are in the first place after the 'grand narrative'. . . . Postmodernity is in every respect 'parasitic' on modernity; it lives and feeds on its achievements and on its dilemmas. What *is* new is the novel historical consciousness developed in *post-histoire*; the spreading feeling that we are permanently going to be in the present and, at the same time, after it.[4]

In short, both the powers that be *and* the post-modernists paint the present as 'our sole eternity'. Admittedly, there are significant differences between the stories they tell. Whereas the former advance a grand-governing narrative which announces that we have arrived at the end of history and 'promises' hope in the form of a 'progress' to be characterized by continued economic growth and expansion, the latter proclaim we are 'liberated' from grand-governing narratives, that we find our-selves in the age of post-history, and, rejecting images of both continuity and progress, post-modern currents offer little or no hope at all. Nevertheless, both essentially deny that political action and struggle might possibly change and radically trans-form – for the better – the present order of things, that human and social agency might actually be capable of making *new* history, let alone new *forms* of history. Together, the end-of-history and post-history theses deny reason to hope that the future could actually be different from the present.[5] Reacting to the varied but, ultimately, similar 'post-modern' rhetorics, Daniel Singer's words of exasperation are relevant here:

> The most fashionable word today seems to be the prefix *post-*. We are living in a 'postindustrial' society and admiring 'postmodern art'. The trendy commentators bombard us with futuristic images of nuclear-triggered X-ray lasers, of one-world television beamed from satellites, of robots doing our work and computers our thinking. However, if you dare to ask why it is that a world changing so fantastically in so many respects must somehow be tied forever to the same forms of property and exploitation, you are dismissed as a dinosaur. On reflection, the philosophy behind this futuristic mumbo jumbo is rather old-fashioned. Like all ruling classes, the present-day one admits the existence of history up to its own triumph, although not beyond. Post-everything means capitalist forever. There was history, but time must now have a stop.[6]

There *is* a crisis of history, but not that enunciated by our New Rights. The crisis is not simply that historical education has been reduced and marginalized and, indeed, warrants all the attention it has been receiving. It is, moreover, that after a decade and more of Reaganism and Thatcherism, in which freedoms have been under attack, inequality has been increasing, and democratic activity has become narrower and shallower, our sense of and anxiety about discontinuity and decline not only persist but are now exacerbated and made all the more problematic by the ongoing siege of collective historical memory, consciousness and imagination being waged via a discourse which celebrates the supposed end of history!

For those of us committed as both citizens and historians to the development – nay, the *making* – of societies ever more libertarian, egalitarian and democratic, such a state of affairs is clearly unacceptable. But what should be the response from those of us who do not believe that the contemporary political and social orders, even in their most advanced and humane liberal-democratic forms, represent the culmination of history? Obviously, historians themselves cannot undo or negate the processes which are being experienced and not just imagined; still, they can and must seek to contribute to our comprehension of and, thereby, to our deliberations regarding how to address them. The pursuit of 'contemporary history', however, is a task which only scholars in selected fields can directly undertake. As I have previously stated, first and foremost we must continue to contest – even more energetically than we have – the abuse of 'the past' and its relations with the present by the New Right and political and economic elites, along with that by any others, above *and* below, who would subordinate and rewrite it to suit their own purposes and ambitions. Yet, a still grander initiative is called for.

More broadly, it is a matter of confronting the sense of impotence and the belief that action, especially *political* action, is futile, which together afflict the popular understanding of history, and of challenging both the forces encouraging and cultivating such views and those who benefit from them. As was discussed above (at the close of Chapter 1), there are those historians who have been insisting that new historical syntheses are in order. Faced with the projects and schemes of the New Right, it is arguable that critical historians themselves ought to be seeking to take the lead both in their creation and in conveying them to students and to wider publics, looking towards the development of new grand-governing narratives. Yet, as the New Rights and their intellectual associates may be learning, such a project, as earlier pointed out, depends, at least in democratic polities, on the actual formation of a consensus or movement towards it – a development that appears to be missing thus far, and fortunately so, for given the politics of the day, it would likely be supportive of the conservative powers that be.

To be completely clear about it, the problem we face is not how to restore the old liberal and social-democratic consensuses, the narratives about the triumph of the Keynesian Welfare State (and, remember, the 'end of ideology') and the historical analysis associated with them. The social realities they denied or obscured and the conflicts of the 1960s and 70s persisting in however attenuated fashion today, as well as the many critical and pluralistic historical studies accomplished during the past generation, should warn us against simple syntheses. At the same time,

I am not saying with the post-modernist philosophers and theorists that we have transcended the age of grand narratives; though I would wish they were right about the mortality of those which posit historical predestinations and inevitabilities. Let us not forget that however much the older-style consensuses may not (at present) exist, there is in the end-of-history and, their own, post-history discourse a grand-governing narrative in formation and, possibly, ascendance. I do very well imagine the articulation of (dare I call them) 'grand-governing' narratives envisioning possible futures dependent not on extra- or trans-historical laws or imperatives, but on determined human agency informed by critical historical memory, consciousness and imagination (I shall return to this in the final section of the chapter). In any case, regarding the restoration of the liberal and social-democratic settlements and associated national grand narratives, although a new politics and history will have to start by engaging the persistent values and ideals of liberalism and social-democracy, the current situation does not allow for a return to the *status quo ante*.

As I stated early in this work, confronting the crisis of history, when appreciated in its fullness, entails a more critical conception of historical practice than those being propounded in most discussions.

THE POWERS OF THE PAST

I would argue that it is now time to recall and reassert that vision which drew so many of us to the discipline in the 1960s and early 70s: a vision of historians as citizen-scholars who by their labours contribute directly to public culture and debate, to the democratic formation and re-formation of political and social thought.

It might immediately be retorted that an understanding of historical practice stated merely in terms of its potential contributions to public discourse encompasses, as well, the intentions and aspirations proclaimed for the discipline by the New Rights and their intellectuals. And, ignoring for the moment their persistent reduction and abuse of the past, that is true. However, in contrast to a view of the purpose and promise of history which reduces it to enhancing consensus in favour of the world as it is (or worse), the vision which attracted and inspired us was that of historical study and thought *critically* engaging and challenging the world in favour of what might yet be made of it, especially in support of the further development and making of the ideals and practices of liberty, equality and democratic community.

Of course, such a vision did not belong to our 'generation' of the 1960s and early 70s alone. Arguably, it had always been a part of the historical enterprise. Distinguishing veneration of 'the past' from historical study and celebrating the role of the latter in undermining the former, the senior English historian, J. H. Plumb, reminded us (in 1968): 'from the Renaissance onwards there has been a growing determination for historians to try and understand what happened purely in its own terms and not in the service of religion or national destiny, or morality, or the sanctity of institutions.' 'True history', he said, is 'the attempt to see things as they were, irrespective of what conflict this might create with what the wise ones of one's own society make of the past. . . . Basically history is destructive.'[7] Granted that the 'narrative' of historiography which Plumb provided was far too ideal and innocent, blind to its deference and corruption, to its serving as 'handmaiden to authority'; still, such an ethos can be found as a continual force in its development and, as we observed regarding the development of social history in particular, it has been regularly renewed by scholars of varyingly intense commitments to projects of political and social change.

By no means merely the property of a particular generation, neither is such a vision of historical study and thought solely the possession of any single political tradition. Although it may have seemed (in Chapter 3) that I was belittling Robert Nisbet's claims about the relationship between conservatives and 'the past' by posing them alongside the practices and schemes of Reagan, Thatcher and their associates, it must be acknowledged that conservatives themselves are no less capable of actually respecting the past and pursuing its study for critical purposes than those on the Left (and other books could well be written on the Left's own disrespect for history). In this regard, I must quote Nisbet's concluding lines to his book, *Conservatism*:

Both sets of traditionalists – Burkean conservatives and Marxian socialists – are compelled to live under the liberal welfare state, which they do not like, though for different reasons, and both ideological groups will yield, as they have for some time now, culture-guerrillas whose most obvious future is that of the use of the past in attack on the present.[8]

Nevertheless, having said all of this, there is no denying that the vision of history's purpose and promise which emerged in the 1960s and infused a generation of exuberant scholarship was, as we have already discussed, clearly of the Left (broadly understood) and its spirit was radical. It was significantly influenced and shaped by the Western Marxist tradition – in fact, the encounter actually entailed the recovery, working-through and elaboration of this tradition of thought as an alternative to the encrusted, orthodox, dogmatic and 'official' doctrine of Marxism, or Marxism-Leninism, dictated and propagated by Soviet ideologues and those of their ilk. Traceable to Marx and Engels themselves, the Western Marxist tradition is itself hardly singular, including such diverse figures as Georg Lukács, Rosa Luxemburg, Karl Korsch, the Frankfurt School thinkers such as Herbert Marcuse and Walter Benjamin, and, the most historically orientated, Antonio Gramsci. However, as varied as their ideas about history and politics were, they were all drawn to the same problematic regarding the persistence of industrial capitalism, the consciousness of working people and the possible role of the intellectual in bringing about political and social change and, in contrast to the economism of both 'Second-International' socialism and Soviet Communism, many of the Western Marxists concerned themselves with questions of culture and ideology.[9]

At the same time, there was the previously noted influence of the British Marxist historical tradition (referred to in both the Prolegomena and Chapter 1). More than any others, the British Marxists and the works they were accomplishing provided a model and seemed to offer an original orientation and direction for aspiring critical historians. The 'vision' of which I speak, therefore, is not merely of historians contributing to public debates but of their scholarly and pedagogical activities revealing the structures and relations of exploitation and oppression past and present *and* recovering 'from the bottom up' the lives and voices of those who have suffered and resisted them. Stated romantically, we saw historians acting in the manner of Robin Hood, that is, 'reappropriating' the past from the powers that be past and present.[10]

It should be made clear that however 'committed' politically is this conception of historical practice, it is no less committed to scholarly *objectivity*. However, it recognizes and is sensitive to the structures, practices, and intentions of power. As Barrington Moore, Jr, explained at the time:

> Objectivity is not the same thing as conventional judiciousness. A celebration of our own society which leaves out its ugly and cruel features, which fails to face the question of a connection between its attractive and its cruel ones, remains an apologia even if it is spoken in the most measured academic tones. There is a strong tendency to assume that mild-mannered statements in favour of the *status quo* are 'objective' and that anything else is a form of 'rhetoric' . . . any simple straightforward truth about political institutions or events is bound to have polemical consequences. It will damage some group interests. In any society the dominant groups are the ones with most to hide about the way society works.

Thus, to maximize objectivity *and* to write critical history, he recommended the following: 'For all students of human society, sympathy with the victims of historical processes and skepticism about the victors' claims provide essential safeguards against being taken in by the dominant mythology. A scholar who tries to be objective needs those feelings as part of his ordinary equipment.' Or, in the more evocative words of Walter Benjamin: 'Only that historian will have the gift of fanning the spark of hope in the past who is firmly convinced that *even the dead* will not be safe from the enemy if he wins. And this enemy [the ruling class] has not ceased to be victorious.'[11]

This objectivity/scepticism is not only an academic or professional obligation. It is also absolutely crucial to realizing one's political, especially *democratic*, aspirations. As the French historian, Jean Chesneaux, has insisted: 'Here as elsewhere the stakes are political. Scientific accuracy is not an abstract intellectual demand, but the precondition of a coherent political analysis: "Whoever invents false revolutionary legends for the people, amuses them with lyrical tales, is no less guilty than a geographer who draws up misleading maps for navigators."[12]

In an age of celebrated relativism we ought not to pass over this particular issue too quickly. Considering the never-ceasing use and abuse of the past by the powerful and the oppressive on a global scale, we must recognize, without at all denying our critical perspectives, that the most radical aspiration of students of history is that of 'keeping the record straight' or, in the too-often ridiculed words of Leopold von Ranke: 'to show what really happened' (although he no doubt intended things quite different than those I am proposing). As Yosef Hayim Yerushalmi has admonished:

> The essential dignity of the historical vocation remains, and its moral imperative seems to me now more urgent than ever. . . . Against the agents of oblivion, the shredders of documents, the assassins of memory, the revisers of encyclopedias, the conspirators of silence, against those who, in Kundera's wonderful image, can airbrush a man out of a photograph so that nothing is left of him but his hat – only the historian, with his austere passion for fact, proof, evidence, which are central to his vocation, can effectively stand guard.[13]

One cannot help but re-record the observation of the late deposed Soviet leader, Nikita Khrushchev, that 'Historians are dangerous people. They are capable of upsetting everything!' Starting here, our vision nevertheless demanded more, it demanded a more extensive engagement (a word which the intellectual servants of the political and economic elites love to belittle). It compelled us, in view of the world in which we lived, to see historians not as consensus-builders but as political and social critics invoking the *powers of the past* – perspective, critique, consciousness, remembrance and imagination – both to comprehend and consider the present and to help chart new directions for the future. By *perspective* I mean the awareness that the way things are is not the way they have always been nor the way they will, or must, necessarily be in the future. 'The problem is precisely that of seeing things historically', Gramsci wrote, and Karl Korsch dubbed it the 'principle of historical specification'. Eric Hobsbawm expressed it like this:

> It does seem to me, particularly at present, that you've got to recognize what is new in a situation and what is, therefore, unprecedented and to what extent old ways of handling it are inadequate or not. . . . Now all these things [referring to the global changes and developments of the post-WWII period] require historical perspective that is essentially the capacity to see how society changes and when things are different and when things are the same.[14]

Perspective as historical specificity was a foremost imperative and objective of both French *annalistes* and British Marxists, no more brilliantly developed perhaps than in the studies of the social structures and mentalities of European feudalism by the great medievalist and founding figure of the *Annales*, Marc Bloch. Though he may have given too much weight to foresight and prescience in this instance, Bloch's remarks in *Strange Defeat* are worth recalling: 'History is, in its essentials, the science of change . . . the lesson it teaches is not that what happened yesterday will necessarily happen tomorrow, or that the past will go on reproducing itself. By examining how and why yesterday differed from the day before, it can reach conclusions which will enable it to foresee how tomorrow will differ from yesterday.' (*Strange Defeat* was written in 1940 following the fall of France and its occupation by the Germans. Bloch, who had served in the French army, already a veteran of the First World War, had been evacuated to England, but chose to immediately return to France, to his family, to his work and to join the Resistance. Tragically, in 1944 he was captured and executed by the Gestapo.)[15]

More recently, the American social and cultural historian of early modern France, Natalie Zemon Davis, who was herself clearly influenced by both the *Annales* and Marxist traditions, voiced the spreading aspiration to invoke this particular power of the past, perspective, in a possibly even more original way. Noting her disavowal of that kind of Marxism which had proclaimed its own grand narrative of historical 'stages' and guarantees, she went on to say:

> But I do use the past in another way. I let it speak and I show that

things don't have to be the way they are now. I want to show
how different the past was. I want to show that even when times
were hard, people found ways to cope with what was happening
and maybe resist it. I want people today to be able to connect
with the past by looking at the tragedies and sufferings of the
past, the cruelties and the hatefulness, the hope of the past, the
love people had, and the beauty they had. They sought for power
over each other, but they helped each other, too. They did things
out of both love and fear – that's my message. Especially, I want
to show that it could be different, that it was different and there
are alternatives.[16]

Critique is more specific, entailing a deliberate effort at
debunking and demystifying the contemporary world. In
particular this means unveiling and revealing the *social* origins of
the present especially those of the structures and relations of
power, exploitation and oppression which have come to be
represented and conceived of as *natural* and inevitable. Theistic,
biological, psychological, economic and technological deter-
minisms: these are not merely scholastic and academic theories
and paradigms. They abound and are reproduced in public and
private conversation and thought. Marx spoke of this problem as
a 'fetishism'; and, following him, Georg Lukács explored it as
'reification': 'man in capitalist society confronts a reality "made"
by him (as a class) which appears to him to be a natural
phenomenon alien to himself' – which Max Horkheimer and
Theodor Adorno encapsulated in the phrase 'All reification is a
forgetting'. Thus, the task of the critical historian becomes that
of 'breaking the tyranny of the present' through 'anamnesis'. It is
necessary, in the words of Walter Benjamin, to 'brush history
against the grain'.[17] David Noble, American historian and the
author of pioneering works on the 'second industrial revolution'
and the social determination of its managerial practices and
technologies has articulated the potential, or threat, of history as
*de*reification:

> It is the primary task of the historian to demystify history, to
> render it intelligible in human rather than in super-human or non-
> human terms, to show that history is a realm of human freedom
> as well as necessity. By describing how people have shaped
> history in the past, the historian reminds us that people continue
> to shape history in the present.[18]

Walter Benjamin may have been right when he reflected that political struggle is 'nourished more by the image of enslaved ancestors than liberated grandchildren'.[19] Nevertheless, if we are to comprehend the manifold expression of human agency and its effects, and confront the prevailing sense of futility in action, then we must attend to action and agency above *and* below. *Consciousness*, therefore, refers to an even fuller appreciation of the making of history. It recalls the aspirations for education expressed by Gramsci (quoted earlier in the Prolegomena) regarding the development of a 'historical dialectical conception of the world, which understands movement and change, which appreciates the sum of effort and sacrifice which the present has cost the past and which the future is costing the present, and which conceives the contemporary world as a synthesis of the past, of all past generations, which projects itself into the future.' And there is no question but that Gramsci himself had in mind the recovery of the actions and agency of the elites and statemakers, their powers, impositions and exactions, *and*, to the extent possible, the actions and agency of those whom he referred to in what were to be his *Prison Notebooks* as the 'subaltern classes'. Indeed, throughout the *Notebooks* he urges the exploration and investigation of the lives and movements of working people *within the context*, and as part of the dynamic, of the social orders that they both maintained and resisted and against which they occasionally rebelled.[20]

The starting point, or framework, for such work was well articulated by the English critic, Terry Eagleton: 'What is meant by reading history from the standpoint of the oppressed is not that the oppressed are the concealed, forgotten, inarticulate, abandoned "subject" of history; it means, rather, grasping history as constructed from within the constraints that the oppressed by their very existence impose.'[21] As we know, following the lead of the British Marxists and others in their efforts to reappropriate the experiences and struggles of peasants, yeomen, slaves, artisans and workers, and moving out in original directions and fashions from them, historians transatlantically (and beyond) have accomplished much and we are now provided with an impressive (to some, excessive) scholarship on both the triumphs and the, far more usual, defeats ensuing from the conflicts of class, race and ethnicity, and gender which have been variably expressed in resistance, rebellion and revolutionary-rising, not to mention accommodation and the modes of resistance and survival which go on within it.

Far more remains to be done, but let us not be naïve or foolish. To invoke the powers of the past is to call forth a chronicle of tragedy, what Christopher Hill has called 'the experience of defeat'. And where it is not tragic it is ironic. As the nineteenth-century English writer and socialist, William Morris, observed in his novel, *The Dream of John Ball*: 'I pondered how men fight and lose the battle, and the thing they fought for comes about in spite of their defeat, and when it comes turns out to be not what they meant, and other men have to fight for what they meant under another name.' None of which negates the fact that 'nothing is gained without a struggle.'[22]

Remembrance acknowledges that while 'the past is not for living in, it is a well of conclusions from which we draw in order to act.'[23] The power of the past in this respect actually begins with the chronicling of defeat, tragedy and, even, horror. It is motivated by 'the will to bear witness' with all due and sincere respect to those who have suffered and were, or were not, able themselves to testify. Herbert Marcuse explains:

> To forget is . . . the mental faculty which sustains submissiveness and renunciation. To forget is also to forgive what should not be forgiven if justice and freedom are to prevail. Such forgiveness reproduces the conditions which reproduce injustice and enslave-ment: to forget past suffering is to forgive the forces that caused it – without defeating those forces. . . . Against this surrender to time, the restoration of remembrance to its rights, as a vehicle of liberation, is one of the noblest tasks of thought.

Moreover, within the chronicle there is both tragedy and grounds for hope: 'Remembrance of the past may give rise to dangerous insights, and the established society seems to be apprehensive of the subversive contents of memory. . . . Memory recalls the terror and the hope, but whereas in reality, the former recurs in ever new forms, the latter remains hope.' It is not a question of religious inspiration and/or a belief in divine intervention, nor one of weights and measures, that is, posing the 'progress' of science, technology and material advancement alongside the record of humanly enacted suffering. It is a matter of standing *in* history and, without losing touch with the record and experience of defeat, recognizing that human action and agency from below in opposition to the powers that be, are not always beaten and that even those which were, warrant our attention for in their own ways they have been consequential. The philosopher, Ronald Aronson, in seeking reasons to hope in the face of the 'dialectics of disaster', turned to look again at the past and exclaimed that 'we have accomplished so much':

> The real historical advances in human social morality have occurred through . . . struggles. Slavery has been abolished, democratic rights won, certain elements of dignity and equality promised and achieved, wars ended, other wars forestalled – only because we have acted. Projected now desperately, now with confidence, in collective visions by movement after movement, sacrificed for, agitated for, partially achieved, then legitimized by law and custom, social progress has been *made true* each step of the way.[24]

It must be insisted that this is *not* to provide for the restoration of an optimistic and progressive narrative: 'Not only is there no overarching progress, in the sense of one force operating behind the backs of human beings and imposing itself on and through them – neither is there any decisive human tendency leading towards the improvement of the human lot.' Critical historians know this, but it does not leave them without resources and treasures in the face of the 'progress' of the end-of-history ideologues or the *anomie* of the post-modernists. 'Hope does not demand a belief in progress', Christopher Lasch has written, 'It demands a belief in justice: a conviction that the wicked will suffer, that wrongs will be made right. . . .' Though it is not our task *as* historians to exact retribution, in our invocation of remembrance we help to realize the idea that the 'antonym of "forgetting" is not "remembering", but *justice*', as Yerushalmi has suggested in reflection on the 1987 trial in France of the Nazi 'butcher of Lyons', Klaus Barbie.[25]

There is more. Remembrance recalls not only the experience and the struggle but the hopes themselves – the aspirations, the visions and the dreams. Armed with these, our capacity to consider critically the present order of things and imagine alternatives to it is renewed and enhanced. The political theorist, John Keane, has reiterated the importance of a 'democratic remembrance of things past': 'An active democratic memory recognizes that the development of fresh and stimulating perspectives on the present depends upon criticisms that break up habitual ways of thinking, in part through types of criticism which remember what is in danger of being forgotten.' Capturing the tragic nature of history, Barrington Moore wrote in *Social Origins of Dictatorship and Democracy*, reflecting on the struggles of peasants and artisans in the making of the modern world: 'From these facts one may conclude that the wellsprings of human freedom lie not only where Marx saw them, in the aspirations of classes about to take power, but perhaps even more in the dying wail of a class over whom the wave of progress is about to roll.' Indeed, although he would later make statements seeming to disclaim such 'younger' thinking, Marx himself once romantically proposed that: 'It will then be clear that the world has long possessed the dream of a thing which it needs only to possess the consciousness in order to really possess it. It will be clear that the problem is not some great gap between the thoughts of the past and those of the future, but the completion of the thoughts of the past.'[26]

Finally, *imagination* is to comprehend that the present *is* history, *not* its end or its afterwards and, thus, it insists that we consider the structure, movement and possibilities of the contemporary world and how we might *act* to prevent the barbaric and develop the humanistic. As E. P. Thompson has seen it: 'Historical consciousness ought to assist one to understand the possibilities of transformation and the possibilities within people'; and, similarly, Herbert Gutman: 'Historical understanding teaches us to transform the seemingly fixed and eternal in our lives into things that can be changed. It teaches working people that the structures surrounding them have been made and remade, over and over. It teaches that we live in history.'[27]

Imagination recalls us to another aspect of the 'democratic' vision of history which our generation made its own: that historical labours were to be linked with not only the experiences and struggles of working people and the oppressed of the past, but, also, those of the present – that the purpose and promise of historical study and thought were bound up with the *making* of history not only in the past tense but in those of the present and future as well.

MAKING HISTORY

I have not restated the vision of the purpose and promise of historical study and thought which drew so many of us to the discipline merely for 'historical' reasons, because of its importance to a generation, an exceptional generation, of historical scholarship. I have done so, first, because it remains unfulfilled, and, second, because in the face of the crisis of history, so imperative. Moreover, it is an act of recollection and of redemption made all the more necessary, it would seem, by the amnesia apparently suffered by many of the editorial 'gate-keepers' of social historiography. Astonishingly (as we saw in Chapter 1), their recent calls for new ideas and approaches with which to 'refresh' the field were essentially devoid of any recognition of the political and critical impulse motivating the phenomenal growth and development of social history in the 1960s or, more importantly, the need to revive such an impulse today (and this, in spite of the commanding presence which 'critical' and 'adversarial' historians are supposed to possess in the profession!).

In his book on the 'academicization' of intellectual life in America, *The Last Intellectuals*, Russell Jacoby has appreciatively and sympathetically acknowledged that selected 'radical' historians more than their counterparts in other disciplines have 'informed, even influenced public discussions'; but he rightly warns that historians, too, have been increasingly subject to a process of self-enclosure within university departments and professional associations, a process for which they themselves, that is, *we* ourselves, no less than others, are ultimately responsible. (It is, apparently, no less the case in Britain.) Paralleling the spreading and deepening sense of hopelessness and futility, we have splendidly succeeded through hard work and accomplishment in commencing the 'reappropriation' of the past, but it might be asked, for *whom*? (I am here reminded of the question which Marc Bloch proffered regarding his own generation: 'The real trouble with us professors was that we were absorbed in our day-to-day tasks. Most of us can say with some justice that we were good workmen. Is it equally true to say that we were good citizens?')[28]

It must not be forgotten that our subscription to a radical-democratic vision of history's purpose and promise was inspired not only, nor even originally, as my words thus far in this chapter might too readily imply, by our intellectual encounters with the work of more senior and earlier scholars and thinkers, but also by our active involvements, or aspirations to become so involved, in the struggles and movements of the day and our intentions to contribute to them by enlarging historical memory, consciousness and imagination. Against the reduction of history to the status of servant of the powers that be and in support of the world as it is we not only need to recall the radical-democratic purpose and promise of historical study and thought, but also to redeclare and revitalize our commitment to it. I find others of my generation realizing the same. American social historian, Roy Rosenzweig writes:

> the initial energy of the new social history came from its emergence, and connection to, the social and political movements of the 1960s. Conversely, the problem of the 'new' history today is not so much fragmentation as an intense and depoliticized professionalization . . . current social history has lost the political and social questions and concerns that originally animated it and along the way has lost any relevance to a nonacademic public. Resolving the crisis of history may require that historians not only write about the making of our public culture in the past, but also take a more active role in remaking it in the present.

We have witnessed a tremendous growth in popular interest and demand for 'the past'. It is time for us to establish, or *re*-establish, the connections between 'history' and 'the people', which means taking to heart the words of Gerda Lerner: 'We must be open to the ways in which people now relate to the past, and we must reach out to communicate with them at their level.'[29] The 'pragmatic' proposals to address the crisis and alienation of history discussed in Chapter 1 might well be reconsidered and reconceived in the light of this discussion, along with developing plans and ideas even more activist in character. This entails working at the grassroots through labour unions, women's centres, churches and synagogues, and community organizations; involving ourselves with these groups in the creation and recreation of historical museums and their exhibits; and seeking new avenues of publication and communication, including the writing of stories and columns in local and national newspapers and magazines. At the same time, it means learning and relearning how to address 'publics' intelligently and smartly but not so 'academically', through our writing and speaking, as well as media-production, and teaching our students in h2istory to be able to do the same. Indeed, we should foster in our students and ourselves the recognition that the historian, however scholarly, can also be a public intellectual and critic. However much such talk seems naïvely optimistic, experience dictates both the necessity and the possibility of such endeavours; as Gramsci used to remind: 'Pessimism of the intellect, optimism of the will'.

Yet, whatever else we undertake in this regard, our efforts must commence with and, ultimately, return to the terrain of schooling, education and the determination of historical curricula for it is through its schools that a people articulates and communicates its public values, identities and aspirations. Here, I would argue – perhaps, against the grain of my colleagues and comrades – that even as we contest and reject the New Rights' use and abuse of the past and their ambitions for history, we must not only enthusiastically endorse their calls for the reinvigoration and restoration of historical education but, even, seek to *critically* appropriate their projects, including the re-development of coherent syntheses and 'narratives'. However, and this, of course, is crucial, in contrast to renditions of our 'significant pasts' which entail stories defining the present order of things as the culmination of Western and world-historical development, the end of history, we must begin to fashion and cultivate, from the perspective of the bottom up, a narrative of tragedy *and* hope which speaks of the contemporary world not as a termination point (or an 'afterwards') but as a moment of contradictions and dangers and, also, imperatives and possibilities including those which might be engaged for *democratic* development and the making of freer and more equal social orders. As I have said, such syntheses must eschew guarantees and predestinations and encourage hope, not so much in 'progress' as in the possibility, *if* individual and collective agency struggle for it, of 'justice'.[30]

I would extend our appropriation of supposedly 'conservative' projects even further by demanding that we actually redeem the 'classical' ideal of education, that is, as preparation to *rule* – historically, the preparation and outfitting of the ruling *elite*. Schooling in history and the humanities were central features of this process, intended, as Elizabeth Fox-Genovese recounts, 'to provide selected individuals with a collective history, culture, and epistemology so that they could run the world effectively'.[31] Contrary to the more simplistic of radical positions, it is not a matter of rejecting such a conception of education and, with it, the fundamental role which history played within it, but of radically transforming it. *Democratic* schooling must also be about the preparation and outfitting of 'rulers' – as Gramsci put it: 'forming [the child] during this time as a person capable of thinking, studying, and ruling – or controlling those who rule'. However, as Gramsci well knew, it must be bound to a polity, *or* a struggle for such, in which it is not an 'elite' that rules, but 'the people': 'democracy, by definition, cannot mean merely that an unskilled worker can become skilled. It must mean that every "citizen" can "govern" and that society places him, even if only abstractly, in a general condition to achieve this.'[32]

Moreover, it is not simply a question of replacing the old 'elitist' stories with new 'populist' ones. The redemption of the classical ideal of education should also include the critical appropriation of the 'traditions of Western Civilization' and their rearticulation within the narratives we would develop. This would entail their comprehension and representation not as 'heritage' but as 'inheritances' (along the lines proposed, and for the reasons indicated, in the surprisingly welcome Final Report of the British National Curriculum History Working Group). Asserting that Marxism – the 'philosophy of praxis' – did not involve a disavowal of Western civilization, but its incorporation, Gramsci wrote: 'The philosophy of praxis presupposes all this cultural past ['this entire movement of intellectual and moral reformation']: Renaissance and Reformation, German philosophy and the French Revolution, Calvinism and English classical economics, secular liberalism and historicism which is at the root of the whole modern conception of life.' And, in these terms, it is not surprising that he insisted upon a 'classical' historical education for the working class: 'If it is true that universal history is a chain made up of the efforts man has exerted to free himself from privilege, prejudice and idolatry, then it is hard to understand why the proletariat, which seeks to add another link to that chain should not know how and by whom it was preceded, or what advantage it might derive from this knowledge.' At the same time, Gramsci also called for a fuller understanding, a *social* history, of intellectual and cultural traditions:

> From our point of view, studying the history and the logic of the various philosophers' philosophies is not enough. At least as a methodological guideline, attention should be drawn to the other parts of the history of philosophy; to the conceptions of the world held by the great masses, to those of the most restricted ruling (or intellectual) groups, and finally to the links between these various cultural complexes and the philosophy of the philosophers.[33]

Truly critical study of this sort must also be imbued with the tragic sensibility and historical realism insisted upon by Walter Benjamin:

> Whoever has emerged victorious participates to this day in the triumphal procession in which the present rulers step over those who are lying prostrate. According to traditional practice, the spoils are carried along in the procession. They are called cultural treasures, and a historical materialist views them with cautious detachment. For without exception the cultural treasures he surveys have an origin which he cannot contemplate without horror. They owe their existence not only to the efforts of the great minds and talents who have created them, but also to the

anonymous toil of their contemporaries. There is no document of
civilization which is not at the same time a document of
barbarism.[34]

Nevertheless, such an understanding of past and present does
not entail the wholesale rejection of Western civilization as the
more nihilistic currents of post-modernism suggest. In fact, as
Gramsci recognized: 'In the accumulation of ideas transmitted to
us by a millennium of work and thought there are elements
which have eternal value, which cannot and must not perish. The
loss of consciousness of these values is one of the most serious
signs of degradation brought about by the bourgeois regime; to
them everything becomes an object of trade and a weapon of
war.' The challenge for critical historians is, therefore, that 'of
taking them up . . . making them glow with new light'.[35] But it
does not cease there, for as Benjamin warned: 'The danger affects
both the content of that tradition and its receivers. The same
threat hangs over both: that of becoming a tool of the ruling
classes. In every era the attempt must be made anew to wrest
tradition away from a conformism that is about to overpower
it.'[36]

In this vein, we must remind ourselves of what our historical
scholarship has been revealing for some time (and increasingly so
today!): that which has been called *European* or *Western*
civilization is not only *not* as 'singular', 'bright' and 'progressive'
as had long been taught by ideologues and pedagogues but not so
simply 'European' or 'Western'. Contrary to the exclamations of
the Right, 'Western culture' is a product of a complex history of
adaptation, origination, innovation and incorporation resulting
both from the interactions among 'Western' peoples themselves
and from those with non-Western peoples by way of exploration,
exchange, theft, conflict, conquest and migration (elected and
coerced) – all of which must be treated as deftly and
imaginatively as our *historical* literary and teaching skills allow.[37]
It is not a question of fairness, or at least not that alone; it is a
question of accuracy and it is crucial if we are to comprehend the
continuities, changes *and* discontinuities in our 'national' and
'international' experiences. Indeed, it becomes all the more
urgent if we are to begin to address the implications of the

ongoing globalization of the capitalist world economy, offering possibilities both of good and of evil depending upon the kinds of collective agency mobilized and advanced from above and/or below both nationally *and* transnationally. Tom Bender may be correct in saying that our historical syntheses must be articulated as *national* narratives given the contemporary form and nature of *political* life, but inasmuch as our 'national' histories and 'Western Civilization' always have been, and are ever increasingly, entangled in an even 'larger' set of developments and experiences, we should keep in mind the words of the historian and French patriot, Marc Bloch, to the effect that there can be 'no national history, only world history' and, in the same spirit, those of Ronald Aronson:

> There are many histories, but [t]here is also a world history, among whose decisive events are numbered the rise of Christianity, the Reformation, the Industrial Revolution, the French, American and Russian and Chinese Revolutions. Such world-historic events affect all societies sooner or later, influencing the lives of the most remote peoples. In this sense, whoever may have been our antecedents and whatever is our history, Spartacus and the bourgeois revolutions have become a part of our distant past and the American Black and Civil Rights movements have shaped our present being and possibilities. However abstract these links may appear we are indeed affected by an interrelated process of human struggle unfolding through, and creating, human history.[38]

The 'significant pasts' and 'selective traditions' to be articulated and rendered in historical curricula must not be considered frozen or permanent fixtures, nor presented as self-evident (points stated, we should again appreciate, in the Report of the National Curriculum History Working Group). It must always be made clear that these historical narratives are constructs based upon (objective) historical scholarship and interpretation informed by particular values and visions – let us hope, and work to assure, that they are those of liberty, equality and democratic community (themselves historically *made*) – and, thus, subject to *historically* determined revision in response both to new and original studies of the past *and* to what we make of history, that is, to the extent that 'Action in the present will determine the meaning of the past'.[39]

Perhaps, what we must actually do is make clear that our vision for history and historical study represent not so much a 'break' with educational 'tradition' as the reclamation and reaffirmation of the most critical and, potentially, democratic aspects of it. As the political scientist, Benjamin Barber, observed not long ago, at one and the same time reflecting on the aspirations of the 1960s and recalling the most classical intentions of pedagogical practice: 'all education is or ought to be radical – a reminder of the past, a challenge to the present, and a prod to the future.'[40]

Am I, then, arguing for the development of new grand-governing narratives? Clearly so. However, that I not be misinterpreted I would repeat once again that the kind of narrative we should seek to articulate and advance must be one which speaks not of guarantees about the course of history, but of possibilities for the *making* of history, including the possibility of new *forms* of history characterized by the abolition of class and the liberation of race, ethnic, national and gender identities and relations.

Yet, have I not repeatedly declared that the making of grand-governing narratives requires the establishment of a 'consensus' or, at least, movement towards it? Once more, yes; and, thus, even as we work towards the development of a grand narrative alternative, in both form and content, to that of the New Right and the powers that be, we should also be attempting to articulate and advance a conception of 'consensus' alternative, here, too, in form and content, to that to which they aspire. We might commence by considering the idea that 'Social solidarity does not rest on shared values or ideological consensus, let alone on an identity of interests; it rests on public conversation. It rests on social and political arrangements that serve to encourage debate instead of foreclosing it. . . .'[41]

Nevertheless, however much we may endeavour to contribute by our labours and invocations of the powers of the past to collective historical thinking, we cannot on our own engender consensus and a new grand narrative. The making of consensus and a grand narrative, hegemonic or democratic, remains a matter of politics *and* struggle. And, here, we necessarily move beyond schooling and education. Better said, we move to a broader notion of education entailing the formation of a dialectical relationship between historical study and thought *and* the experience and agency of working people and the oppressed today, one in which the pasts we recover, critically inform collective historical memory, consciousness and imagination and, out of which, we ourselves, as historians, gain fresh insights and ideas with which to approach our dialogue with the past anew. Securing the *connections* between 'the people', of whom we ourselves are a part, and historical scholarship and teaching will require great energy, sensitivity and imagination – not to mention skills of public communication.[42]

All along I have said that what is at stake in our response to the crisis of history is not just the status of the discipline, but the very purpose and promise of historical study and thought and, ultimately, the visions of past, present and possible futures to prevail in our public cultures. Engaged in a radical-democratic fashion, our labours might yet contribute to the development of a politics and struggle out of which there could be engendered a new, more original narrative envisioning not the end of history, not post-history, but the extension and continuing development of the ideals and relations of liberty, equality and democratic community.

NOTES

PROLEGOMENA

1. These opening paragraphs are a revised and extended version of those at the outset of my article, 'E. P. Thompson, the British Marxist historical tradition and the contemporary crisis', in H. J. Kaye and K. McClelland (eds), *E. P. Thompson: Critical debates* (Oxford, 1990).
2. Barrington Moore, Jr, *Social Origins of Dictatorship and Democracy* (Boston, 1966) and Eugene Genovese, *The Political Economy of Slavery* (New York, 1967), *The World the Slaveholders Made* (New York, 1971), *In Red and Black* (New York, 1972) and *Roll, Jordan, Roll* (New York, 1974). On the British historians, see Harvey J. Kaye, *The British Marxist Historians* (Oxford, 1984).
3. The *historical* 'education of desire' is adapted from E. P. Thompson, *William Morris* (New York, 1976 rev. edn), p. 723. The quote from Gramsci is from *Selections from the Prison Notebooks*, edited and translated by Q. Hoare and G. Nowell Smith (London, 1971), pp. 34–5.
4. Walter Benjamin's 'Theses' are included in his collection, *Illuminations*, edited with an Introduction by Hannah Arendt (New York, 1968), pp. 255–66. Gramsci's writings are *The Prison Notebooks* and *The Prison Letters* – for the former in English see above, note 3, and for the latter see *Gramsci's Prison Letters* edited with an Introduction by Hamish Henderson (London, 1988). Also, in the period in which this book began to take shape there were two essays that I found most helpful: Gerda Lerner's 'The necessity of history and the professional historian', *Journal of American History*, vol. 69, no. 1 (1982), pp. 7–20; and Alan Bullock's 'Breaking the tyranny of the present', *Times Higher Education Supplement*, 24 May 1985, pp. 18–19.
5. Yosef Hayim Yerushalmi, *Zakhor* (New York, 1989), pp. 85–6.

1. Fritz Stern, *The Varieties of History* (New York, 1972 edn), p. 9.
2. On the French schoolchildren's 'ignorance' of the Revolution, see 'More heroes: s'il vous plait', *The Economist*, 24 September 1983, p. 61.
3. See the National Commission on Excellence in Education Report, *A Nation at Risk* (Washington, D.C., 1983) commissioned by the US Department of Education, and Diane Ravitch and Chester Finn, Jr, *What Do Our 17-Year-Olds Know?: A report on the first national assessment of history and literature* (New York, 1987). The numbers of history degrees awarded are from the Center for Education Statistics, US Department of Education. On the crisis in history textbooks, see Frances Fitzgerald, *America Revised* (New York, 1979). On the crisis in Britain (which also connects with the politics of historical education to be discussed in Chapter 3), see the 'Conservative' argument presented by Alan Beattie in *History in Peril* (London, 1987), a pamphlet produced by the Centre for Policy Studies.
4. Warren Sussman, 'History and the American intellectual' (1964), in his *Culture as History* (New York, 1984), p. 23; Hayden White, 'The burden of history' (1966) in his *Tropics of Discourse* (Baltimore, Md., 1978), pp. 27–58; and J. H. Plumb, 'The historian's dilemma', in his edited *Crisis in the Humanities* (Harmondsworth, 1964), pp. 26–8. See also J. H. Plumb, *The Death of the Past* (New York, 1969).
5. C. Vann Woodward, 'The future of the past' (1969), in his collection *The Future of the Past* (New York, 1989), pp. 3–26.
6. Henry A. Giroux, 'Schooling and the culture of positivism: notes on the death of history', in his *Ideology, Culture and the Process of Schooling* (Philadelphia, Pa., 1981), pp. 37–62; John Berger, *Pig Earth* (New York, 1979), p. 213; and Walter Adamson, *Marx and the Disillusionment of Marxism* (Berkeley, Calif., 1985), pp. 229–30.
7. Russell Jacoby, *Social Amnesia* (Boston, 1975), p. 4; Marshall Berman, *All That is Solid Melts Into Air: The experience of modernity* (New York, 1982), p. 15.
8. John Lukacs, 'American History? American history', *Salmagundi*, nos. 50–1 (1980–1), pp. 172–80.
9. On *American Heritage*, see Roy Rosenzweig, 'Marketing the past: *American Heritage* and popular history in the United States, 1954–1984', *Radical History Review*, no. 32 (1985), pp. 7–29.
10. David White, 'The born-again museum', *New Society*, 1 May 1987, p. 10. On the heritage phenomena in Britain, see Robert

Hewison, *The Heritage Industry* (London, 1987), and Patrick Wright, *On Living in an Old Country* (London, 1985).

11. Christopher Lasch, 'Introduction' to R. Jacoby, *Social Amnesia*, p. viii; David Lowenthal, *The Past is a Foreign Country* (Cambridge, 1985), p. 7; and Christopher Lasch, 'The politics of nostalgia', *Harper's*, November 1984, p. 69. Also, C. Lasch, *The Culture of Narcissism* (New York, 1978).

12. C. Lasch, 'The politics of nostalgia', pp. 65–6, 70.

13. Such work is underway. For examples in Britain, see above note 10; and in the United States see the work published in recent issues of *Radical History Review* and, also, Susan Porter Benson, Stephen Brier and Roy Rosenzweig (eds), *Presenting the Past* (Philadelphia, Pa., 1986).

14. David Sutton, 'Radical liberalism, Fabianism and social history', in Richard Johnson, Gregor McLennan, Bill Schwarz and David Sutton (eds), *Making Histories* (London, 1982), pp. 15–42; J. M. Winter, 'Introduction: Tawney the historian', in J. M. Winter (ed.), *History and Society: Essays by R. H. Tawney* (London, 1978), pp. 1–40 and Ross Terrill, *R. H. Tawney and His Times* (Cambridge, Mass., 1973); and Luther Carpenter, *G. D. H. Cole: An intellectual biography* (Cambridge, 1973).

15. Traian Stoianovich, *French Historical Method: The Annales paradigm* (Ithaca, N.Y., 1976) and Georg Iggers, *New Directions in European Historiography* (Middletown, Conn., 1975; with additions, 1984), pp. 43–79, 146–52. See also, on Marc Bloch, Carole Fink, *Marc Bloch: A life in history* (Cambridge, 1989) and, on Georges Lefebvre and the historiography of the French Revolution, several of the earlier chapters in H. J. Kaye (ed.), *The Face of the Crowd: Selected essays of George Rudé* (London, 1988).

16. David W. Noble, *The End of American History* (Minneapolis, Minn., 1985), Chapters 2 and 3, pp. 16–64 on Turner and Beard; and Peter Novick, *That Noble Dream: The 'objectivity question' and the American historical profession* (Cambridge, 1988), pp. 92–108.

17. T. Stoianovich, *French Historical Method*; G. Iggers, *New Directions in European Historiography*, pp. 43–79; and Fernand Braudel, *On History* (Chicago, 1980).

18. Harvey J. Kaye, *The British Marxist Historians* (Oxford, 1984), esp. pp. 8–17. See also the articles in the 100th issue of *Past & Present*: Christopher Hill, Rodney Hilton, and Eric Hobsbawm, 'Origins and early years', and Jacques Le Goff, 'Later history' (August 1983), pp. 3–13, and 14–28.

19. Sean Wilentz, 'The new history and its critics', *Dissent*, Spring 1989, pp. 244–5, and P. Novick, *That Noble Dream*, pp. 383, 404.

20. Raphael Samuel, 'History Workshop, 1966–80', in R. Samuel (ed.), *People's History and Socialist Theory* (London, 1981),

pp. 410–17, and Editors, 'History Workshop Journal', *History Workshop Journal*, no. 1 (Spring 1976), pp. 1–3.

21. Paul Buhle, 'Madison: an introduction', in P. Buhle (ed.), *History and the New Left: Madison, Wisconsin, 1950–1970* (Philadelphia, Pa., 1970); P. Novick, *That Noble Dream*, p. 420; and Jonathan Weiner, 'Radical historians and the crisis in American history, 1959–1980', *Journal of American History*, vol. 76, no. 2 (September 1989), pp. 399–434.

22. James Green, 'Introduction', in J. Green (ed.), *Workers' Struggles Past and Present: A 'Radical America' reader* (Philadelphia, Pa., 1983), pp. 3–20. See also Paul Buhle (ed.), *Fifteen Years of Radical America: An anthology, radical America*, vol. 16, no. 3 (May 1982), and Paul Berman, 'Spirit of '67: radical Americanism and how it grew', *Village Voice Literary Supplement*, no. 19 (September 1983). *Radical America* moved to Boston in the early 1970s, where it continues to be published.

23. J. Weiner, 'Radical historians and the crisis in American history, 1959–1980', p. 427 and MARHO, 'A draft statement of principles' (1974), reprinted in *The Journal of American History*, vol. 76, no. 2 (September 1989), pp. 487–8.

24. There are innumerable references. For example: Felix Gilbert and Stephen Graubard (eds), *Historical Studies Today* (New York, 1972); Geoffrey Barraclough, *Main Trends in History* (New York, 1979); Georg Iggers and Harold Parker (eds), *International Handbook of Historical Studies* (Westport, Conn., 1979), esp. the introductory essay by Iggers; Michael Kammen (ed.), *The Past Before Us: Contemporary historical writing in the United States* (Ithaca, N.Y., 1980); Theodore Rabb and Robert Rothberg (eds), *The New History: The 1980s and beyond* (Princeton, N.J., 1982); and Eric Foner (ed.), *The New American History* (Philadelphia, Pa., 1990). See also Thomas Schlereth, 'Material culture studies and social history research', *Journal of Social History*, vol. 16, no. 1 (1983), pp. 111–45; and the special issue of *The Journal of Interdisciplinary History*: 'The evidence of art: images and meanings in history', vol. 17, no. 1 (1986).

25. Examples of such historical-social science centres are the programmes established at the universities of Cambridge and Essex in England, and in the United States at the University of Michigan, the New School for Social Research (New York), the University of California-Los Angeles, and SUNY-Binghamton. On historical sociology, see Peter Burke, *Sociology and History* (London, 1980); Charles Tilly, *As Sociology Meets History* (New York, 1981), Philip Abrams *Historical Sociology* (Somerset, 1982) and Theda Skocpol (ed.), *Vision and Method in Historical Sociology* (Cambridge, 1984).

26. Arthur Marwick, *The Nature of History* (London, 1989 edn),
     pp. 138–9. See also Juliet Gardner (ed.), *What is History Today?*
     (London, 1988) for a sense of the 'pluralism' of historical studies
     in the 1980s. And, on the two modes of 'environmental history',
     see, for examples, Donald Worster (ed.), *The Ends of the Earth:
     Perspectives on modern environmental history* (Cambridge, 1988) and
     Donald M. Lowe, *The History of Bourgeois Perception* (Chicago,
     1982).

27. Barrington Moore, Jr, *Social Origins of Dictatorship and Democracy*
     (Boston, 1966), pp. 522–3.

28. Olivier Zunz (ed.), *Reliving the Past: The worlds of social history*
     (Chapel Hill, N.C., 1985). For evidence of the rise of
     global/world history see the new journal *World History* published
     by the rapidly growing World History Association. See also
     Philip D. Curtin, 'World historical studies in a crowded world',
     Perspectives, vol. 24, no. 1 (January 1986), pp. 19–20 and Donald
     Kagan, 'The changing world of world histories', *The New York
     Times Book Review*, 11 November 1984, pp. 1, 41–2.

29. The term 'people's history' is from Raphael Samuel (ed.), *People's
     History and Socialist Theory* (London, 1981). Gerda Lerner's
     remark is in her article 'The necessity of history and the
     professional historian', *Journal of American History*, vol. 69, no. 1
     (1982), p. 19. For a critical examination of the subject, see Kent
     Blaser, 'What happened to new left history?', *South Atlantic
     Quarterly*, vol. 85, no. 3 (1986), pp. 283–96, and vol. 86, no. 3
     (1987), pp. 209–28.

30. See, for Geoffrey Elton, 'The historian's social function', *Royal
     Historical Society Transactions*, 5th Series, vol. 27 (1977),
     pp. 197–211; *The Practice of History* (London, 1969); 'Second
     thoughts on history at the universities', *History*, vol. 54 (1969),
     pp. 60–7; *The History of England* (Cambridge, 1984); and, with
     R. W. Fogel, *Which Road to the Past?* (New Haven, Conn., 1983).
     For Gertrude Himmelfarb, see the essays collected in *The New
     History and the Old* (Cambridge, Mass., 1987). In response to
     Himmelfarb see, for example, Sean Wilentz, 'The new history
     and its critics'.

31. Elizabeth Fox-Genovese and Eugene Genovese, 'Political crisis of
     social history' (1976) revised and reprinted in their *The Fruits of
     Merchant Capital* (New York, 1983), pp. 179–212. See also Tony
     Judt, 'A clown in regal purple: social history and the historians',
     History Workshop, no. 7 (Spring 1979), pp. 66–94.

32. Lawrence Stone, *The Past and the Present Revisited* (London, 1987),
     p. 30; O. Zunz, *Reliving the Past*, p. 3; Peter Stearns (Editor),
     'Social history and history: a progress report', *Journal of Social
     History*, vol. 19, no. 2 (1985), pp. 319–34; Keith Nield and Janet

Blackman, 'Editorial', *Social History*, vol. 10, no. 1 (1985), pp. 1–7; and the Editors, 'Histoire et sciences sociales. Un tournant critique?', *Annales ESC*, no. 2 (1988), pp. 291–3.

33. See P. Evans, D. Rueschmeyer and T. Skocpol (eds), *Bringing the State Back In* (Cambridge, 1985); and, for example, J. Morgan Kousser, 'Restoring politics to social history', *The Journal of Interdisciplinary History*, vol. 12, no. 4 (1982), pp. 569–96 and the responses to the article in vol. 15, no. 3 (1985), pp. 459–500; the special issue of *Journal of Social History* on 'Social and political history', vol. 16, no. 3 (1983), and the special issue of *The Journal of Interdisciplinary History*, 'The origin and prevention of major wars', vol. 18, no. 4 (1988). For discussions and examples of the 'new cultural history', see the essays in Lynn Hunt (ed.), *The New Cultural History* (Berkeley, Calif., 1989); and for a critical discussion of this development, see Bryan Palmer, *Descent into Discourse* (Philadelphia, Pa., 1990).

34. See, for example, the essays in Paul Gagnon (ed.), *Historical Literacy: The case for history in American education* – the Bradley Commission on History in Schools (New York, 1989); and Bernard Gifford (ed.), *History in the Schools: What shall we teach?* – the Clio Project (New York, 1990); James Fitzgerald, 'History in the curriculum: debate on aims and values', *History and Theory*, Beheft no. 22 (1983), pp. 81–100; Christopher Lucas, 'Toward a pedagogy of the useful past for teacher preparation', *Journal of Thought*, vol. 20, no. 1 (1985), pp. 19–33.

35. See James Turner, 'Recovering the uses of history', *Yale Review*, vol. 70, (Winter 1971), pp. 221–33, and Richard Kohn, 'The future of the historical profession', *AHA Perspectives*, November 1989, p. 8.

36. Anthony Sutcliffe, 'Past tense . . . future imperfect', *Times Higher Education Supplement*, 11 May 1984, p. 13 and his contribution to 'Forum', *History Today*, November 1984, pp. 3–4; Richard Neustadt, 'Uses of history in public policy', *Humanities*, vol. 2, no. 5 (1981), pp. 1–3 (along with related essays in the same issue) and, with Ernst May, *Thinking in Time: The uses of history for decision makers* (New York, 1986); Alan Kantrow (ed.), 'Why history matters to managers: a roundtable discussion', *Harvard Business Review*, January–February 1986, pp. 81–8; Donald Warren, 'A past for the present: history education and public policy', *Educational Theory*, vol. 28, no. 4 (1978), pp. 253–65; and Anthony Seldon, 'Detachment, myth and the up-to-date taboo', *Times Higher Education Supplement*, 31 July 1987, p. 12.

37. Theodore S. Hamerow, *Reflections on History and Historians* (Madison, Wis., 1987), pp. 33, 238.

38. Marc Bloch, *The Historian's Craft* (New York, 1953), p. 5 (my italics), and Yosef Hayim Yerushalmi, *Zakhor* (New York, 1989),

pp. 91, 99. See also the review of Hamerow's book by Alan Megill in *History and Theory*, vol. 27, no. 1 (1988), pp. 94–106 and my own in *The Times Higher Education Supplement*, 30 March 1987, p. 17.

39. Yet, I must acknowledge that soon after the first draft of this chapter was written, a symposium was published in the *American Historical Review* which in part began to address the question of aspirations. See 'AHR forum: the old history and the new', in vol. 94, no. 3 (1989), pp. 654–98.

40. On the making of a 'global' synthesis see, for example, William H. McNeill, 'Mythistory, or truth, myth, history and historians', *American Historical Review*, vol. 91, no. 1 (1986), pp. 1–10; and for a critical discussion of particular models of it, see Craig Lockard, 'Global history, modernization and the world-system approach: a critique', *The History Teacher*, vol. 14, no. 4 (1981), pp. 489–515. Also on 'world history' see Geoffrey Barraclough's *An Introduction to Contemporary History* (Harmondsworth, 1967). On the call for 'national' syntheses in the USA, see: Herbert Gutman, 'The missing synthesis: what happened to history?', *The Nation*, 21 November 1981, pp. 521, 553–4; Thomas Bender, 'Making history whole again', *New York Times Book Review*, 6 October 1985, pp. 1, 42–3 and 'Wholes and parts: the need for synthesis in American history', *Journal of American History*, vol. 73, no. 1 (1986), pp. 120–36; and Michael Zuckerman, 'Myth and method: the current crisis in American historical writing', *The History Teacher*, vol. 17, no. 2 (1984), pp. 219–45. And for such a call in Britain, see David Cannadine, 'The state of British history', *Times Literary Supplement*, 10 October 1986, pp. 1139–40 and 'British history: past, present – and future?', *Past & Present*, no. 116 (August 1987), pp. 169–91. For the critical responses to Bender, see the contributions to 'A round table': synthesis in American history', *Journal of American History*, vol. 74, no. 1 (1987), pp. 107–30; and for those in response to Cannadine, see 'Debate: British history: past, present – and future?', *Past & Present*, no. 119 (May 1988), pp. 171–203. My own contribution to the British debate, written as a piece of 'criticism' in the aftermath of the re-election of Margaret Thatcher and the Conservatives in June 1987, is 'Our island story retold', *The Guardian*, 3 August 1987, p. 7; also, towards a dialogue between American and British critical historiographies which looks towards the idea of historical syntheses, see my 'E. P. Thompson, the British Marxist historical tradition and the contemporary crisis', in H. J. Kaye and K. McClelland (eds), *E. P. Thompson: Critical perspectives* (Oxford, 1990).

41. Roy Rosenzweig, 'What is the matter with history?', in 'A round table', (i.e. the responses to Bender cited in note 40), p. 121.

CHAPTER 2

1. Christopher Lasch, *The Culture of Narcissism* (New York, 1979), p. xiii.
2. Terrence Des Pres, 'On governing narratives: the Turkish-American case', *The Yale Review*, vol. 75, no. 4 (1986), p. 517.
3. See the discussions in: V. G. Kiernan, *America: The new imperialism* (London, 1978), pp. 151–225; Kees van der Pijl, *The Making of an Atlantic Ruling Class* (London, 1984); and Richard B. DuBoff, *Accumulation and Power* (New York, 1989), pp. 143–63.
4. Samuel Bowles and Herbert Gintis, *Democracy and Capitalism* (New York, 1986), pp. 57–8. The term 'post-war charter' is from Richard Flacks, *Making History* (New York, 1988), pp. 53–8; see also the articles in Steve Fraser and Gary Gerstle (eds), *The Rise and Fall of the New Deal Order, 1930–1980* (Princeton, N.J., 1989).
5. Allen Hunter, 'The politics of resentment and the construction of middle America' (unpublished paper, 1987), quoted in Michael Apple, 'Redefining equality: authoritarian populism and the conservative restoration', *Teachers College Record*, vol. 90, no. 2 (Winter 1988), pp. 173–4.
6. Frances Fitzgerald, *Fire in the Lake* (New York, 1973), p. 9 and Frances Fitzgerald, *America Revised: History schoolbooks in the twentieth century* (New York, 1980), p. 10. See also on the American 'Jeremiad', Enrico Augelli and Craig Murphy, *America's Quest for Supremacy and the Third World* (London, 1988), esp. pp. 35–58; Sacvan Bercovitch, *The American Jeremiad* (Madison, Wis., 1978); and Donald W. White, 'History and American internationalism: the formulation from the past after world war II', *Pacific Historical Review*, vol. 63, no. 2 (1989), pp. 145–72.
7. Peter Novick, *That Noble Dream: The 'objectivity question' and the American historical profession* (Cambridge, 1988), pp. 332–3.
8. William L. Langer, 'The United States role in the world', in *Goals for Americans: The report of the president's commission on national goals* (Englewood Cliffs, N.J., 1960), pp. 299, 301; quoted in Godfrey Hodgson, *America In Our Time* (Garden City, N.Y., 1976), p. 13, which provides an excellent discussion of the American consensus (see Chapter 4, 'The ideology of the liberal consensus', pp. 67–98).
9. Peter Jenkins, *Mrs. Thatcher's Revolution: The ending of the socialist era* (Cambridge, Mass., 1988), p. 33.
10. *ibid.*, p. 31.
11. Kenneth O. Morgan, 'The twentieth century (1914–1984)', in K. Morgan (ed.), *The Oxford Illustrated History of Britain* (Oxford, 1984), p. 568. See also Kenneth O. Morgan, *Labour in Power, 1945–1951* (Oxford, 1984) and Bob Jessop, 'The transformation

of the state in postwar Britain', in R. Scase (ed.), *The State in Western Europe* (London, 1980), pp. 23–93.

12. Joel Krieger, *Reagan, Thatcher and the Politics of Decline* (New York, 1986), p. 23.

13. J. W. Burrow, *A Liberal Descent: Victorian historians and the English past* (Cambridge, 1981), p. 3; John Tosh, *The Pursuit of History* (London, 1984), p. 5; and Valerie Chancellor, *History for Their Masters: Opinion in English history textbooks, 1800–1914* (Bath, 1970), pp. 49, 127–8. See also Peter J. Bowler, *The Invention of Progress: The Victorians and the past* (Oxford, 1989); R. W. Johnson, *The Politics of Recession* (London, 1985), esp. 'Pomp and circumstance', pp. 224–55; V. G. Kiernan, 'Working class and nation in nineteenth-century Britain', in H. J. Kaye (ed.), *History, Classes and Nation-States: Selected writings of V. G. Kiernan* (Oxford, 1988), pp. 186–98; and V. G. Kiernan, 'Labour and the literate in nineteenth-century Britain', in H. J. Kaye (ed.), *Poets, Politics and the People: Selected writings of V. G. Kiernan [II]* (London, 1989), pp. 152–77.

14. T. H. Marshall, 'Citizenship and social class' in *Class, Citizenship and Social Development* (New York, 1964). See also on Marshall's arguments: Anthony Giddens, 'Class division, class conflict and citizenship rights', in his *Profiles and Critiques in Social Theory* (Berkeley, Calif., 1982); Bryan S. Turner, *Citizenship and Capitalism* (London, 1986); and J. M. Barbalet, *Citizenship* (London, 1988).

15. J. Krieger, *Reagan, Thatcher and the Politics of Decline*, p. 189 and S. M. Lipset, *Political Man* (1960; New York, 1963 edn), pp. 441–2. See also Chaim Waxman (ed.), *The End of Ideology Debate* (New York, 1968) and Anthony Arblaster, *The Rise and Decline of Western Liberalism* (Oxford, 1984), esp. 'Cold War liberalism', pp. 309–32.

16. Alan Wolfe, *America's Impasse: The rise and fall of the politics of growth* (New York, 1981), p. 10 and P. Jenkins, *Mrs. Thatcher's Revolution*, p. 5. On the United States, see also: David P. Calleo, *The Imperious Economy* (Cambridge, Mass., 1982).

17. See Juan Williamson, *Eyes on the Prize: America's civil rights years, 1954–1965* (New York, 1987); Taylor Branch, *Parting the Waters: America in the King years* (New York, 1988); James Miller, *' mocracy is in the Streets'* (New York, 1987); and Todd Gitlin, *The Sixties: Years of hope, days of rage* (New York, 1987).

18. Barbara Ehrenreich, *Fear of Falling* (New York, 1989), pp. 121–2. See also Mike Davis, *Prisoners of the American Dream* (London, 1986), pp. 126–7ff.

19. See Sara Evans, *Personal Politics: The roots of women's liberation in the civil rights movement and the new left* (New York, 1979).

20. Colin Leys, *Politics in Britain* (London, 1989 rev. edn), pp. 73, 84; David Caute, *The Year of the Barricades: A journey through 1968* (New York, 1987); Ronald Fraser, *1968: A student generation in revolt* (London, 1988); and Sheila Rowbotham, *The Past Before Us: Feminism in action since the 1960s* (London, 1989). See also David Boucher, *The Feminist Challenge: The movement for women's liberation in Britain and the USA* (London, 1983).

21. See Colin Leys, *Politics in Britain*, pp. 84–5 and Tom Nairn, *The Break-Up of Britain* (London, 1981 rev. edn).

22. J. Krieger, *Reagan, Thatcher and the Politics of Decline*, p. 127; Walter Russell Mead, *Mortal Splendor: The American empire in transition* (Boston, 1987); C. Leys, *Politics in Britain*, pp. 79–80; and Glyn Williams and John Ramsden, *Ruling Britannia: A political history of Britain, 1688–1988* (London, 1990), esp. Chapter 25: 'Going for growth, 1961–1974', pp. 456–74.

23. W. R. Mead, *Mortal Splendor*, pp. 44–5.

24. P. Jenkins, *Mrs. Thatcher's Revolution*, p. 18 and G. Williams and J. Ramsden, *Ruling Britannia*, esp. pp. 462–86.

25. James O. Connor, *Accumulation Crisis* (New York, 1984), p. 1. Essential reading is Joyce Kolko, *Restructuring the World Economy* (New York, 1988).

26. W. R. Mead, *Mortal Splendor*, p. 89, and P. Jenkins, *Mrs. Thatcher's Revolution*, pp. 12–13, 17.

27. Bennett Harrison and Barry Bluestone, *The Great U-Turn* (New York, 1988), pp. 7–11 and Andrew Glyn and Bob Sutcliffe, *British Capitalism, Workers and the Profits Squeeze* (Harmondsworth, 1972). See also F. Frobel, J. Heinrichs and O. Kreye, *The New International Division of Labour* (Cambridge, 1980) and Nigel Harris, *The End of the Third World* (London, 1986).

28. Andrew Gamble, *The Free Economy and the Strong State* (London, 1988), pp. 3–4.

29. *ibid.*, p. 3.

30. See: Anthony King, 'Overload: problems of governing in the 1970s', *Political Studies*, vol. 23 (1975), pp. 284–96; Alan Wolfe, *The Limits of Legitimacy: The political contradictions of contemporary capitalism* (New York, 1977); Jurgen Habermas, *Legitimation Crisis* (orig. German edn 1973; New York, 1975); Michael Crozier, Samuel P. Huntington and Joji Watanuki, *The Crisis of Democracy* (New York, 1975); Daniel Bell, *The Cultural Contradictions of Capitalism* (New York, 1976); Samuel Brittan, 'The economic contradictions of democracy', *British Journal of Political Science*, vol. 5 (1975), pp. 129–59; Robert Nisbet, *The Twilight of Authority* (New York, 1975); and Michael Harrington, *The Twilight of Capitalism* (New York, 1976). Additionally, see

Anthony H. Birch, 'Overload, ungovernability, and delegitima-tion: the theories and the British case', *British Journal of Political Science*, vol. 14 (1984), pp. 135–60.

31. Peter N. Carroll, *It Seemed Like Nothing Happened: America in the 1970s* (New Brunswick, N.J., 1990 rev. edn), pp. 135, 235.

32. J. Krieger, *Reagan, Thatcher and the Politics of Decline*, pp. 4–5 and Christopher Lasch, 'Democracy and the "crisis of confidence" ', *democracy*, vol. 1, no. 1 (1981), pp. 25–40.

33. R. Emmett Tyrrell, Jr (ed.), *The Future that Doesn't Work: Social democracy's failure in Britain* (New York, 1977); James Walvin, *Victorian Values* (London, 1987), p. 5; and P. Jenkins, *Mrs. Thatcher's Revolution*, pp. 48–9. See, also, the contributions to both Isaac Kramnick (ed.), *Is Britain Dying?* (Ithaca, N.Y., 1979) and David Coates and John Hilliard (eds), *The Economic Decline of Modern Britain: The debate between left and right* (Hemel Hempstead, 1986), and Alan Sked, *Britain's Decline* (Oxford, 1987).

34. P. Carroll, *It Seemed Like Nothing Happened*, pp. 297–301, and Robert Hewison, *The Heritage Industry: Britain in a climate of decline* (London, 1987), pp. 9, 10, 47. See also Patrick Wright, *On Living in an Old Country: The national past in contemporary Britain* (London, 1985).

35. Christopher Lasch, 'The politics of nostalgia', *Harper's*, November 1984, p. 69 (Lasch is quoting a remark by Anthony Brandy in an essay of 1978). Also, see the contributions to Christopher Shaw and Malcolm Chase (eds), *The Imagined Past: History and nostalgia* (Manchester, 1989), esp. David Lowenthal, 'Nostalgia tells it like it wasn't', pp. 33–46.

36. Sven Birkerts, 'The nostalgia disease', *Tikkun*, vol. 4, no. 2 (1989), p. 22.

37. David Harvey, *The Condition of Postmodernity* (Oxford, 1989), pp. 54–6. See also Fredric Jameson, 'Postmodernism, or the cultural logic of late capitalism', *New Left Review*, no. 146 (July–August 1984), pp. 52–111.

CHAPTER 3

1. F. Stirton Weaver, *Class, State and Industrial Structure* (Westport, Conn., 1980); and see Ralph Miliband, *The State in Capitalist Society* (New York, 1969) on the persistence and centrality of *class* in the post-war period.

2. Ralph Miliband, *Divided Societies* (Oxford, 1989), pp. 139–40.

3. Antonio Gramsci, *Selections from the Prison Notebooks*, edited and translated by Q. Hoare and G. Nowell Smith (London, 1971),

p. 334. Also, on the problem of hegemony, see Enrico Augelli and Craig Murphy, *America's Quest for Supremacy and the Third World* (London, 1988), pp. 121–4, Anne Showstack-Sassoon, *Gramsci's Politics* (London, 1980), pp. 134–46, and, especially, Joseph V. Femia, *Gramsci's Political Thought* (Oxford, 1981).

4. A. Gramsci, *Selections*, p. 161 (my italics) and E. Augelli and C. Murphy, *America's Quest*, pp. 121–4.

5. David Sallach, 'Class domination and ideological hegemony', *Sociological Quarterly*, vol. 15, no. 1 (Winter 1974), p. 41.

6. Raymond Williams, *Marxism and Literature* (New York, 1977), pp. 115–16.

7. For examples of such work, see Susan Porter Benson, Stephen Brier and Roy Rosenzweig (eds), *Presenting the Past* (Philadelphia, Pa., 1986); Richard Johnson, Gregor McLennan, Bill Schwarz and David Sutton (eds), *Making Histories* (London, 1982); Donald Horne, *The Re-presentation of History* (London, 1984); Patrick Wright, *On Living in an Old Country* (London, 1985); and Volker R. Berghahn and Hanna Schiesler, *Perceptions of History: International textbook research* (Oxford, 1987). Also, see Eric Hobsbawm and Terence Ranger (eds), *The Invention of Tradition* (Cambridge, 1983).

8. Michael Wallace, 'Visiting the past: history museums in the United States', in S. Benson, S. Brier and R. Rosenzweig (eds), *Presenting the Past*, pp. 137–61.

9. Of interest is that the development of social history and, especially, history from the bottom up have influenced recent initiatives to develop a more critical museology; however, as curator Gary Kulik notes: 'Most museums remain shrines. . . . For too many visitors, and even staff members, museums remain places of celebration, even veneration.' See Gary Kulik, 'Designing the past: history-museum exhibitions from Peale to the present', in Warren Leon and Roy Rosenzweig (eds), *History Museums in the United States: A critical assessment* (Urbana, Ill., 1989), pp. 3–37. Also, see the other articles in this collection on history museums.

10. A. Gramsci quoted in E. Augelli and C. Murphy, *America's Quest*, p. 124.

11. R. Williams, *Marxism and Literature*, p. 112.

12. A. Gramsci, *Selections*, p. 210.

13. On the problem of 'decades', see Christopher Lasch, 'Counting by tens', *Salmagundi*, no. 81 (Winter 1989), pp. 51–61.

14. David Vogel, *Fluctuating Fortunes* (New York, 1989), p. 145 and Leonard Silk and David Vogel, *Ethics and Profits* (New York, 1976), pp. 57–8.

15. Colin Leys, *Politics in Britain: From Labourism to Thatcherism* (London, 1989 rev. edn), pp. 94–6.

16. Colin Leys, 'Thatcherism and British manufacturing', *New Left Review*, no. 151 (May–June 1985), p. 17. Also, see Michael Useem, *The Inner Circle: Large corporations and the rise of political activity in the U.S. and U.K.* (New York and Oxford, 1984), p. 158.

17. Bennett Harrison and Barry Bluestone, *The Great U-Turn: Corporate restructuring and the polarizing of America* (New York, 1988), p. 51. Also, see Mike Davis, *Prisoners of the American Dream* (London, 1986), p. 131.

18. C. Leys, *Politics in Britain*, pp. 136–7 and Colin Crouch, 'The intensification of industrial conflict in the United Kingdom', in Colin Crouch and Alessandro Pizzorno (eds), *The Resurgence of Class Conflict in Western Europe since 1968* (New York, 1978), pp. 191–256.

19. D. Vogel, *Fluctuating Fortunes*, pp. 193–213. Also, see Kim McQuaid, *Big Business and Presidential Power* (New York, 1982), pp. 284–306 and Thomas Byrne Edsall, *The New Politics of Inequality* (New York, 1984), pp. 107–41.

20. M. Useem, *The Inner Circle*, pp. 71, 132–4, 157–60 and C. Leys, 'Thatcherism and British manufacturing', pp. 16–17.

21. On 'policy regimes' in American history, see Edward Greenberg, *Capitalism and the American Political Ideal* (New York, 1985).

22. See Stephen Gill, *American Hegemony and the Trilateral Commission* (Cambridge, 1990), pp. 156–60. Also, see the volume, Holly Sklar (ed.), *Trilateralism* (Boston, 1980) and, on the pre-Trilateral period, Kees Van der Pijl, *The Making of an Atlantic Ruling Class* (London, 1989).

23. Michael Crozier, Samuel P. Huntington and Joji Watanuki, *The Crisis of Democracy: Report on the governability of democracies to the Trilateral Commission* (New York, 1975), p. 9; Samuel Huntington, 'The United States', pp. 113–15. Also, see the comments of S. Gill, *American Hegemony*, pp. 52–3, and Alan Wolfe, *The Limits of Legitimacy* (New York, 1977), pp. 321–34.

24. I cannot resist noting that Huntington himself actually defines the American 'governing class' for us in his chapter of the Trilateral Report (see *The Crisis of Democracy*, p. 92).

25. M. Crozier, S. Huntington and J. Watanuki, *Crisis of Democracy*, pp. 6–7.

26. *ibid.*, pp. 183–4.

27. A. Wolfe, *Limits of Legitimacy*, pp. 326–7.

28. The Trilateralists were especially well represented in the Carter and second Reagan Administrations. Also, we should note that a leading British Trilateralist has been David Owen, an important figure in the Labour Party and Governments of the 1970s, and a founder of the now-defunct Social Democratic Party.

29. S. Gill, *American Hegemony*, pp. 163–8.

30. On the 'international' character of the New Right, see Simon Gunn, *Revolution of the Right: Europe's new conservatism* (London, 1989).

31. On the New Right in Britain, see Andrew Gamble, *The Free Economy and the Strong State: The politics of Thatcherism* (London, 1988); Stuart Hall, *The Hard Road to Renewal* (London, 1988); and Bob Jessop, Kevin Bonnett, Simon Bromley and Tom Ling (eds), *Thatcherism* (Cambridge, 1988). On the United States, see Gillian Peele, *Revival and Reaction: The right in contemporary America* (Oxford, 1984) and Jerome Himmelstein, *To the Right: The transformation of American conservatism* (Berkeley, Calif., 1990). Also, for comparative studies of the British and American New Rights, see Desmond S. King, *The New Right: Politics, markets and citizenship* (London, 1987); Kenneth Hoover and Raymond Plant, *Conservative Capitalism in Britain and the United States* (London, 1989); and R. Miliband, L. Panitch and J. Saville (eds), *Socialist Register 1987: Conservatism in Britain and America, rhetoric and reality* (London, 1987).

32. Peter Riddell, *The Thatcher Government* (Oxford, 1985 rev. edn), p. 24.

33. Andrew Gamble, 'The political economy of freedom', in Ruth Levitas (ed.), *The Ideology of the New Right* (Cambridge, 1986), p. 30. Also, see K. Hoover and R. Plant, *Conservative Capitalism*, pp. 15–42 and Anthony Arblaster, *The Rise and Decline of Western Liberalism* (Oxford, 1984), pp. 339–49.

34. P. Riddell, *The Thatcher Government*, p. 24. On the organizations and institutes of the New Right, see Nigel Williamson, *The New Right: The men behind Mrs. Thatcher* (London, 1984).

35. Sir Keith Joseph, 'This is not the time to be mealy-mouthed: intervention is destroying us' (June 1974), in K. Joseph, *Reversing the Trend* (London, 1975).

36. These points are treated more fully in K. Hoover and R. Plant, *Conservative Capitalism*, pp. 134–42. Also, see Dennis Kavanagh and Peter Morris, *Consensus Politics from Attlee to Thatcher* (Oxford, 1989), pp. 18–22.

37. K. Joseph, 'The politics of political economy', in *Reversing the Trend*, p. 60. Curiously, this view had been expressed previously in a Marxist version: Perry Anderson and Tom Nairn, 'The origins of the present crisis' (1964) reprinted in P. Anderson and R. Blackburn (eds), *Towards Socialism* (London, 1965), pp. 11–52. For a work of cultural history sympathetic with the Joseph/Anderson–Nairn thesis see Martin J. Weiner, *English Culture and the Decline of the Industrial Spirit* (Cambridge, 1981). Also, for a critical review of the literature – critical, especially, of the practice of allowing Tory politicians to set the historiographical agenda! –

see James Raven, 'British history and the enterprise culture', *Past & Present*, no. 123 (May 1989), pp. 178–204.

38. K. Joseph, 'The quest for common ground', in K. Joseph, *Stranded in the Middle Ground?* (London, Centre for Policy Studies, 1976), pp. 19–36.

39. K. Joseph, 'The politics of political economy', pp. 56–7 and 'The Quest for Common Ground', pp. 27–8.

40. Keith Joseph and Jonathan Sumption, *Equality* (London, 1979), pp. 1, 42.

41. On Roger Scruton, see Anthony Arblaster, 'Scruton: intellectual by appointment', *New Socialist*, November 1985, pp. 16–20. On the Conservative Philosophy Group, see Hugo Young, *One of Us: A biography of Margaret Thatcher* (London, 1989), pp. 406–7.

42. Ferdinand Mount, *The Subversive Family* (London, 1982) and, on Mount, see Miriam David, 'Moral and maternity: the family in the right', in R. Levitas (ed.), *The Ideology of the New Right*, pp. 154–5.

43. See Stuart Hall, Charles Critcher, Tony Jefferson, John Clarke and Brian Roberts, *Policing the Crisis: Mugging, the state, and law and order* (New York, 1978) and Peter Jenkins, *Mrs. Thatcher's Revolution* (Cambridge, Mass., 1988, US edn), pp. 66–77.

44. A. Arblaster (quoting Roger Scruton), 'Scruton: intellectual by appointment', p. 17 and David Edgar, 'The free or the good', in R. Levitas (ed.), *The Ideology of the New Right*, pp. 74–5.

45. William Simon, *A Time for Truth* (New York, 1978), pp. 222, 228–33. On Simon and the Olin Foundation, see Jon Wiener, 'Dollars for neo-con scholars', *The Nation*, January 1990, pp. 12–14.

46. See Sidney Blumenthal, *The Rise of the Counter-Establishment* (New York, 1986). Also, see D. Vogel, *Fluctuating Fortunes*, pp. 213–27 and Joseph G. Peschek, *Policy-Planning Organizations: Elite agendas and America's rightward turn* (Philadelphia, Pa., 1987).

47. See Peter Steinfels, *The Neoconservatives* (New York, 1979) and S. Blumenthal, *The Rise of the Counter-Establishment*, esp. pp. 122–65. On Irving Kristol in particular, see Steinfels, pp. 81–108 and, for Kristol's own writings, his books *Two Cheers for Capitalism* (New York, 1978) and *Reflections of a Neoconservative* (New York, 1983). Also, for a critical set of reflections on the 'culture and politics of Reaganism' see Irving Howe, 'The spirit of the times: greed, nostalgia, ideology and war whoops', *Dissent*, Fall 1986, pp. 413–25.

48. See Joseph G. Peschek, ' "Free the Fortune 500!" The American Enterprise Institute and the politics of the capitalist class in the 1970s', *Critical Sociology*, vol. 16, nos. 2–3 (Summer–Fall 1989), pp. 165–80 and S. Blumenthal, *The Rise of the Counter-Establishment*, pp. 38–45.

49. On Daniel Bell, see P. Steinfels, *The Neoconservatives*, pp. 161–88, and on Norman Podhoretz, see S. Blumenthal, *The Rise of the Counter-Establishment*, pp. 133–47.

50. On Daniel Patrick Moynihan, see P. Steinfels, *The Neoconservatives*, pp. 108–61.

51. See Walter LaFeber, 'The last war, the next war and the new revisionists', *democracy*, vol. 1, no. 1 (January 1981), pp. 93–103; Theodore Draper, 'Neoconservative history', *New York Review of Books*, 16 January 1986, pp. 5–15; and Jonathan Alter, 'A new war over Yalta', *Newsweek*, 28 April 1986, p. 49.

52. Jeane J. Kirkpatrick, 'Dictatorships and double standards' (1979), in J. Kirkpatrick, *Dictatorships and Double Standards* (New York, 1982), pp. 10, 31, 32; 'Ideas and institutions' (1981), in J. Kirkpatrick, *The Reagan Phenomenon and Other Essays* (Washington, D.C., 1983), p. 44; and 'Reagan policies and black American goals for Africa' (1981), in *The Reagan Phenomenon*, p. 27.

53. G. Peele, *Revival and Reaction*, pp. 52–5, 77–8.

54. Michael S. Joyce, 'The National Endowments for Humanities and the Arts', in Charles L. Heatherly (ed.), *Mandate for Leadership: Policy management in a conservative administration* (Washington, D.C., 1981).

55. See G. Peele, *Revival and Reaction*, pp. 80–119 and J. Himmelstein, *To the Right*, pp. 63–128; Peter Steinfels, 'Neoconservative theology', *democracy*, vol. 2, no. 2 (April 1982), pp. 18–27; and Sean Wilentz, 'The trials of televangelism: Jerry Falwell and the enemy', *Dissent*, (Winter 1990), pp. 42–8. By one of the movement's top organizers, fund-raisers and spokespersons, see Richard A. Viguerie, *The New Right: We're ready to lead* (Falls Church, Va., 1980). Also, see Steve Bruce, *The Rise and Fall of the New Christian Right* (Oxford, 1990).

56. S. Blumenthal, *The Rise of the Counter-Establishment*, pp. 207–9. Also, see G. Peele, *Revival and Reaction*, pp. 33–6 and Walter Russell Mead, *Mortal Splendor* (Boston, 1987), pp. 143–6. And, of course, George Gilder, *Wealth and Poverty* (New York, 1981).

57. Margaret Thatcher interviewed, 'Programmes for the 1980s', *Illustrated London News*, May 1983, p. 24 (my emphases) and 'Let me give you my vision' (1975), in M. Thatcher, *Let Our Children Grow: Selected speeches, 1975–77* (London, Centre for Policy Studies, 1977), p. 29. By the way, I must note here that on this very day – 22 November 1990 – as I was putting the final touches to this chapter, Margaret Thatcher announced that she would step down from the posts of Prime Minister and leader of the Conservative Party.

58. Margaret Thatcher, 'Dimensions and conservatism', in *Let Our Children Grow*, pp. 110–11.

59. Margaret Thatcher, 'Those good old days, by Maggie', *The Standard*, 15 April 1983.

60. See, for examples, the special supplement, 'Victorian values', in *New Statesman*, 27 May 1983, which includes: Raphael Samuel, 'Soft focus nostalgia' and 'Cry God for Maggie, England and St. George'; Michael Ignatieff, 'Law and order in a city of strangers'; Gareth Stedman Jones, 'Poor law and market forces'; and Leonore Davidoff and Catherine Hall, 'Home sweet home'. Also, see James Walvin, *Victorian Values* (London, 1987).

61. In Ronald Reagan, *A Time for Choosing: The speeches of Ronald Reagan, 1961–82* (Chicago, 1983), pp. 73–84.

62. Paul D. Erickson, *Reagan Speaks: The making of an American myth* (New York, 1985), pp. 45, 48–9.

63. Laurence I. Barrett. *Gambling with History: Ronald Reagan in the White House* (New York, 1984 edn), pp. 55–7.

64. 'Interview with President Reagan', 27 December 1981, in *Public Papers of the Presidents of the United States: Ronald Reagan, 1981* (Washington, D.C., 1982), p. 1197.

65. Ronald Reagan, 'Encroaching control – the peril of ever-expanding government' (1961), in *A Time for Choosing*, p. 38.

66. Robert Dallek, *Ronald Reagan: The politics of symbolism* (Cambridge, Mass., 1984), pp. 4–8.

67. R. Reagan, 'A time for choosing' (1964), in *Ronald Reagan Talks to America* (Old Greenwich, Conn., 1983), p. 4; 'Text of President's Address to Congress on State of the Union', *New York Times*, 5 February 1986, p. A-20; and 'Remarks at the Conservative Political Action Conference Dinner', in *Public Papers . . . 1981*, p. 278. Also, see Barbara Ehrenreich, 'The new right attack on social welfare', in Fred Block, Richard A. Cloward, Barbara Ehrenreich and Frances Fox Piven, *The Mean Season* (New York, 1987), pp. 161–96.

68. Ronald Reagan, 'Second Inaugural Address', in *Vital Speeches*, 1 February 1985, p. 228, and 'Remarks at the "Prelude to Independence" celebration', 31 May 1985, in *Weekly Compilation of Presidential Documents*, 3 June 1985, p. 718.

69. Anthony Barnett, *Iron Britannia* (London, 1982), p. 18.

70. Margaret Thatcher, 'Speech to a conservative rally at Cheltenham Race Course' (3 July 1982), reprinted in A. Barnett, *Iron Britannia*, pp. 149–50.

71. An apt phrase to describe Thatcherism offered by Ralph Miliband in 'Class war conservatism', *New Society*, 19 June 1980, pp. 278–80. For a critical commentary on Thatcherism and the 'loss of Empire', see Nicholas Boyce, 'Thatcher's dead souls', *New Statesman & Society*, 14 October 1988, pp. 27–30.

72. M. Thatcher, 'Speech to a Conservative Rally at Cheltenham Race Course', pp. 150–52.

73. Ronald Reagan, 'Radio address to the nation', 16 February 1985, in *Weekly Compilation of Presidential Documents*, 25 February 1985, pp. 186–7, and 'Remarks at the Conservative Political Action Conference Dinner', 1 March 1985, in *Weekly Compilation of Presidential Documents*, 8 March 1985, p. 245. And the Editors, 'Reagan cast as King George', *In These Times*, 27 February–12 March 1985, p. 14.

74. Ronald Reagan, 'Interview with representatives of the Scripps-Howard News Service', 25 October 1984 in *Public Papers of the President of the United States: Ronald Reagan, 1984* (Washington, D.C., 1985), p. 1647. On this see the item, 'Remark by President Reagan about Spanish Civil War', in *The New York Times*, 10 May 1985, p. 11. Also, for a critical (and personal) response to Reagan's remark on the Spanish Civil War, see Vicente Navarro, 'The Lincoln Brigade: some comments on U.S. history', *Monthly Review*, September 1986, pp. 29–37.

75. Ronald Reagan, 'Press conference', 18 April 1985, in *Weekly Compilation of Presidential Documents*, 22 April 1985, p. 475. On the Bitburg controversy, see the collections of articles edited by Geoffrey Hartman, *Bitburg in Moral and Political Perspective* (Bloomington, Ind., 1986) and Ilya Levkov (ed.), *Bitburg and Beyond* (New York, 1987). On the New Right German historians and the 'historians' debate', see Richard J. Evans, *In Hitler's Shadow* (New York, 1989); Charles S. Maier, *The Unmasterable Past* (Cambridge, Mass., 1988); Judith Miller, *One, by One, by One* (New York, 1990), esp. pp. 13–60; and the collection of articles in Peter Baldwin (ed.), *Reworking the Past: Hitler, the holocaust and the historians' debate* (New York, 1990).

76. Robert Nisbet, 'The conservative renaissance in perspective', *The Public Interest*, no. 81 (Fall 1985), pp. 140–1. Also, see Nisbet's *Conservatism* (Minneapolis, Minn., 1986), and *The Present Age: Progress and anarchy in modern America* (New York, 1988) in which he offers critical reflections on the Reagan decade.

77. *American Heritage Dictionary of the English Language* (New York, 1979 edn), p. 715.

78. George Orwell, *1984* (New York, 1961), p. 204.

79. Marc Ferro, *The Use and Abuse of History, or, How the Past is Taught* (London, 1984 English edn), p. vii.

80. F. A. Hayek, *The Road to Serfdom* (London, 1944). On the rise of neo-liberalism, see D. Graham and P. Clarke, *The New Enlightenment* (London, 1986).

81. Fritz Machlup, 'Notes from the editor', in F. Machlup (ed.), *Essays on Hayek* (New York, 1976), pp. xii–xiii. Also quoted in Keith Nield, 'Liberalism and history: reflections on the writing of

world histories', *Culture and History*, no. 5 (1989–90), pp. 66–7 (but my italics).

82. F. A. Hayek, 'Introduction', in F. A. Hayek (ed.), *Capitalism and the Historians* (Chicago, 1954), pp. 3–4, 9–10.

83. See, on this question, George Rudé, *Debate on Europe, 1815–1850* (New York, 1972), esp. pp. 60–72.

84. Ronald Max Hartwell, 'Capitalism and the historians', in F. Machlup (ed.), *Essays on Hayek*, pp. 87, 90. Also, see Colin Welch, 'Intellectuals have consequences', in R. Emmett Tyrrell, Jr (ed.), *The Future that Doesn't Work: Social democracy's failure in Britain* (New York, 1977), pp. 42–63.

85. Rhodes Boyson, *Centre Forward: A radical conservative programme* (London, 1978), pp. 188–9. Quoted in J. Raven, 'British history and the enterprise culture', p. 201.

86. Margaret Thatcher's Foreword to Hugh Thomas, *History, Capitalism and Freedom* (London, Centre for Policy Studies, 1979).

87. I. Kristol, *Two Cheers for Capitalism*, pp. 99, 26, and S. Blumenthal, *The Rise of the Counter-Establishment*, p. 151. Also, see Kristol's 'The American Revolution as a successful revolution' in his *Reflections of a Neoconservative*, pp. 78–94.

88. Ronald Reagan, 'What is academic freedom?' (1970), and 'On the function of a university' (1966), in *Ronald Reagan Talks to America*, pp. 186, 188, 173.

89. Sir Keith Joseph, 'Why teach history in schools?', *The Historian*, no. 1 (Spring 1984), pp. 12, 11 (my emphasis).

90. Colin Hughes, 'History teaching should foster pride in Britain, Joseph says', *The Times*, 14 August 1984, p. 4.

91. Christopher Hill, contribution to 'Forum', *History Today*, vol. 34 (May 1984), pp. 6–7.

92. C. Hughes, 'History teaching should foster pride', p. 4.

93. E. Ellsworth-Jones and P. Pringle, 'Tories plan teach-ins in more marginal seats', *The Sunday Times*, 14 January 1973, pp. 1, 3; Margaret Thatcher quoted in 'Conference "bias" seen as a task for teachers', *The Times*, 18 January 1973, p. 6; and 'Ministers kept out of curriculum matters', *The Times*, 14 February 1973, p. 11.

94. G. R. Elton, *The Future of the Past* (Cambridge, 1986), p. 22 and *The History of England* (Cambridge, 1984), pp. 28, 25–6. Also by Elton, see *The Practice of History* (London, 1969) and 'The historian's social function', *Royal Historical Society Transactions*, 5th Series, vol. 27 (1977), pp. 197–211. Note: *The New Statesman* is an independent Left magazine (now titled *New Statesman & Society*).

95. On the National Humanities Center, see David Noble's two-part article 'Corporatist culture ministries', *The Nation*, 21 March 1981, pp. 336–40 and 20 June, pp. 754–7. And, on Bennett's appointment to the NEH, see John S. Friedman, 'The battle for

the NEH', *The Nation*, 19 December 1981, pp. 662–3. Also, see Edward B. Fiske, 'Reagan's man for education', *The New York Times Magazine*, 22 December 1985, pp. 30 . . . 68. After serving as Reagan's Secretary of Education, Bennett was appointed the head of the federal anti-drug campaign ('Drug Czar'), a post he held until late 1990. For a collection of Bennett's speeches as Secretary of Education, see *Our Children and Our Country* (New York, 1988).

96. W. Bennett and T. Eastland, *Counting by Race* (New York, 1979).

97. William J. Bennett, *To Reclaim A Legacy* (Washington, National Endowment for the Humanities, November 1984), p. 30.

98. W. J. Bennett, *To Reclaim A Legacy*, p. 16.

99. *ibid.*, see for examples, p. 11. Also, on the NEH in the 1980s, see Catherine R. Stimpson, 'Federal papers', *October*, no. 53 (Summer 1990), pp. 25–40.

100. Leonard Kriegel, 'Who cares about the humanities?', *The Nation*, 29 December–5 January 1985, p. 714 (my emphasis).

101. William J. Bennett and Chester Finn, *What Works: Research about teaching and learning* (Washington, US Department of Education, 1986), p. 53. Also, on Finn's call for 'national standards', see his Op-Ed piece, 'A seismic shock for education', in *The New York Times*, 3 September 1989.

102. William J. Bennett, 'Lost generation: why America's children are strangers in their own land', in *Policy Review*, no. 33 (Summer 1985), pp. 43, 45. For a critical consideration of Bennett's arguments about the imperative of a 'common culture' and his definition of America's, see David Bromwich, 'Moral education in the age of Reagan', *Dissent*, Fall 1986, pp. 447–69.

103. Gary Bauer, 'Speech to Association of American Publishers', 15 January 1986.

104. Lynne V. Cheney, *American Memory: A report on the humanities in our nation's schools* (Washington, National Endowment for the Humanities, September 1987), p. 7.

105. Lynne V. Cheney, *Humanities in America* (Washington, National Endowment for the Humanities, September 1988), pp. 7, 29.

106. See Joe Conason, 'Return of the inquisition', *Village Voice Supplement: Class action*, 21 January 1981, pp. 3–5. Also, the New Right foundations have been supporting the launching of conservative student newspapers at US colleges and universities which often 'target' Left student groups and professors (see Fox Butterfield, 'The right breeds a college press network', *The New York Times*, 24 October 1990, pp. 1, B9.

107. See Carolyn J. Mooney, 'Conservative scholars call for a movement to "reclaim" academy', *The Chronicle of Higher Education*, 23 November 1988, pp. 1, 11. Also, see Jon Wiener, 'Why the right is losing in academe', *The Nation*, 24 May 1986,

pp. 724–6 and 'Campus voices right and left', *The Nation*, 12 December 1988, pp. 644–6. The journal of the National Association of Scholars is *Academic Questions*.

108. For an example of Meese's rhetoric, see his speech 'The battle for the constitution', in *Policy Review*, no. 35 (Winter 1986), pp. 32–5.

CHAPTER 4

1. See Francis Fox Piven and Richard A. Cloward, *The New Class War: Reagan's attack on the welfare state and its consequences* (New York, 1985, rev. edn); Fred Block, Richard A. Cloward, Barbara Ehrenreich and Frances Fox Piven, *The Mean Season: The attack on the welfare state* (New York, 1987); Sydney Blumenthal and Thomas Byrne Edsall (eds), *The Reagan Legacy* (New York, 1988); and Philip Mattera, *Prosperity Lost* (New York, 1990).

2. See Andrew Gamble, *The Free Economy and the Strong State* (London, 1988) and Dennis Kavanagh and Anthony Seldon (eds), *The Thatcher Effect* (Oxford, 1989).

3. See, on the United States, John Judis, 'The conservative crackup', *The American Prospect*, Fall 1990, pp. 30–42.

4. See, on the United States, Joshua Cohen and Joel Rogers, ' "Reaganism" after Reagan', in R. Miliband, L. Panitch and J. Saville (eds), *Socialist Register 1988* (London, 1988), pp. 387–424, and, on Britain, see the reports in *The Observer*, 22 May 1988, p. 1; Gordon Marshall, David Rose, Howard Newby and Caroline Vogler, *Social Class in Modern Britain* (London, 1988); and *The Guardian*, 17 September 1988, p. 4. Also of relevance, on American public opinion, see Barry Sussman, *What Americans Really Think* (New York, 1988).

5. Paul Kennedy, *The Rise and Fall of the Great Powers* (New York, 1987). For examples of the concerns being expressed about 'national' developments in the United States see: George Will, *Suddenly: The American idea abroad and at home, 1986–1990* (New York, 1990); Robert Nisbet, *The Present Age: Progress and anarchy in modern America* (New York, 1988); Lewis Lapham, *Imperial Masquerade* (New York, 1990) along with his essay, 'Democracy in America?', *Harper's*, November 1990, pp. 47–56; and P. Mattera, *Prosperity Lost*. Also, see the symposia in: *Tikkun*, July–August 1990; *Commentary*, September, 1990; and *The National Interest*, no. 21 (Fall 1990). On Britain, see, for example, Zygmunt Bauman, 'Britain's exit from politics', *New Statesman & Society*, 29 July 1988, pp. 34–8, the essays in Geoff Andrews

(ed.), *Citizenship* (London, 1990), and *Encouraging Citizenship: Report of the speaker's commission* (London, HMSO, 1990).

6. See above, Chapter 1, note 34, for references to such commissions' reports. On the 'multiculturalism' debate in New York State, see Alan Singer, 'Multicultural education is good education – but it can't perform miracles', *AHA Perspectives*, December 1990, pp. 14–16; Diane Ravitch, 'Remaking New York's history curriculum', in 'Where we stand' (American Federation of Teachers Weekly Advertisement) in *The New York Times*, 12 August 1990, p. E7; and 'A campus forum on multiculturalism: opening academia without closing it down', *The New York Times*, 9 December 1990, p. E5. Also, regarding the idea of 'national tests' in the United States, see Karen De Witt, 'The push to consider a once taboo subject: national school tests', *The New York Times*, 3 February 1991, p. E5.

7. *National Curriculum History Working Group: Final report* (London, Department of Science and Education and the Welsh Office/HMSO, April 1990), p. ix.

8. See Judith Judd, 'Thatcher changes course of history', *The Observer*, 20 August 1989, p. 1, and 'History dons object to PM's interference', *The Observer*, 27 August 1989, p. 2; and Celia Weston, 'British bias on history endorsed', *Manchester Guardian Weekly*, 20 August 1989, p. 5. Also, see the letter of the Working Group's chairman which opens the Final Report.

9. *National Curriculum History Working Group: Final Report*, pp. 9–11. Also, see the following discussions of the Final Report: Keith Thomas, 'The future of the past', *Times Literary Supplement*, 8 June 1990, pp. 610, 621; Raphael Samuel, 'The return of history', *London Review of Books*, 14 June 1990, pp. 9–12 and Bernard Crick, Book Review (untitled), *The Political Quarterly*, vol. 61, no. 4 (October–December, 1990), pp. 486–91.

10. R. W. Johnson, 'Paul Johnson', in his *Heroes and Villains: Selected essays* (London, 1990), pp. 119–20.

11. A. Gamble, *Free Economy and Strong State*, p. 208 (my italics).

12. G. Will, *Suddenly*, pp. 108–9.

13. See, on the United States, Michael Omi and Howard Winant, *Racial Formation in the United States* (New York, 1986), pp. 131–5; and, on Britain, see the several essays in Ruth Levitas (ed.), *The Ideology of the New Right* (Cambridge, 1986).

14. See Kevin Phillips, *The Politics of Rich and Poor* (New York, 1990). The book treats the 'aftermath of Reagan' but also discusses Thatcher's reign (esp. pp. 146–50). Also, see the interesting and entertaining book by John Taylor, *Circus of Ambition: The culture of wealth and power in the eighties* (New York, 1989).

15. See, on the United States, several of the chapters in S.

Blumenthal and T. B. Edsall (eds), *The Reagan Legacy* and, on
Britain, see A. Gamble, *The Free Economy and the Strong State*,
esp. pp. 216–20.

16. See, on the United States, Thomas Byrne Edsall, 'The Reagan
    legacy' in S. Blumenthal and T. B. Edsall (eds), *The Reagan
    Legacy*, esp. pp. 31–4 and, on Britain, see B. C. Roberts, 'Trade
    unions', in D. Kavanagh and A. Seldon (eds), *The Thatcher Effect*,
    pp. 64–80.
17. See for example, on the United States, L. Lapham, 'Democracy
    in America?' and, on Britain, Z. Bauman, 'Britain's exit from
    politics'.
18. P. Mattera, *Prosperity Lost*, p. 187.
19. Stephen Gill, *American Hegemony and the Trilateral Commission*
    (Cambridge, 1990), p. 107 (my italics).
20. Nigel Harris, *The End of the Third World* (London, 1986), p. 199.
    Also, see Joyce Kolko, *Restructuring the World Economy* (New
    York, 1988).
21. On this possibility, I recommend Michael Harrington, *Socialism:
    Past and future* (New York, 1990). On the 'problem' of the
    globalization of capital for labour and 'national' development see
    Jeff Faux, 'Labour in the new global economy' and Walter Russell
    Mead, 'The world economic order', *Dissent*, Summer 1990,
    pp. 376–82, 383–93.
22. With reservations regarding his view of our contemporary
    period, I recommend J. H. Plumb, *The Death of the Past* (London,
    1969).
23. Daniel Singer, 'Dancing on the grave of the Revolution', *The
    Nation*, 6 February 1989, pp. 165–8.
24. Scott Malcolmson, 'Not everyone loves a parade', *Village Voice*,
    25 July 1989, pp. 29–32.
25. See Daniel Singer, *Is Socialism Doomed?: The meaning of Mitterrand*
    (New York, 1988). Also, for the elites' view of France's
    contemporary 'maturity' see 'Seminar on France', in The
    Trilateral Commissions' *Paris Plenary, April 1989* (New York,
    1989), pp. 6–38.
26. By François Furet, see *La Revolution, 1780–1880* (Paris, 1989)
    and, with Mona Ozouf, *The Critical Dictionary of the French
    Revolution* (Cambridge, Mass., 1989). Also, see his article 'From
    1789 to 1917 and 1989' in *Encounter*, September 1990, pp. 3–7.
    On Furet's links to the Olin Foundation, see Jon Wiener, 'Dollars
    for neocon scholars', 1 January 1990, p. 13. On the historio-
    graphy of the French Revolution from a *historical*-Marxist
    perspective, see George Comninel, *Rethinking the French Revolu-
    tion* (London, 1989). And, for an interesting set of discussions on
    the current thinking on the Revolution, see the two symposia in
    French Historical Studies, vol. 16, no. 4 (Fall 1990), pp. 741–802:

'The origins of the French Revolution: a debate' and 'François Furet's interpretation of the French Revolution'.

27. Simon Schama, *Citizens* (New York, 1990); E. J. Hobsbawm, *Echoes of the Marseillaise: Two centuries look back on the French Revolution* (New Brunswick, N.J., 1990). Also, on Schama, see Bernard Barber, 'The most sublime event', *The Nation*, 12 March 1990, pp. 351–60; and for Schama himself on 'revisionism', see his review essay, 'The nightmares of reason', *The New Republic*, 31 July 1989, pp. 26–33.

28. E. P. Thompson, *Whigs and Hunters* (London, 1975), p. 258.

29. D. Singer, 'Dancing on the grave of the Revolution', p. 166.

30. For a chronicle of 1989, see Bernard Gwertzman and Michael T. Kaufman (eds), *The Collapse of Communism by the Correspondents of the New York Times* (New York, 1990).

31. See, on the history of the concept, Raymond Williams, 'Democracy' in his book, *Keywords: A vocabulary of culture and society* (New York, 1976), pp. 82–7 and Anthony Arblaster, *Democracy* (Minneapolis, Minn., 1987).

32. B. Gwertzman and M. T. Kaufman (eds), *The Collapse of Communism*.

33. Mobil Corporation Advertisement on Op-ed page, 'And the walls came tumbling down', *The New York Times*, 7 December 1989, p. 31. Noted also in P. Mattera, *Prosperity Lost*, p. 1.

34. On the question of the 'third way' and other related issues, see Bogdan Denitch, *The End of the Cold War* (Minneapolis, Minn., 1990). Also, see the contributions to the special issue of *Dissent* on 'Revolution in Europe' (Spring 1990) and Fred Halliday, 'The ends of Cold War', *New Left Review*, no. 180 (March–April 1990), pp. 5–23.

35. See *Encounter* 'Symposium: an inquest on the death of communism', Part I, July–August 1990, pp. 3–38 and Part II, September 1990, pp. 24–32; *New Perspectives Quarterly*, issue on 'The triumph of capitalism', vol. 6, no. 3 (Fall 1989); Jerry Z. Muller, 'Capitalism: the wave of the future', *Commentary*, December 1988, pp. 21–6; Peter Drucker, *The New Realities* (New York, 1989), p. 176; Edward Yardeni, *The Triumph of Capitalism*, Topical Study no. 17, Prudential-Bache Securities (New York, 1989); Robert Heilbroner, 'The triumph of capitalism', *The New Yorker*, 31 January 1989, pp. 98–109; and Ralf Dahrendorf, *Reflections on the Revolution in Europe* (New York, 1990), p. 42 (my italics). Also, see Arthur Seldon, *Capitalism* (Oxford, 1990) for a spirited argument on behalf of capitalism.

36. Stanley Aronowitz, 'On intellectuals', in Bruce Robbins (ed.), *Intellectuals: Aesthetics, politics, academics* (Minneapolis, Minn., 1990), p. 5.

37. J. Kolko, *Restructuring the World Economy*, p. 347 (my italics).

38. Francis Fukuyama, 'The end of history?', *The National Interest*, no. 16 (Summer 1989), pp. 3–18. Responses were published in the same issue and in issue no. 17 (Fall 1989); Fukuyama's 'Reply to my critics', appeared in issue no. 18 (Winter 1989), pp. 3–10. *The National Interest* is published by Irving Kristol with significant support by the Olin Foundation; on this and on Fukuyama's article having been commissioned by Alan Bloom for his Olin Foundation-funded centre at the University of Chicago, see J. Wiener, 'Dollars for neocon scholars', p. 12.

39. See, for one of innumerable examples, James Atlas, 'What is Fukuyama saying? And to whom is he saying it?', *The New York Times Magazine*, 22 October 1989, pp. 38–42, 54–5.

40. F. Fukuyama, 'The end of history?', pp. 3–4. I must note that as I write: war has begun in the Persian Gulf; the Soviets may be 'cracking down' on the Baltic Republics; and the Chinese Government is sending more people to prison for their participation in the Beijing Spring protests.

41. Daniel Singer, 'On revolution', *Monthly Review*, June 1989, p. 33.

CHAPTER 5

1. Gwyn A. Williams, 'The concept of *Egemonia* in the thought of Antonio Gramsci', *Journal of the History of Ideas*, vol. 21, no. 4 (October–December 1960), pp. 586–99.

2. Patrick Wright, *On Living in an Old Country* (London, 1985), p. 7.

3. David W. Noble, *The End of American History: Democracy, capitalism and the metaphor of two worlds in Anglo-American historical writing, 1880–1980* (Minneapolis, Minn., 1985), pp. 144–5; Norman Birnbaum, *The Radical Renewal* (New York, 1988), pp. 194–5.

4. Agnes Heller, *The Postmodern Political Condition* (New York, 1988), pp. 1, 3, 11.

5. See the discussions in Perry Anderson, *In The Tracks of Historical Materialism* (London, 1983), pp. 32–56; Marshall Berman, *All That is Solid Melts into Air* (New York, 1982); Alex Callinicos, *Against Postmodernism* (New York, 1990); and David Harvey, *The Condition of Postmodernity* (Oxford, 1989). Also, see the chapter on the post-structuralist philosopher, Michel Foucault in Michael Walzer, *The Company of Critics* (New York, 1988), pp. 191–209.

6. Daniel Singer, *Is Socialism Doomed?* (New York, 1988), p. 29.

7. J. H. Plumb, *The Death of the Past* (London, 1969), pp. 13–14.

8. Robert Nisbet, *Conservatism* (Minneapolis, Minn., 1986), p. 109.

9. See C. Wright Mills, *The Marxists* (New York, 1962); Perry Anderson, *Considerations on Western Marxism* (London, 1976); Russell Jacoby, *Dialectic of Defeat: Contou.: of Western Marxism* (Cambridge, 1981); and Martin Jay, *Marxism and Totality* (Berkeley, Calif., 1984). For examples of the articulation of the 'vision' which drew a multi-aged 'generation' to historical studies in the 1960s, see, in addition to the references in the discussions of *History Workshop*, *Radical America* and *Radical History Review* in Chapter 1 above: Barton J. Bernstein's 'Introduction' to his edited collection, *A New Past in American History* (New York, 1968), pp. v–xiii; Howard Zinn, *The Politics of History* (Urbana, Ill., 1970, 1990 rev. edn); Gareth Stedman Jones, 'History: the poverty of empiricism', in R. Blackburn (ed.), *Ideology in Social Science* (New York, 1973), pp. 96–118; and Robbie Gray, 'History', in T. Pateman (ed.), *Counter Course* (Harmondsworth, 1972), pp. 281–93.

10. Harvey J. Kaye, *The British Marxist Historians* (Oxford, 1984) and my article, 'Political theory and history: Antonio Gramsci and the British Marxist historians', *Italian Quarterly*, nos. 97–8 (Summer–Fall 1984), pp. 145–66. Also, see the special issue on the 'British Marxist historical tradition' of *Radical History Review*, no. 19 (Winter 1978–9) and MARHO (ed.), *Visions of History* (New York, 1983).

11. Barrington Moore, Jr, *Social Origins of Dictatorship and Democracy* (Boston, 1966), pp. 522–3; Walter Benjamin, *Illuminations* (New York, 1969), p. 157.

12. Jean Chesneaux, *Pasts and Futures* (London, 1978), p. 30.

13. Yosef Hayim Yerushalmi, *Zakhor* (New York, 1989), p. 116. Also, see Peter Carroll, *Keeping Time* (Athens, Ga., 1990), esp. pp. 200–8 and D. M. Schreuder, ' "Keeping the Record Straight": historians and the judgement of history', *The Critical Review*, no. 28 (1986), pp. 100–15.

14. Antonio Gramsci, *Selections from the Prison Notebooks* (London, 1971), p. 369; Karl Korsch, *Three Essays on Marxism* (London, 1971); and 'Interview with Eric Hobsbawm', in MARHO (ed.), *Visions of History*, p. 43.

15. Marc Bloch, *Strange Defeat* (Oxford, 1949), pp. 117–18. Also, see Bloch's *Feudal Society* (Chicago, 1961) and the biography by Carole Fink, *Marc Bloch: A life in history* (Cambridge, 1989).

16. 'Interview with Natalie Zemon Davis', in MARHO (ed.), *Visions of History*, pp. 114–15. Also, see Davis's books, *Society and Culture in Early Modern France* (Palo Alto, Calif., 1975) and *The Return of Martin Guerre* (Cambridge, Mass., 1983).

17. Karl Marx, *Capital: Volume one* (New York, 1976), esp. pp. 163–77; Georg Lukács, *History and Class Consciousness* (London, 1971), p. 145; Max Horkheimer and Theodor Adorno, *The Dialectic of*

Enlightenment (New York, 1972); and W. Benjamin, *Illuminations*, p. 359. The phrase 'Breaking the tyranny of the present' is derived from an article under that title by Alan Bullock (*Times Higher Education Supplement*, 24 May 1985, pp. 18–19).

18. David Noble, *America By Design: Science, technology and the rise of corporate capitalism* (Oxford, 1977), p. xix.
19. W. Benjamin, *Illuminations*, p. 262.
20. A. Gramsci, *Selections*, for examples, see pp. 52–5, 196 and 200.
21. Terry Eagleton, 'Marxism and the past', *Salmagundi*, nos. 68–9 (Fall 1985–Winter 1986), p. 283.
22. Christopher Hill, *The Experience of Defeat* (New York, 1984); William Morris, *A Dream of John Ball* included in *Three Works by William Morris* (New York, 1968), p. 53; and Rodney Hilton, *Bond Men Made Free* (London, 1977), p. 236.
23. John Berger, *Ways of Seeing* (Harmondsworth, 1971), p. 11.
24. Herbert Marcuse, *Eros and Civilization* (New York, 1962), p. 212 and *One-Dimensional Man* (Boston, 1964), p. 98; and Ronald Aronson, *The Dialectics of Disaster* (London, 1983), p. 301. Also, on 'the will to bear witness', see Terrence Des Pres, *The Survivor: An anatomy of life in the death camps* (New York, 1976).
25. R. Aronson, *The Dialectics of Disaster*, p. 207; Christopher Lasch, *The True and Only Heaven* (New York, 1990), pp. 80–1; and Y. H. Yerushalmi, *Zakhor*, p. 117. Also, on the Barbie case and trial in France, see Erna Paris, *Unhealed Wounds: France and the Klaus Barbie affair* (New York, 1985) and Judith Miller, *One by One, by One* (New York, 1990), pp. 112–38.
26. John Keane, *Democracy and Civil Society* (London, 1988), p. 33; B. Moore, Jr, *Social Origins of Dictatorship and Democracy*, p. 505; and Karl Marx, 'A correspondence of 1843' in D. McLellan (ed.), *Karl Marx: Selected writings* (Oxford, 1977), p. 38.
27. 'Interview with E. P. Thompson', in MARHO (ed.), *Visions of History*, p. 17; Herbert Gutman, 'Foreword' to Paul Buhle and Alan Dawley (eds), *Working for Democracy: American workers from the revolution to the present* (Urbana, Ill., 1985), p.xi.
28. Russell Jacoby, *The Last Intellectuals: American culture in an age of academe* (New York, 1987), pp. 164–6; and Marc Bloch, *Strange Defeat*, p. 173. Also, see N. Birnbaum, *The Radical Renewal*.
29. Roy Rosenzweig, 'What is the matter with history?', *Journal of American History*, vol. 74, no. 1 (1987), p. 122; and Gerda Lerner, 'The necessity of history and the professional historian', *Journal of American History*, vol. 69, no. 1 (1982), p. 17. Also, see George Lipsitz, 'The struggle for hegemony', *Journal of American History*, vol. 75, no. 1 (1988), pp. 146–50. Here, I should note my own involvement in the formation and development of the Wisconsin Labor History Society. The experience of this organization attests to the possibility that labour history need not remain an academic

activity. Its membership and leadership is overwhelmingly composed of union and labour movement people. I have learned a great deal from them and, I hope, contributed something in return.

30. A noteworthy initiative in this direction is the projected two-volume text, *Who Built America?*, being produced by the American Social History Project begun under the supervision of the late Herbert Gutman. Volume One was published in 1989 (New York) treating American history to 1877. Earlier efforts of this sort were: Leo Huberman, *We, The People* (New York, 1932); Howard Zinn, *A People's History of the United States* (New York, 1980) and A. L. Morton, *A People's History of England* (London, 1938).

31. Elizabeth Fox-Genovese, 'The claims of a common culture: gender, race, class and the canon', *Salmagundi*, no. 72 (Fall 1986), p. 132. Also, Lawrence Stone, *The Past and the Present Revisited* (London, 1987 rev. edn), pp. 3–5.

32. A. Gramsci, *Selections*, p. 40.

33. *ibid.*, p. 395; Antonio Gramsci, *Selections from Political Writings: 1910–1920* (New York, 1977), p. 13; and A. Gramsci, *Selections from the Prison Notebooks*, pp. 344–5.

34. W. Benjamin, *Illuminations*, p. 256.

35. Antonio Gramsci, *The Modern Prince and Other Writings* (New York, 1957), p. 20.

36. W. Benjamin, *Illuminations*, p. 257.

37. See, for discussions of this, Geoffrey Barraclough, *History in a Changing World* (Oxford, 1955) and *An Introduction to Contemporary History* (London, 1964).

38. Tom Bender, 'Wholes and parts: the need for synthesis in American history', *Journal of American History*, vol. 73, no. 1 (1986), pp. 120–36; Marc Bloch is quoted in Theodore Zeldin, 'Beyond the "new history" ', *London Review of Books*, 16 March 1989, p. 15; R. Aronson, *Dialectics of Disaster*, p. 213. Also, for some excellent propositions for critical historical education, see Marc Ferro, *The Use and Abuse of History* (London, 1984), p. 240.

39. *National Curriculum History Working Group: Final report* (London, Department of Science and Education and the Welsh Office/HMSO, April 1990), pp. 8–11; and R. Aronson, *Dialectics of Disaster*, p. 211.

40. Benjamin R. Barber, 'Cultural conservatism and democratic education: lessons from the sixties', *Salmagundi*, no. 81 (Winter 1989), p. 173.

41. Christopher Lasch, 'The communitarian critique of liberalism', *Soundings*, vol. 69, nos. 1–2 (1986), p. 67.

42. For discussions of 'connected criticism' which are relevant to historians, see C. Wright Mills, *The Sociological Imagination* (New

York, 1959), esp. pp. 177–94 and Michael Walzer, *Interpretation and Social Criticism* (Cambridge, Mass., 1987). Also, on the need to distinguish between our responsibilities as teachers and critics, see Peter Mandler, 'The "double life" in academia: political commitment and/or objective scholarship?', *Dissent*, Winter 1989, pp. 94–9.

INDEX

Abraham Lincoln Brigade, 103
Accuracy in Adaemia (AIA), 118
Accuracy in Media (AIM), 118
Adam Smith Institute, 85
Adamson, Walter, 16–17
Adorno, Theodor, 156
African-Americans, 50–1, 125, 167
American Enterprise Institute (AEI), 90, 93
American Heritage, 19
American Historical Association, 15, 27–8
American Revolutiion (1776), 44, 98, 100,
    102–3, 109, 139, 167
Anderson, Perry, 183
Annales, 22–4, 32, 34, 105, 155
Apple, Michael, 177
Argentina, 92, 100–1
Aronowitz, Stanley, 141–2
Aronson, Ronald, 159, 167

Barber, Benjamin, 168
Barbie, Klaus, 159
Barnett, Anthony, 100
Bauer, Gary, 116
Beard, Charles, 23
Bell, Daniel, 90
Beloff, Max, 84
Bender, Thomas, 38–9, 167
Benjamin, Walter, 9, 152–3, 157, 165–6
Bennett, William J., 112–16
Berger, John, 16, 196
Berger, Peter, 90
Berlin Wall, 139–40
Berman, Marshall, 17
Berr, Henri, 22
Birkerts, Sven, 62–3
Birnbaum, Norman, 146–7
Black Britons, 52
Bloch, Marc, 22–3, 37, 155, 162, 167
Bluestone, Barry, 76
Blumenthal, Sidney, 109
Boorstin, Daniel, 24
Boyson, Rhodes, 108–9
Braudel, Fernand, 23
'British disease' (decline), 59
British Empire, 45, 47–8, 52, 55, 58, 104

British Marxist historians, 3, 7, 9, 23–4,
    152–3, 155, 157–8
Brzezinski, Zbigniew, 79
Buckley, William F., Jr, 93
Buhle, Paul, 26
Bulgaria, 139
Bullock, Alan, 170
Burke, Edmund, 95, 141
Burrow, J.W., 47
Bush Administration, 136, 137
Business Roundtable, 76–7
'Butskellism' (R.A. Butler–Hugh
    Gaitskell), 47

Cambridge University, 87
Campaign for Nuclear Disarmament
    (CND), 52
Cannadine, David, 38–9
capital (business and corporate), 56–7,
    74–82, 86, 89, 132–5
Carroll, Peter, 58, 61–2
Carter Administration, 57–9
Center for Policy Studies, 85, 96
Central America, 102–3
Central Intelligence Agency (CIA), 44, 102
Chancellor, Valerie, 48
Cheney, Lynn, 116–18
Chesneaux, Jean, 153–4
China, 135, 139, 167
Churchill, Winston, 101, 104
citizenship, 124, 150, 162, 164
Civil Rights struggle, 50–1, 167
Cold War, 42–5, 48–9, 66, 90–2, 136, 140,
    142
Cole, G.D.H., 22
Commentary, 90
Commons, John R., 26
Confederation of British Industries (CBI),
    77
consciousness, 157–8
consensus historians, 24–5, 44, 146
Conservative Party (Tories), 46, 50, 53,
    54, 66, 77, 83–9, 95, 108–9, 123–4, 128,
    130–1
Conservative Philosophy Group, 87

contras (Nicaraguan), 102–3, 122
Coors, Joseph, 93
critique, 156
Cuba, 102

Dahrendorf, Ralf, 141
Dallek, Robert, 99
Davis, Natalie Zemon, 155–6
Dector, Midge, 90
democracy, 3–4, 30, 43–5, 48–9, 59, 79–81,
    142–3, 153–4, 164–5, 168–9
Democratic Party, 47, 53–9, 78, 91, 130–1
Depression (1930s), 41, 85, 96
Des Pres, Terrence, 41
Deutsh, Karl, 16–17
Dobb, Maurice, 3
Dolan, Terry, 93
Drucker, Peter, 141
Duby, George, 23

Eagleton, Terry, 157
Eastern Europe, 7, 40, 42, 91, 135–6,
    139–43, 146
Edgar, David, 88–9
education (historical), 5, 12–18, 60–2,
    105–19, 121, 124–8, 163–8
Ehrenreich, Barbara, 51
Elton, Geoffrey, 32, 112
Engels, Friedrich, 22, 24
Equal Rights Amendment, 54
Erickson, Paul, 97

Falklands War, 100–1, 112
Falwell, Jerry, 94
Fascism (European), 41, 103, 136
Febvre, Lucien, 22–3
Ferro, Marc, 105
Finn, Chester, 115, 171
Fitzgerald, Frances, 43–4
Ford, Henry, 12
Foucault, Michel, 63
Fox-Genovese, Elizabeth, 32–3, 164
Frankfurt School, 152
French Revolution (1789), 13, 22, 135–8,
    145, 165, 167
Friedman, Milton, 84, 94
Fukuyama, Francis, 142–3
Furet, François, 23, 137–8

Gamble, Andrew, 57–8, 84
Genovese, Eugene, 3, 32–3
Germany, 57, 100, 103–4, 124, 136–7,
    139–40, 155
Gilder, George, 94
Gill, Stephen, 133
Giroux, Henry, 9, 16
Glazer, Nathan, 90
globalization of capital, 56, 133–5, 140–3,
    167
Goldwater, Barry, 93, 99
Gorbachev, Mikhail, 139
Goubert, Pierre, 23

Gramsci, Antonio, 1, 4, 9, 13, 40, 65,
    67–74, 83, 120, 145, 152, 157, 163–6
Greater London Council (GLC), 122
'Great Society', 53, 91
Greenberg, Edward, 182
Grenada, 122
Gutman, Herbert, 38, 160

Hamerow, Theodore, 36–7
Hammond, John and Barbara, 22
Handlin, Oscar, 24
Harrison, Bennett, 76
Hartwell, R.M., 108
Harvey, David, 63
Hayek, Friedrich, 84, 94, 106–8
Heath Government, 83, 110–11
Hegel, Georg Friedrich, 142
hegemony, 65–74, 82–4, 94–5, 117, 123–5,
    130–5, 145–7
Heilbroner, Robert, 141
Heller, Agnes, 147
heritage *see* National Heritage
Heritage Foundation, 93, 113
Hewison, Robert, 62
Hill, Christopher, 3, 24, 110, 158
Hilton, Rodney, 3, 23–4
Himmelfarb, Gertrude, 32
Hispanic-Americans, 125
'historians' debate' (German), 104
Historical Association, 110
history from the bottom up, 30–1, 153–61
History Workshop, 25–6, 28–9, 97
Hitler, Adolf, 103–4
Hobsbawm, Eric, 3, 24, 138, 155
Hofstadter, Richard, 24, 44
Hollywood and the film industry, 98
Holocaust, 18, 41, 103–4
Horkheimer, Max, 156
Hungary, 102, 139–40
Hunter, Allen, 42–3
Huntington, Samuel, 79–81

Iggers, Georg, 22
imagination, 160–1
Industrial Revolution, 107, 167
Institute of Economic Affairs, 84
intellectuals, 49, 68–70, 79–80, 82–4,
    87–90, 106–9, 152, 161–9
Iran, 92
Irish Republican Army (IRA), 53
Irvine, Reed, 118
Islamic fundamentalism, 57

Jacoby, Rusell, 17, 161
James, C.L.R., 27
Japan, 57, 78–82, 124
Jenkins, Peter, 46–50, 56, 59–60
Jews, Jewish history, 1, 10–11, 91, 103
Johnson Administration, 53–4, 91
Johnson, Paul, 84, 127–8
Johnson, R.W., 127–8
Joseph, Sir Keith, 85–7, 96, 110–12, 114,
    125

Keane, John, 160
Kennedy, Paul, 124
Kennedy Administration, 53–4, 99, 100
Keynesianism, 42, 45–50, 53, 84–5, 121, 123, 149
Kruschev, Nikita, 154
Kiernan, Victor, 9, 24
King, Martin Luther, Jr, 54, 115
Kirkpatrick, Jeane, 90, 92–3
Kohl, Helmut, 136
Kolko, Joyce, 142
Korsch, Karl, 152, 155
Kriegel, Leonard, 115
Krieger, Joel, 49, 53
Kristol, Irving, 109
Kulik, Gary, 181

La Feber, Walter, 91
Labour Party, 46–7, 50, 53–7, 74, 78, 130–1
labour (working class), 42, 46, 51, 56–7, 74–7, 81, 129, 131–4, 157, 165–9
Langer, William, 44–5
Lasch, Christopher, 20–1, 40–1, 62, 159
Lefebvre, Georges, 22–3
Le Goff, Jacques, 23
Lerner, Gerda, 162–3, 170
Le Roy Ladurie, Emmanuel, 23
liberalism, 43, 45–50, 53, 130–1, 145, 149
Lincoln, Abraham, 99
Leys, Colin, 75
Lipset, Seymour Martin, 24, 49, 90
Lockard, Craig, 9, 176
Lowenthal, David, 9, 20
Lukacs, Georg, 152, 156
Lukacs, John, 18
Luxemburg, Rosa, 152

MacGregor, John, 126
Magna Carta, 92
Manifest Destiny, 43
Marcuse, Herbert, 152, 158
Marshall, T.H., 48
Marwick, Arthur, 30
Marx, Karl, 22, 24, 69, 115, 152, 156, 160
McCarthyism, 91
Mead, Walter Russell, 54
media and television, 69–70, 136–7, 140, 142–3, 163
Meese, Edwin, III, 118
memory, 69–72, 158–9
Miliband, Ralph, 9, 67
Mills, C. Wright, 2
miners' strike (1984–5), 101
Mitterrand, François, 136–7
Mont Pelerin Society, 106–8
Moore, Barrington, Jr, 3, 30, 153, 160
Moral Majority, 88, 94, 116
Morris, William, 158
Mount, Ferdinand, 88
Moynihan, Daniel Patrick, 90–1
multiculturalism, 125
museums, 18–21, 71, 163

Mussolini, Benito, 103

Nairn, Tom, 179, 183
National Association of Scholars, 118
National Center for the Humanities, 112
National Conservative Political Action Committee, 93, 99, 102
National Curriculum History Working Group, 125–7, 165, 167
National Endowment for the Arts (NEA), 93
National Endowment for the Humanities (NEH), 93, 112–18
National Front, 53
National Heritage (British), 19–20, 62, 127
National Interest, 142
National Review, 93
nationalism, 43–5, 53, 82, 100–2, 110–12, 115–16, 125–6, 134–5
Nazism, 103–4, 136
neoconservatives (intellectuals), 89–93, 142
New Deal, 42, 47, 90, 98, 100
New Left, 27, 51–2, 152
New Right, 5, 7, 39, 65–6, 82–119, 143, 145–9, 163–4
Nicaragua, 92, 102–3, 122
Nisbet, Robert, 40, 104, 118, 151–2
Nixon Administration, 45–5, 58, 76, 83, 133
Noble, David, 156
Noble, David W., 146
nostalgia, 20–1, 62–4, 70–1
Notre Dame University, 97
Novak, Michael, 90
Novick, Peter, 24–5, 44

objectivity, 153–4
Olin Foundation, 89, 138
Orwell, George, 105, 139
Owen, David, 182

Paine, Tom, 99
Past & Present, 24
perspective, 154–6
Phillips, Howard, 93
Plaid Cymru (Welsh nationalists), 53
Plumb, J.H., 15, 151
Podhoretz, Norman, 90
Poland, 139–40
post-modernism, 34, 62–3, 147–8, 150
progress, 41–50, 146–8, 159
Progressive historians, 23–4, 27
Protestantism, 43, 94, 167
Public Interest, 90

race and ethnicity, 30, 50–3, 93, 102, 125, 129, 131, 168
Radical America, 25–8
Radical History Review and MARHO, 25, 27–8, 172
Ranke, Leopold von, 22, 154
Ravitch, Diane, 171

Reagan, Ronald and 'Reaganism', 7, 66, 74, 83, 96–101, 102–5, 110, 113–19, 121–30, 132–3, 137, 148
reification, 156
remembrance, 158–60
Republican Party, 47, 53–5, 66, 83, 90, 94, 99, 123–4, 130–1
Riddell, Peter, 84
Robin Hood, 153
Robinson, James Harvey, 23
Rockefeller, David, 78
Romania, 139
Roosevelt Administration, 91, 99, 100
Rosenzweig, Roy, 39, 162
Rude, George, 3, 24

Salisbury Group and *Salisbury Review*, 87
Samuel, Raphael, 26
Saville, John, 9, 24
Scaife, RIchard, 93
Schama, Simon, 138
Scottish Nationalist Party (SNP), 53
Scruton, Roger, 87–8
Second World War, 37, 41–6, 85, 98, 100–4, 159
selective tradition, 70, 124, 166–8
Simon, William, 89, 109, 138
Singer, Daniel, 9, 136, 138–9, 143, 148
social history and historiography, 21–34, 107, 114, 150–69
socialism (social democracy), 45–50, 53, 108, 131–2, 136–44
Soviet Union (and Russia), 7, 40, 42, 91, 98, 102, 136–7, 139–40, 142, 152, 167
Spanish Civil War, 103
Statue of Liberty, 19, 139
Stern, Fritz, 12
Stone, Lawrence, 33
Students for a Democratic Society (SDS), 26
Studies on the Left, 27
Sumption, Jonathan, 87
Susman, Warren, 14
Sweden, 140

Tawney, R.H., 22
Tebbit, Norman, 129
Thatcher, Margaret and 'Thatcherism', 7, 66, 74, 83–9, 94–7, 100–1, 104, 109–12, 118–19, 121–30, 136–7, 148

think-tanks, 85, 90
Third World, 2–3, 31, 56–7, 92, 133, 138
Thomas, Hugh, 84, 87, 112
Thompson, E.P., 3, 4, 24, 27, 138, 160
Tosh, John, 48
Trilateral Commission, 78–82, 89, 135, 141
Trump, Donald, 129
Turner, Frederick Jackson, 23, 26–7

union-busting, 76

Victorian Age, 47–8, 86–9, 96–7
Vietnam War, 18, 41, 51–2, 54, 58, 91
Vogel, David, 74–5

Wallace, Michael, 71
Walvin, James, 59
Weaver, F. Stirton, 67
Webb, Sydney and Beatrice, 22
Weber, Max, 34–5
Weiner, Martin J., 183
Welfare State, 42, 45–50, 85–8, 99, 121, 123, 149
Werner, Jon, 173, 192, 194
Western Civilization, 37, 113–18, 164–7
Western Europe, 41, 45–6, 55–6, 58, 78–82, 103, 139, 166
Western Marxism, 152–61
Weyrich, Paul, 93
White, Hayden, 14
Wilentz, Sean, 24
Will, George, 129
Williams, Raymond, 70, 72
Williams, William Appleman, 27
Wilson Government, 53–7, 75, 78
Wisconsin, University of, 26–7
Wolfe, Alan, 49
women's movement and feminism, 51–2, 55, 129, 131
world history, 38, 125, 126, 147, 163–7
Woodward, C. Vann, 15
Wright, Patrick, 146

Yalta, 91
Yardeni, Edward, 141
Yerushalmi, Josef Hayim, 10–11, 37, 154, 159
Young Americans for Freedom, 93